DESIGN D&T MAKE IT !

food
technology
revised edition

Jill Robinson ■ Helen Roberts ■ Elizabeth Barnard
Tristram Shepard

Text © Jill Robinson, Helen Roberts, Elizabeth Barnard and Tristram Shepard 1997, 2001
Original illustrations © Nelson Thornes Ltd 2001

First edition published in 1997 by Stanley Thornes (Publishers) Ltd
Second edition published in 2001 by:

Nelson Thornes Ltd
Delta Place
27 Bath Road
CHELTENHAM
GL53 7TH
United Kingdom

05 / 10 9 8 7 6

A catalogue record for this book is available from the British Library

ISBN 0 7487 6084 9

Designed and typeset by Carla Turchini
Picture research by Jennie Karrach and John Bailey
Artwork by Tristram Ariss, John Fowler, Andrew Loft, Hardlines and Tristram Shepard
Printed and bound in China by Midas Printing International Ltd

The authors would like to thank family and friends for their support and encouragement and also thank Roy Ballam, Julie Booker, Hazel King and Barbara Monks for their contributions to the second edition.

The publishers would like to thank:
Palethorpes – manufacturers of quality savoury products: p.60;
Flour Information Bureau: pp. 31 and 42;
Snugbury's Ice Cream: p.110;
Mrs Claire M Abbott MIFST, MSoFHT: pp.120 and 158;
Hazelwood Frozen Foods: p.137;
A J Boon Family Butcher: p.78;

The publishers are grateful to the following for permission to reproduce photographs or other illustrative material:
Anthony Blake: pp. 19 (Soe Atkinson), 32 (Kieran Scott), 110 (top), 129, 138;
APV: pp. 146, 147 (bottom);
Beamish Open Air Museum: p. 154 (centre);
BOC Gases: p. 98 (bottom);
Boots company PLC: p.6 (bottom left);
Cephas: pp. 59 (top – Peter Barr), 90 (Nigel Blythe);
Frijj: p.6 (top left);
Format: pp. 78, 139 (bottom – Brenda Prince), 161 (Mo Wilson);
Hulton Getty Picture Collection: p. 154 (top);
Hutchison Picture Library; p.8 (top – Robert Aberman);
Impact Photos: p. 139 (top – Michael Gover);
Marks and Spencer: p. 9 (bottom right);
Martyn Chillmaid: pp. 38, 47, 50, 51, 53, 54, 55, 58, 67, 82 (bottom), 111, 120, 121 (centre, bottom), 125, 134, 147 (top), 152, 154 (bottom), 160, 162, 163, 164, 165, 166, 167, cover;
Peter Gould: p. 153 (left);
Pizza Express: p. 152;
Powerstock Zefa: pp. 29 (top), 86, 97 (H Dombrowski);
Robert Harding Picture Library: pp. 37 (bottom), 151;
Safeway: pp. 73 (top), 162 (centre);
Science Photolibrary: pp. 8 (top and bottom left – David Parker), 23 (Rosenfeld Images Limited), 24 (top – Philip Goutier, Eurelios), 33, 51 (bottom), 57 (bottom – James King-Holmes, Farmer Giles Foods), 67 (Rosenfeld Images Limited), 79, 83 (Shiela Terry, Anne Sheasby, Home Economist), 84 (Andrew Syred), 87, 103 (left – Ed Young, Agstock), 106 (Food and Drug Administration), 113 (top – James King-Holmes, Pasta Company), 114 (Rosenfeld Images Limited), 137 (James King-Holmes, Northern Foods), 153 (right – R Maisoneuve, Publiphoto Division);
Science Pictures Ltd: pp. 24 (middle), 71, 150, 151;
Still Pictures: p. 6 (bottom right – Wolfgang M Weber);
Stone: p.6/7 (top – Rex Butcher);
Tesco Photographic Unit: pp. 69, 74, 102 (top), cover;
Topham Picture Point: p. 82 (top);
TRIP: p. 21 (Ask Images);
Tristram Ariss: p. 2.

Contents

Introduction

Welcome to Design & Make: Food Technology. *This book has been written to support you as you work through your GCSE course in Design and Technology. It will help guide you through the important stages of your coursework, and assist your preparation for the final examination paper.*

■ ACTIVITY

Make sure that as part of your design folder you include evidence of having completed a number of short-term focused practical tasks as suggested in the Activity sections.

Long or short?

If you are following a short course, check with your teacher which sections of the book you do not need to cover.

Making it

Whatever your project remember that the final realisation is particularly important. It is not enough just to hand in your design folder. You must have a food product which you have made.

The quality of your final realisation must be as high as possible as it counts for a large proportion of the marks.

During your course you will need to develop practical skills in using food ingredients and processing equipment. This is something you can't do just by reading a book! The best way is to watch carefully as different techniques and procedures are demonstrated to you, and practise them as often as possible.

How to Use this Book

There are two main ways you might use the book.

1   Follow the six units in sequence over the whole course. As you cover each unit undertake a selection of the suggested activities (i.e. focused practical tasks) and then the design and make task which is presented at the start. This will ensure you cover the syllabus completely. You may decide not to take all of the units as far as the production of a finished food product.
2   Undertake alternative tasks to one or more of those provided. Where appropriate, refer to those pages which cover the related specific areas of knowledge and understanding defined in the examination syllabus and the KS4 National Curriculum.

Contents

Project guide
The book begins with a coursework guide which summarises the design skills you will need for extended project work. Refer back to these pages throughout the course.

The units
Each unit starts with a general introduction and an outline of a design and make task. Before tackling this task you will need to work through the unit to cover the knowledge and understanding you will need.

Informing the consumer
This is a separate section on packaging and labelling. You can refer to this during any of the units if you have been asked to make suggestions for packaging your food product.

Glossary
As you work through the text it is important that you begin to use the correct technical terms. Many of these are listed in the Glossary at the back of the book, and printed in **bold type** the first time they are used in the text.

IN YOUR PROJECT

Special 'In Your Project' paragraphs help you to think about how you could apply the content of the pages to your current work.

KEY POINTS

Use the 'Key Points' paragraphs to revise from when preparing for the final examination paper. Three specimen papers are included at the end of Units 2, 3 and 6.

Beyond GCSE

There are good opportunities for skilled people to work in the food industry – in product development, manufacturing, microbiology and product engineering. Such people need to be flexible, good communicators, willing to work in teams, and to be computer literate. Further courses and training opportunities are available at various levels which you might like to find out more about.

The Food Industry

Not so long ago there was a very limited choice of food products available to us. What we ate was produced locally and didn't keep fresh for very long.

Thanks to developments in food technology we can now buy a wide choice of produce from around the world, and eat it when we want.

Food for Thought

Why do you eat food? Is it because you enjoy it? Because you feel hungry? Or are there more subtle reasons such as to cheer you up when you're feeling down?

In the past we would not have had the luxury of such considerations, we had to eat to survive and we had to eat whatever was available. Today, we have a huge choice of food products, places to eat and methods of cooking.

Regarding food as a commercial commodity rather than a necessity has seen the development of a huge food industry and the idea of **Food Technology**.

Food technology is about the development of new food products in order to satisfy consumer demand. This new technology did not appear overnight; it has developed in the western world gradually over a number of years and for a variety of reasons.

What is a Food Technologist?

The role of the **Food Technologist** has emerged from our food industry; that is, someone who designs new products using food as their material. A food technologist needs a sound knowledge of the science of food as well as a flair for creating exciting new flavours, textures and aromas.

Consumer voices

The 'voice' of the consumer has become an integral part of our evolving food industry. A new food product would just not be launched without extensive market research to ensure it was meeting the needs of a particular consumer group.

Market research determines what it is that consumers really want; not just in terms of the food but the packaging, the price, the quantity and even where it should be placed on the shelves.

This market research has spotted consumers' recent demand for foods that are of organic origin and those that have been produced without exploiting farmers and workers involved in their production (known as 'fairtrade' products).

Changes in society

There is no single reason for the development of our food industry in Britain. Society has changed over a long period of time due to a range of influences that are inextricably linked. Some of those influences can be listed as:

▷ the Industrial Revolution
▷ our growing population
▷ the changing role of women
▷ advances in technology such as transportation, canned food and microwaves
▷ rising standards of living and an increase in disposable income
▷ the use of market research within food technology
▷ the increasing popularity of convenience foods
▷ changing styles of shopping, from supermarket to internet
▷ advances in food production such as biotechnology (GM foods)
▷ an increasing knowledge of food-related diseases.

The result of these and other influences is what you see today in our supermarkets, shops, homes and restaurants and cafes.

The things we demand of our food today will probably be different to our demands in another ten or twenty years time. The food industry moves at a fast pace in order to keep up with the latest developments and consumer trends.

Veggie needs
The vegetarian food market was estimated at £1.1 billion in 1997. Vegetarian food products have become more and more popular over the last ten years and many non-vegetarians now choose them as an alternative to meat. The development of products such as tofu, soya and Quorn™ have helped to meet this consumer demand.

Single market
In 1961 only 4% of households were classed as 'one person'. Today the figure is 12% and is set to continue to rise, with people living longer and more people choosing to live independently. Consequently, the food industry has responded by providing a wider range of single portion readymeals.

Kids market
In 2000, KP spent £7 million on the launch of a new brand character for their snack Hula Hoops, Hoopy McHula. Many people are concerned about the amount of advertising aimed at children that is for foods high in fat, sugar and salt.

Food for thought
Today's food industry is the largest manufacturing industry in Britain. The sandwich industry alone employs over 320,000 people (both full- and part-time).

Working with Food

Food Technology involves the study of food as a material. A food technologist needs to understand how food 'works'.

Food Components

During the development of new food products it is essential to know about the **components** of food. Generally speaking foods include one or more of the following compounds; water, carbohydrate, protein, fat, vitamins and minerals. However, their composition is likely to change over a period of time. For example, vegetables may become soft as they age and their vitamin content will decrease. Processed foods are also likely to contain additional substances such as flavourings, preservatives or gelling agents.

Functions of Food

After studying the components of a food, food technologists also need to understand how different foods **function**. An egg, for example, can be whisked to create a foam or used as a binding agent. It plays a significant role in the production of an emulsion and, when separated, its culinary possibilities are extended even further. When engineering new recipes to test, a food technologist must be aware of the way foods function both on their own and together with other ingredients.

Food Processing

Food as a material should not be studied in isolation; individual foods and the process of making food products are interlinked. These processes may be relatively simple such as the milling of wheat to produce flour, or highly complex such as creating a pizza that can be cooked in a toaster.

Developing new products today involves a lot of research, experimentation, testing and trialling. A small-scale recipe for a chicken korma cannot simply be multiplied up and used on a production line to create tens of thousands of meals! Large-scale machinery may affect food in a different way to a domestic cooker, causing meat to become tough or a sauce too runny. The changes that are needed may only be subtle but they can make the difference between a profitable new product and a costly failure.

Processing foods can also involve preserving them and the latest techniques include accelerated freeze-drying, irradiation and the production of dried fruits that do not require soaking. Some preservation methods stem from the past when people had to preserve foods in order to have sufficient food all year round. Fruits were turned into jam, onions were pickled and meats were cured. Processed food has changed dramatically as the needs of consumers have altered and as advances in food technology have occurred.

Food Safety

Food safety is not a new phenomenon but its emphasis has definitely changed. In the past a lack of knowledge caused problems such as sour milk or inedible meat and some unscrupulous food producers would add cheap ingredients to bulk out products like bread. However, today it is the scale of food production that has the potential to cause a food safety issue.

In 1990 a Food Safety Act was introduced that placed a much greater emphasis on temperature control, monitoring and the maintenance of records. 'Quality' is now a key word in the food industry and it has become everyone's responsibility. Total Quality Management is a system often employed to involve all workers in the quality assurance procedure. Food hygiene courses have also become highly popular with employers who want their staff to be fully informed about food safety.

Microwave food contamination test. French fries and hamburgers are cooked in a microwave oven during an experiment into the contamination of food by chemicals in its packaging. Once cooked the food is liquidised and the chemicals extracted using a solvent. Research has shown that designs that improve airflow through the package reduce food contamination.

Healthy foods

Since we now have such a wide choice of foods available to us in the western world, consumers have started to become concerned about the healthiness of those foods.

In 1998 the Government published *Saving Lives: Our Healthier Nation* which outlined ways in which the risk of diet-related diseases could be reduced or avoided.

Healthy eating has now become quite an issue with the British public and the food industry has had to respond accordingly with low-fat, low-sugar, low-salt and high-fibre versions of many foods. In addition, we have seen the advent of 'nutriceuticals' or functional foods which contain naturally occurring components with specific nutritional attributes. For example, some margarines now contain Omega 3 because these fatty acids from oily fish have been found to lower the risk of cardiovascular disease.

A Food Standards Agency was set up in April 2000. This is an independent agency run by people with expertise in food safety. It has the role of raising the standard of food in the UK, and exists to:

▷ provide advice and information to the public and to the Government on food safety from farm to fork, nutrition and diet

▷ protect consumers through effective enforcement and monitoring

▷ support consumer choice through promoting accurate and meaningful labelling.

Using ICT in Food Technology (1)

ICT (Information and Communication technology) is widely used in the food industry, as you will discover. You can considerably enhance your Food Technology GCSE coursework with the effective use of ICT.

Using ICT in your Work

To gain credit for using ICT you don't have to become a computer expert! What you do need to know is when best to use a computer to help with your work. Sometimes it is easier to use ICT to help with parts of your coursework than to do it another way, e.g. nutritional analysis. However, it is sometimes far easier to write some notes on a piece of paper than use a computer – this saves you time and helps you to do the job more effectively.

Following are some ideas showing you how using ICT could enhance your coursework. Some can be used at more than one stage. You do not have to use all the ideas – and you may have many more!

Identifying the Problem

The internet could be used to search food manufacturers and retailers web-sites for new food products – indicating new product trends. For example, **www.newfoods.com** searches for the latest food product launches in the UK.

Project Planning

A time chart can be produced showing the duration of the project and what you hope to achieve at each stage using a word processor or DTP program. Some programs allow you to produce a Gantt chart (See page 123).

Investigation

Information
The internet can be used to perform literature searches and communicate with other people around the world via e-mail.

Survey
A questionnaire can be produced using a word processor or DTP.

Presentation of research
Results from a survey can be presented using a spreadsheet as a variety of graphs and charts.

Product analysis
Food products can be analysed to gather information about their sensory qualities. This information can be used to present charts using a spreadsheet.

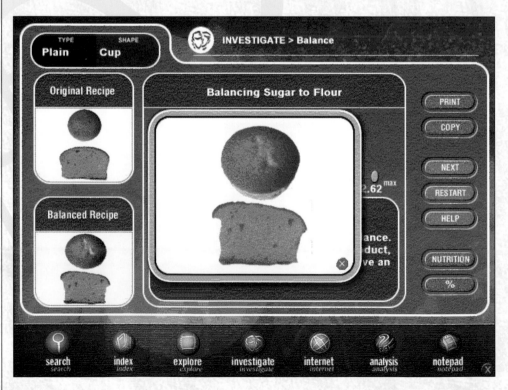

Specification

The specification can be written in a word processor. Visual images of the product, sensory diagram and other illustrations could also be added. Information can be easily modified at a later date.

Developing Initial Ideas

Physical design

Images of your product could be produced using a simple graphics program or a DTP package. New software from the food industry show you photographs of products you have designed before you make them.

Nutrition

Modelling of the energy and nutrients provided by the product can be tested and modified easily.

Cost

Likely costs of new products can be modelled using a spreadsheet. Different ingredient costs can be modelled quickly and easily allowing you to see the consequences of your design ideas.

	A	B	C
1	Cost		
2			
3	Ingredients	Weight (g)	Cost (£)
4	SR Flour	200	£0.11
5	Margarine	200	£0.25
6	Egg	200	£0.45
7	Caster Sugar	200	£0.32
8			
9		Total	£1.13
10			

Sensory

Diagrams showing the proposed sensory attributes for your product can be produced using a spreadsheet. These could be in the form of a radar or a pie-chart, depending on the type of test performed, e.g. preference or discrimination.

Planning and Testing

Sensory

A radar diagram can be used as a guide for testing prototype products.

Function

Digital scans of bakery products could be taken to analyse the effect of different ingredients in a product.

Datalogging

A temperature probe could be used to record the time taken to reduce the temperature of a cook-chill meal to safe levels.

Quality

Digital photographs could be taken for analysis, or used for quality comparison.

Final Ideas and Production

Final idea

A show report showing the specification, images, sensory attributes, production method and ingredients can be word-processed.

Production plan

A detailed flow diagram, including HACCP, could be produced using a DTP program. Images could also be added to show important stages, e.g. a critical control point.

Quality

Digital images from the testing stage can be used in the production plan as a guide to show how the product should be assembled or to indicate its colour.

CAM

Pre-programmed equipment could be used to replicate manufacture, e.g. bread machine.

Packaging

Packaging nets can be produces using graphics package or by using templates, e.g. **www.dtonline.org**. Scanned or digital photographs can then be placed within the templates to produce instant food packaging.

Evaluation

When undertaking a product analysis scanned images or digital photographs can be analysed and compared to your original specification. In addition, results from sensory evaluation could be presented.

ICT

Using ICT in Food Technology (2)

Using the internet and using CAD-CAM programs are two particularly appropriate uses of ICT in Food Technology.

Using the World Wide Web

The internet is a vast network of computers linked together around the globe. The World Wide Web is a series of documents that are linked together via the internet. Most people use the internet to access web-sites and to communicate via e-mail.

The number of web-sites is increasing everyday, providing a vast array of information as text, video, audio, illustrations and photographs. Web-site addresses for food manufacturers and retailers often appear in advertising and on packaging.

Although the internet can provide large amounts of information for coursework, you need to be selective and choose items that will help you with the task at hand – do not print out everything, be selective and summarise important points.

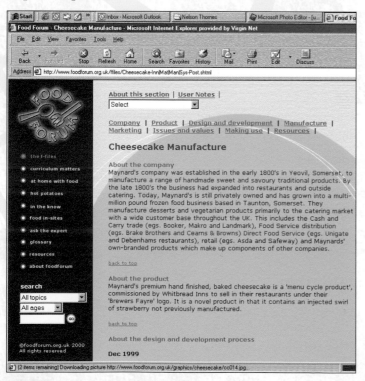

Here are the address of some web-sites that are particularly relevant to Food Technology:

➤ **www.nutrition.org.uk**
Information on food and nutrition – e.g., the dietary needs for a specific target group.

➤ **www.foodforum.org.uk**
Information on a variety of food technology topics – e.g. smart foods.

➤ **www.foodtech.org.uk**
Examine food functions, manufacturing and the use of ICT in industry – e.g. pasta manufacture.

➤ **www.newfoods.com**
Search for new food products being launched in the UK, e.g. new vegetarian products designed for children.

➤ **www.j-sainsbury.co.uk/partnerships/education**
Explore how products are development in the food industry – e.g. review the quality control procedures in place in the manufacture of a cook-chill product.

▷ If you use a web-site for your coursework, make sure that you record its name and the date you visited it.
▷ You need to check that the information you find is accurate and reliable.

ICT

Search engines

To help you find the information you need you can use a Search engine. A search engine is a web-site that allows you to type in a key word/s for a specific subject. It then scans the internet for web-sites that match what you are looking for. Here are the addresses of some popular search engines:

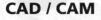

www.excite.co.uk
www.yahoo.co.uk
www.netscape.com
www.hotbot.co.uk
www.msn.co.uk
www.searchtheweb.com

E-mail

E-mail is a fast method of communicating with other people around the world. Text, photographs and computer files can be attached and shared. Some web-sites have e-mail addresses – you could try to contact experts to see if they could help with your coursework. It is important to be as specific as you possibly can, as these experts may be very busy people.

CAD / CAM

Computer Aided Design (CAD) and Computer Aided Manufacture (CAM) are terms used for a range of different ICT applications that are used to help in the process of designing and making products. CAD and CAM will help you enhance your coursework.

CAD is a computer aided system for creating, modifying and communicating a plan for a product or components of a product. In Food Technology CAD is used to:

▷ design the physical appearance of a product
▷ calculate the energy and nutrients provided by a product using nutritional analysis
▷ model the cost, or portion size, of a single or batch of products using a spreadsheet
▷ calculate expected shelf-life
▷ present sensory attribute data
▷ show the assembly procedure for a product
▷ produce packaging designs.

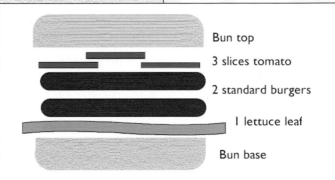

CAM is a broad term used when several manufacturing processes are carried out at one time aided by a computer. These may include process control, planning, monitoring and controlling production. For example, in Food Technology, CAM can be used to:

▷ monitor production of a process in relation to a specification, e.g. the temperature must be between 75°C and 80°C
▷ control changes to production in relation to the feedback from the monitoring, e.g. reduce or increase the heat to make sure it is between 75°C and 80°C.

In school you may be able to include the use of:

▷ flow-charting software to plan production, with Critical Control Points
▷ data-logging devices to record temperature, pH, etc
▷ pre-programmed equipment to manufacture products, e.g. bread-maker, microwave oven, ice-cream machine
▷ electronic scales for accuracy in weight tolerances.

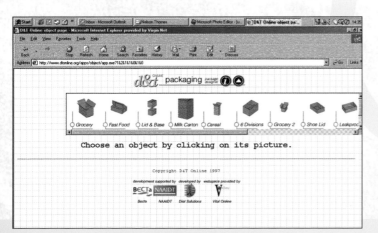

Choosing and Starting Projects

Identifying suitable design and make projects for yourself is not easy. A carefully chosen project is much more likely to be interesting and easier to complete successfully. Investing time and effort choosing a good project makes progress a lot easier later on.

Project Feasibility Studies

Possible projects

Make a start by making a list of:

▷ local food manufacturers, food retailers and catering outlets you could visit to do some research into the sort of new food products which customers are looking for

▷ people you know outside school who might be able to help by providing information, access and/or advice.

The next stage is to get up and get going. Arrange to visit some of the places you've listed. Choose the sorts of food products which you would be interested in finding out some more about. Make contact with the people you know, and get them interested in helping you. Tell them about your D&T course, and your project.

Alternatively, you could use the internet to search food manufacturers' and retailers' web-sites for new food products. Try using **www.newfoods.com** to search for the latest products in the UK.

With a bit of luck, after you've done the above you should have a number of ideas for possible projects.

starting points

There are different ways in which you might start a project. Your teacher may have:

● told you exactly what you are required to design
● given you a range of possible design tasks for you to choose from
● left it up to you to suggest a possible project.

If you have been given a specific task to complete you can go straight on to page 16.

If you are about to follow one of the main units in this book, you should go straight to the first page of the task.

If you have been given a number of possible tasks to choose from you should go straight to the section on page 15 entitled 'Making your Choice'.

However, if you need to begin by making some decisions about which will be best task for you, then the first stage is to undertake some project feasibility studies as described on this page.

Final outcomes

Try to identify what the possible outcomes of your projects might be – not what the final food product would be like, but the form your final realisation might take, such as a batch of bread products or a range of cook-chill cold desserts. Think carefully about the following:

▷ Might it be expensive or difficult to make in school?
▷ Do you have access to the equipment and food items which would be required?
▷ Will you be able to find out how the food product could be processed and manufactured?
▷ Does the success of the project depend on important information you might not be able to get in the time available?
▷ Are there good opportunities for you to use your ICT skills effectively?

Making your Choice

For each of your possible projects work through pages 16 and 17 (Project Investigation) and list your starting questions and sources of information.

Look back over your starting questions and sources of information, and consider:

▷ Could you think of only one or two areas for further research?
▷ Did you find it difficult identifying a range of sources of information?

If this has been the case, then maybe it is not going to prove to be a very worthwhile project.

Ideally, what you're looking for is a project which:

▷ is for a nearby situation you can easily use for research and testing
▷ you can get some good expert advice about
▷ provides good opportunities for you to do a range of research activities
▷ show a good use of ICT
▷ has an outcome which will make it possible for you to make and test a prototype food product
▷ will not be too difficult finally to produce
▷ is suitable for manufacture.

Finally, one of the most important things is that you feel interested and enthusiastic about the project!

don't forget...

A very important consideration is the testing of a prototype of some sort, and of your final design. How would you be able to do this? Could ICT be used?

Remember it's important that what you design is suitable for production. It can't be just a one-off food product. You will need to show some plans for your product to be factory made.

Don't forget to record all your thoughts and ideas about these initial stages of choosing and starting your project.

In your project folio provide a full record of the ideas you reject, and the reasons why. This helps provide important evidence of your decision-making skills, and of the originality of your project.

If you come up with more than one good idea, find out how many projects you have to submit at the end of your course. You might be able to do one or more of your other ideas at a later date.

Make sure you discuss your project ideas with a teacher.

in my design folder

✓ My project is to design a...
✓ I am particularly interested in...
✓ I have made a very good contact with...
✓ My prototype can be tested by...
✓ My final outcome will include...
✓ I can use ICT to...

Project Investigation

You will need to find out as much as you can about the people and the situation you are designing for. To do this you will need to identify a number of different sources of information into which you could research.

Starting Questions

Make a list of questions you will have to find answers to.

You should find the following prompts useful:

Why...?
Where...?
How many...?
How much...?
When...?
What...?
How often...?

- Who is the product aimed at?
- What are their likes and dislikes?
- How much could it cost?
- Where could it be sold?
- How could it be manufactured in quantity?
- How could the existing range be extended?

Sources of Information

Next, carefully consider and write down potential sources of information you might be able to use to discover the answers to your starting questions.

Work through the research methods on the opposite page. Be sure to give specific answers as far as possible (i.e. name names!).

Across your research, aim to obtain overall a mixture of:

▷ factual information: e.g. size, shape, weight, cost, nutrition
▷ information which will be a matter of opinion: e.g. what people think and feel about what they eat and where and how they eat it, what are their likes and dislikes, what they find important, pleasing, annoying, etc.

don't forget...

Write down what you need to find out more about, and how you could obtain the information.

Make sure your research work is clearly and attractively presented.

The more you plan your research, the more different methods of research you use (such as product appraisal, surveys, literature search, internet, CD-ROM, etc), and the more detail you discover, the more marks you will get.

in my design folder

✓ The key things I need to find out about are...
✓ The research methods I am going to use are...
✓ I will be talking to the following people about my project...
✓ I will need to have it all completed by...

Research Methods

User-research
Which people could you observe and talk to who are potential customers? Do you think you will be able to find out about:

- the type of foods they like and dislike?
- the textures, colours and flavours they look for?
- how they like them to be prepared?
- where and when they like to eat?
- where and when they shop for food?

Shop-keepers and serving staff might provide some useful information about which products sell quickest, and the things customers most often ask about.

As well as asking individuals, you could also undertake a small survey or questionnaire.

Existing solutions
Are there any similar existing solutions you could evaluate? You could comment on their:

- taste
- appearance
- texture
- nutritional value
- cost
- packaging
- production methods.

As well as your opinions, maybe you could set up a 'taste-testing' panel (see page 112)?

Expert opinion
Are there any people you know of who could give you 'expert' professional advice on any aspects of the project? If you don't know immediately of anyone, how might you set about finding somebody?

Information search
Has any information about the food product, or a similar product, been documented already in books, magazines, TV programmes, on the internet or CD-ROMs, etc? You might be able to discover things like:

- market size and trends
- social and cultural factors
- dietary requirements
- source and availability of ingredients
- industrial processing and production methods
- health and safety requirements.

If you don't already know that such information exists, where could you go to look for it? Don't forget to consider the possibility of using information stored on a computer database.

In Conclusion

When most of your investigation work has been completed you will need to draw a series of conclusions from what you have discovered. What have you learnt about the following things:

▷ What sort of people are likely to buy the product?
▷ Where and when will they eat it?
▷ What particular ingredients and qualities will it need to have?
▷ What quantity should be made?

Of all the research methods, user-research tends to be the most effective and useful, so you are highly recommended to include some in your investigation. Some form of personal contact is essential to a really successful project.

It is also highly advisable to conduct some form of questionnaire. If you have not done one to submit as part of your coursework, make sure that you will have the opportunity to do so this time.

It isn't necessary to use all the research methods in any one project, but you certainly must show that you have tried a selection of them.

in my design folder

✓ From my research I discovered that...
✓ I kept my research relevant by...
✓ ICT helped me to...
✓ I concluded that...

Design and Product Specification

A design specification is a series of statements which describe the possibilities and restrictions of the product. A product specification includes details about the features and appearance of the final design, together with its ingredients, manufacturing processes and quantities.

Writing a Design Specification

The **design specification** is a very important document. It describes the things about the design which are fixed and also defines the things which you are free to change.

Your research conclusions should form the starting point for your design specification. For example, if you wrote in your conclusions:

'From my survey of finishes for biscuits I discovered that 80% of people preferred chocolate coating.'

In the specification you would simply write:

'The biscuits should be chocolate coated'.

The contents of the specification will vary according to the particular product you are designing, but on the opposite page is a checklist of aspects to consider. Don't be surprised if the specification is quite lengthy. It could easily contain 20 or more statements.

Fixing It

Some statements in the specification will be very specific. For example, *'The snack bar must have a raspberry flavour'*

Other statements may be very open-ended. For example, *'The snack bar can be any shape or size.'*

Most will come somewhere in between. For example, *'It should be have a high fibre content and a long shelf-life.'*

In this way the statements make it clear what is already fixed (e.g. the flavour), and what development is required through experimentation, testing, and modification (e.g. shape, size, fibre content and shelf-life.

Writing a Product Specification

After you have fully developed your food product you will need to write a final more detailed **product specification**. (see also page 46). This time the precise statements about the ingredients, quantities and processes will help ensure that the manufacturer is able to make a repeatable, consistent product.

Your final food product will need to be evaluated against your design specification to see how closely you have been able to meet its requirements, and against your product specification to see if you have made it correctly.

don't forget...

Make sure you include as much numerical data as possible in your specifications. Try to provide data for anything which can be measured, such as size, weight, quantity, time and temperature.

After you've written the design specification, new information may come to light. If it will improve the final product, you can always change any of the statements.

You might find it helpful to start to rough out the design specification first, and then tackle the conclusions to your research. Working backwards, a sentence in your conclusion might need to read:

'From my survey, I discovered that young children are particularly attracted by food made in animal shapes.'

Specification Checklist

The following checklist is for general guidance. Not all topics will apply to your project. You may need to explore some of these topics further during your product development.

Use and performance

Write down the main purpose of the product – what it is intended to do. Also define any other particular requirements, such as time to make, special features, nutritional profile, cost, etc.

Size and weight

The minimum and maximum size and weight will be influenced by things like the ingredients needed and the situations in which the product will be used, kept and served.

Generally the smaller something is, the less ingredients it will use, reducing the production costs. Smaller items can be more difficult to make, however, increasing the production costs.

Appearance

What shapes, colours and textures will be most suitable for the type of person who is likely to buy and eat the product? Remember that different people like different things.

These decisions will have an important influence on the ingredients and manufacturing processes, and are also crucial to ensure final sales.

Safety

A product needs to conform to all the relevant safety standards.

- What warning instructions and labels need to be provided?
- What Hazard Analysis and Critical Control Point (HACCP) procedures will be needed?

Conforming to the regulations can increase production costs significantly, but is an area that cannot be compromised.

Shelf-life

Preservatives are needed to increase shelf-life. However, many consumers prefer additive-free products.

- How does your food product need to be maintained in good quality?
- What are the acceptable food safety risks?

Manufacturing cost

This is concerned with establishing the maximum total manufacturing cost which will allow the product to be sold at a price the consumer or client is likely to pay.

The specification needs to include details of:

- the total number of products likely to be made
- the rate of production
- the size of batches (if appropriate).

Economic considerations

To keep manufacturing costs to a minimum, you may need to specify the use of low-cost ingredients or processing methods.

Environmental requirements

In your specification you will need to take into account how your product and its packaging can be made in the most environmentally friendly way.

Packaging

Food packaging is an essential part of the product. You will need to prepare a separate specification for the packaging. It will need to cover type, size, shape, materials, labelling, etc.

Making the packaging environmentally friendly is important.

You might decide to:

- specify maximum amounts of packaging materials
- avoid a particular material because it can't easily be recycled.
- state the use of a specific printing or packaging process because it consumes less energy.

in my design folder

✓ The people who my product is aimed are...
✓ Their particular needs are...
✓ The nutritional requirements are...
✓ The ingredients should include...
✓ The portion size will need to be...

✓ The shape, colours and textures should...
✓ The following health and safety considerations are essential...
✓ The packaging will need to...

Generating and Developing Ideas

When you start designing you need lots of ideas – as many as possible, however crazy they might seem. Then you need to narrow things down a bit by working in more detail and evaluating what you are doing.

Work towards making a sample to test some specific features of your design. Record the results and continue to refine your ideas as much as you can. Sorting out the final details often requires lots of ideas too.

First Thoughts

Start by exploring possibilities at a very general level. Spend time doing some of the following:

▷ brainstorming, using key words and phrases or questions which relate to the problem

▷ completing spider-diagrams which map out a series of ideas

▷ using random word- or object-association to spark off new directions

▷ thinking up some good analogies to the situation (i.e. What is it like?)

▷ working from an existing food product by changing some of its ingredients and mixing methods

▷ experimenting with some ingredients.

Continue doing this until you have at least three possible approaches to consider. Make sure they are all completely different, and not just a variation on one idea.

Go back to your design specification. Which of your approaches are closest to the statements you made? Make a decision about which idea to take further, and write down the reasons for your choice.

As you work through this section it is important to remember the following sequence when considering potential solutions:

● record a number of different possibilities

● consider and evaluate each idea

● select one approach as the best course of action, stating why.

There are lots of different visual techniques which you can use to help you explore and develop your ideas, such as spider-diagrams, sketches, graphs and tables. Try to use as rich a mixture of them as possible.

don't forget...

As usual, it is essential to record all your ideas and thoughts.

Much of your work, particularly early on, will be in the form of notes. These need to be neat enough for the examiner to be able to read.

Remember to record your ideas, experiments and conclusions. Try to include notes, graphs and tables, test results, flow-diagrams, production plans and photographs. These could be simply recorded on paper, or on a computer using a word processor or spreadsheet.

As you develop your ideas, make sure you are considering the following:
- Design – flavour, texture, colour, shape, smell, etc.
- Dietary requirements
- Viability – if it could be made
- Manufacturing potential – how it could be made economically in quantity
- Health and Safety concerns – how can risk be minimised?

Second Thoughts

Begin to develop your ideas in more detail. Think about and experiment by adapting the ingredients, volumes and method of making for existing recipies. Make sure you keep the initial design specification in mind. Remember who your target group is, and what their particular tastes and dietary needs are.

Wherever possible consider using a computer to experiment with your ideas and analyse and display your and findings. Keep a print-out and keep a copy on a disk of what you do.

Planning the Testing

You will need to experiment with different parts of your product, e.g. the pastry base, the fillings or sauce, the toppings, etc.

At some stage you will be in a position to make some sample (or prototype) products to test. Think carefully about what aspect of your product you want to test. It might be:

▷ volume: does the raising agent work?
▷ shape: have the right ingredients and cooking methods been used?
▷ flavour: does it taste the way it should?
▷ colour: does it look the way it should?
▷ palatability: does it have the right texture?
▷ costing: could cheaper ingredients be used?

Which test methods will be most appropriate? You might decide to plan a sensory evaluation session and/or a 'fair test' with a control sample to measure against. People's opinions can be helpful, but you can't rely on them.

Afterwards you need to write up:

▷ what you wanted to test
▷ how you carried out the test
▷ what the results of the test were
▷ how you intend to develop your product as a result.

Following your first prototype, you may decide to modify it in some way and test it again, or maybe make a second, improved version. Make sure you keep details about all the prototypes you make, and ideally take photographs of them being tested, perhaps using a digital camera.

Sometimes you will need to go back to review the decisions you made earlier, and on other occasions you may need to jump ahead for a while to explore new directions or to focus on a particular detail. Make sure you have worked at both a general and a detailed level.

At some stage you will need to try some things out using actual ingredients.

in my design folder

✓ I got my ideas from...
✓ I chose these ideas because...
✓ I developed my design by...
✓ I made prototypes by...
✓ I tested my prototypes by...
✓ From my tests I discovered...

Planning the Making and the Manufacturing

The final realisation is very important. It presents your proposed design solution. Careful planning is essential.

You will also need to be able to explain how your product could be reproduced or manufactured in quantity.

How many?

What you have designed should be suitable for manufacture. You should discuss with your teacher how many products you should attempt to make. This is likely to depend on the complexity of your design, the cost of ingredients and the equipment available for you to use. It may be that you only make one item, but also provide a clear account of how a larger quantity of them could be manufactured.

keeping a record

Write up a diary record of the progress you made while making. Try to include references to:

- things you did to ensure safety
- the appropriate use of materials
- minimising wastage
- choosing tools
- practising making first
- checking that what you are making is accurate enough to work
- asking experts (including teachers) for advice explaining why you had to change your original plan for making.

A Plan of Action

Before you start planning you will need to ensure that you have a detailed specification for your product. This should include full details about how it will be made. These should be clear enough to enable someone else to make the product from your specification.

Next work out a production flow-chart as follows.

1   List the order in which you will prepare the final product. Include as much detail as you can (see page 52).

2   Divide the list up into a number of main stages, e.g. initial preparation of ingredients (peeling, chopping, stewing), processes and methods used (saucemaking, rubbing in, creaming), assembling (putting in filling, adding pasta to sauce) and finishing (brushing with milk, applying patterns).

3   Identify operations which might be done in parallel. For example, a simmering sauce may be left but stirred occasionally while bread is being made into breadcrumbs in a processor.

4   Work out how long each stage will take and show how the timings will fit into the time you have available.

Time can be saved by making good use of tools and equipment. There may be occasions when it is suitable to use components that have been previously frozen or stored.

Quality Counts

As your making proceeds you will need to check frequently that your work is of acceptable quality.

How accurately will you need to work? What tolerances will be acceptable (see page 60)? How can you judge the quality of the finish?

don't forget...

You may find you have to change your plans as you go. There is nothing wrong with doing this, but you should explain why you have had to adjust your schedule, and show that you have considered the likely effect of the later stages of production.

If you are making a number of identical items you should try to work out ways of checking the quality through a sampling process.

Making It!

While you are in the process of making you must ensure that you use equipment correctly and that you work safely and hygienically. Pay particular attention to safety instructions and guidelines.

Try to ensure that you have a finished item at the end. If necessary you may need to develop and practise certain skills beforehand in order to produce a quality end-product.

Keeping a Record

Write up a diary record of the progress you made while making. Try to include references to:
▷ things you did to ensure safety and hygiene
▷ the appropriate use of ingredients
▷ minimising waste
▷ choosing tools and equipment
▷ practising making first
▷ checking that what you are making is accurate enough to be successful
▷ asking experts (including teachers) for advice
▷ why you had to change your original plan for making.

You could use a digital camera to show changes to your product.

Planning for Manufacture

Remember you may use diagrams to help plan and explain your production method. You can draw these using a graphics program.

What needs to be done by:
next month
next week
next lesson
the end of this lesson?

Manufacturing matters

Try asking the following questions about the way your product might be made in quantity:

- What process is being carried out, and why?
- Are there any alternatives?
- Where is the process carried out, and why?
- When is it carried out and why?
- Who carries it out, and why?
- How is it undertaken, and why?

Remember that manufacturing is not just about making things. It is also about making them better by making them:

- simpler
- quicker
- cheaper
- more efficient
- less damaging to the environment.

You should try to explain how your product would be manufactured in quantity. Work through the following stages of planning for production:

1 Break up the production process into its main parts.
2 Organise the parts into a logical order to produce a production line flow-chart.
3 Specify each stage of the production line clearly. Make sure each stage leads straight into the next.
4 Identify any standard components which will need to be bought in ready-made from outside suppliers.
5 Design the production line, including details of the various manufacturing processes. Make clear where and when different ingredients or components are introduced.
6 Decide how the workforce and workspace should be arranged for maximum efficiency.
7 Decide how and when quality control systems will be applied.
8 Identify hygiene and safety issues, and apply HACCP procedures to exclude or minimise risks.
9 Calculate the manufacturing costs of the product.
10 Review the design of the product and how it is made to see how quality could be improved and costs could be reduced.

in my design folder

✓ I planned the following sequence of making...
✓ I had to change my plan to account for...
✓ I used the following equipment and processes...
✓ I paid particular attention to safety by...
✓ I paid particular attention to hygiene by...
✓ I worked to the following tolerances...
✓ I monitored the quality of my product by...
✓ The way my product could be manufactured in quantity is...

Testing and Evaluation

You will need to find out how successful your final solution is. How well does it match the design specification? How well have you worked? What would you do differently, if you had another chance?

Testing the Final Solution

To find out how successful your design is you will need to test it out. Some of the ways in which you might do this are by:

▷ trying it out yourself
▷ asking other people to use it
▷ asking experts what they think about it.

Sensory evaluation will form an important part of this process. Use techniques such as triangle tests, paired comparison or rating tests to collect information about:

▷ taste
▷ appearance
▷ texture
▷ aroma.

To help you decide what to test, you should look back to the statements in your brief, and focus on the most important ones. If for example it stated that the product should be a main meal for two adults that can be re-heated in a microwave, then you will need to provide evidence to show that it does so. Make sure you use your target consumer group when carrying out the tests. Include as much information and detail as you can.

A food additives researcher tasting naturally-occurring chemicals from food by brushing them onto her tongue. The test is compared to the flavour of the original food to see if it is one that contributes to the flavour. Of the hundreds of chemicals that can be extracted from food, only a few are responsible for its taste. Those chemicals that make up a component of the flavour can be manufactured to make artificial flavours to be added to food.

don't forget...

Don't be too surprised or worried if your design isn't perfect – the important thing is that you can identify what needs improving. Can you make some simple suggestions about how it might be improved?

Final Evaluation

There are two things you need to discuss in the final evaluation: the quality of the **product** you have designed and made, and the **process** you went through while designing and making it.

The product

How successful is your final product? Comment on things like:

▷ how it compares with your original intentions
▷ how well solves the original problem
▷ the function, nutrition and price of the ingredients you used
▷ the results of sensory evaluation
▷ your suggestions for packaging
▷ what a potential consumer said
▷ what experts said
▷ whether it could be manufactured cheaply enough in quantity to allow profit
▷ the ways in which it could be improved
▷ the controls used to ensure a quality product
▷ the use of ICT to assist manufacture.

Justify your evaluation by including references to what happened when you tested it.

If you had more time, what aspects of the product would you try to improve?

The process

How well have you worked? Imagine you suddenly had more time, or were able to start again, and consider:

▷ Which aspects of your investigation, design development work and making would you try to improve, or approach in a different way?
▷ What did you leave to the last minute, or spend too much time on?
▷ Which parts are you most pleased with, and why?
▷ How well did you make the final realisation?
▷ How effective was your use of ICT? How did it enhance your work?

in my design folder

✓ Comparison of my final product specification with my design specification showed...
✓ The people I showed my ideas (drawings and final product) to said...
✓ I was able to try my product out by...
✓ I discovered that...
✓ I could improve it by...
✓ I didn't do enough research into...
✓ I spent too long on...
✓ I should have spent more time on...
✓ The best aspect is...
✓ I have learnt a lot about...
✓ ICT helped me to...

Try to identify a mixture of good and bad points about your final proposal and method of working. You will gain credit for being able to demonstrate that you are aware of weaknesses in what you have designed and the way that you have designed it.

If people have been critical of aspects of your design, do you agree with them? Explain your response.

Don't forget to write about both the product and the process.

Project Presentation

The way you present your project work is extremely important. Remember you won't be there to explain it all when it's being assessed! You need to make it as easy as possible for an examiner to see concise and understand what you have done.

Telling the Story

All your investigation and development work needs to be handed in at the end, as well as what you have made. Your design folder needs to tell the story of the project. Each section should lead on from the next, clearly show what happened, and explain why. Section titles and individual page titles can help considerably.

There is no single way in which you must present your work, but the following suggestions are all highly recommended.

▷ Securely bind all the pages together in some way. Use staples or treasury tags. There is no need to buy an expensive folder.
▷ Add a cover with a title and an appropriate illustration.
▷ Make it clear which are the main sections.
▷ Add in titles or running headings to each sheet to indicate what aspect of the design you were considering at that particular point in the project.
▷ Remember to include evidence of ICT work and other Key Skills. Carefully check through your folder and correct any spelling and pronunciation mistakes.

Presenting your Design Folder Sheets

▷ Always work on standard size paper, either A3 or A4.

▷ Aim to have a good mixture of text and visual images. These could be produced by hand, or on a computer.

▷ You might like to design a special border to use on each sheet.

▷ Include as many different types of graphs, tables, charts and diagrams as possible, preferably using a graphics or spreadsheet program.

▷ When including photographs, use a small amount of adhesive applied evenly all the way around the edge to secure them to your folder sheet.

▷ Think carefully about the lettering for titles, and don't just put them anywhere and anyhow. Try to choose a height and width of lettering which will be well balanced on the whole page. If the title is too big or boldly coloured it may dominate the sheet. If it is thin or light it might not be noticed.

don't forget...

Presentation is something you need to be thinking about throughout your project work.

Make sure you have at least one sheet which covers each of the following headings:

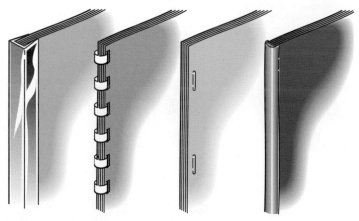

Binding methods

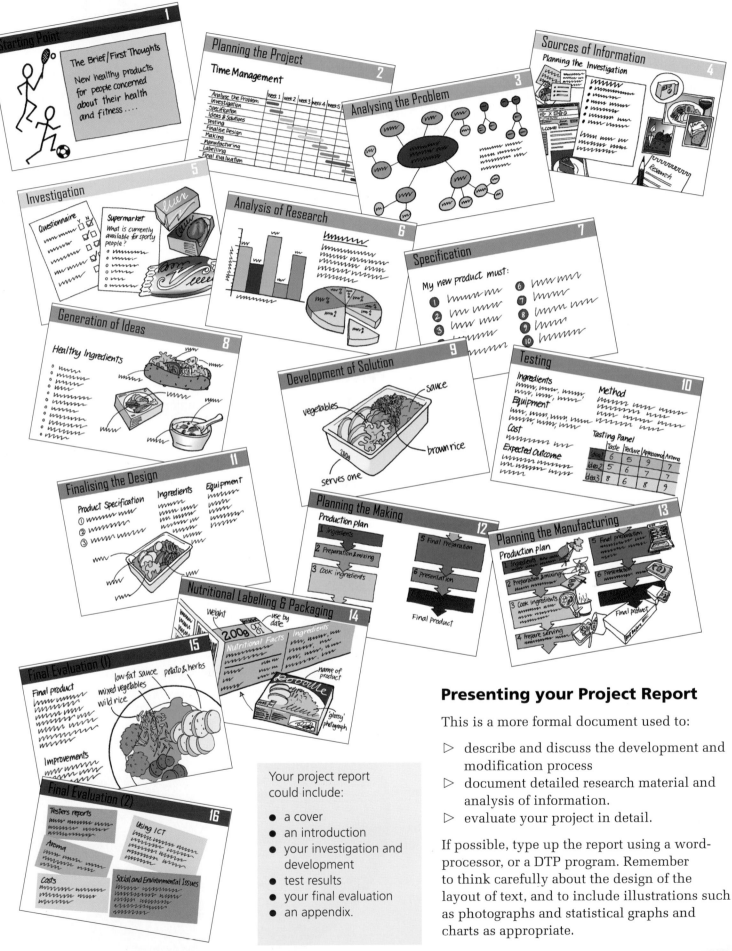

Presenting your Project Report

This is a more formal document used to:

▷ describe and discuss the development and modification process

▷ document detailed research material and analysis of information.

▷ evaluate your project in detail.

If possible, type up the report using a word-processor, or a DTP program. Remember to think carefully about the design of the layout of text, and to include illustrations such as photographs and statistical graphs and charts as appropriate.

Your project report could include:

● a cover
● an introduction
● your investigation and development
● test results
● your final evaluation
● an appendix.

27

Unit One: Introduction

Not so long ago, most of the food we ate was produced locally. There wasn't a lot of choice: many items were available only at certain times of the year, and they didn't keep fresh for very long. Modern food technology has changed all this.

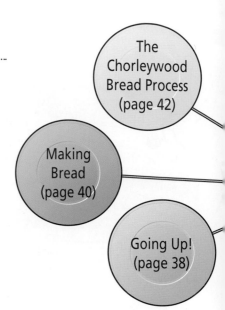

The Chorleywood Bread Process (page 42)

Making Bread (page 40)

Going Up! (page 38)

Introduction

Today we can buy produce from around the world, throughout the year. Thanks to preservatives, packaging and refrigeration, we can also keep it for months.

Food technologists are not just good cooks. They need to be able to identify exactly:

▷ what food products people want
▷ where, when and how they want to buy, prepare and eat these food products
▷ whether the food products can be produced and sold at a price the customer will pay
▷ how many products to produce and over what period of time.

Most of the food we eat has gone through a manufacturing process. The food industry in Britain has a gross output of £42.4 billion and contributes 13.1% of the total manufacturing industry.

The advantages of having processed food products are:

▷ food can be transported to areas of concentrated population
▷ a wider variety of food products is available at different times of the year
▷ increased choice is available to specific dietary groups
▷ food can be distributed to areas of need, so reducing food shortage
▷ worldwide transportation of food is possible, giving greater consumer choice and availability throughout the year
▷ new food products can be created from a wide variety of raw materials, again giving greater choice to the consumer.

Preparing for the Task

Read through the task below. Before you can start to develop and finalise your ideas however, you will need to work through the sections which make up this unit. See the diagram above.

You will also need to refer to the Project Guide at the start of the book.

'Here at Bakewell Bread we concentrate on making standard white and brown sliced loaves.

However, there are signs that sales of these products are beginning to decrease. We would therefore like to develop a range of bread-based products which will appeal to people who are interested in buying bread products that would normally be found in different parts of the world.

We would like to ask you to advise us on:
• what different international bread products we might consider baking, and where they could be sold
• the nutritional profile for one of these products
• how we might organise the production in batches.'

28

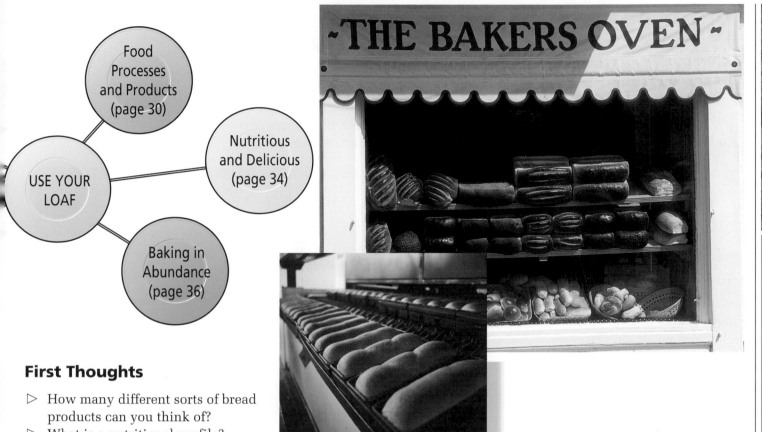

Food Processes and Products (page 30)

Nutritious and Delicious (page 34)

USE YOUR LOAF

Baking in Abundance (page 36)

First Thoughts

▷ How many different sorts of bread products can you think of?
▷ What is a nutritional profile?
▷ What are the main ingredients of bread?
▷ How much do you know about how bread is manufactured?
▷ How is a production line system organised?
▷ How can the quality of a food product be guaranteed?

Getting Started

Before you can begin to make decisions about the sort of bread product you will recommend to Bakewell Bread, you will need to learn a great deal more about how bread is made and manufactured. Most of the information you need is on the following pages.

To begin with you should learn how raw foods are processed, and consider how a single raw food can be used to create a variety of food products.

The **nutritional profile** of a food product is very important to ensure it meets the dietary needs of the consumer.

After finding out about the consumption of bread products, you will need to know more about their ingredients and how they are made, both traditionally and using industrial processes.

Finally you will need to know something about quality control systems, and how production lines are planned.

Developing your Ideas

Start by coming up with ideas for a range of bread products from other countries. Then you must decide which product to develop, and experiment with its ingredients and the baking process. Remember that it will be made on a production line system.

Planning and Making It!

Plan the production of a sample batch of your product to take to Bakewell Breads. You will need to provide precise and clear recommendations about the ingredients and their quantities, as well as baking times and temperatures.

Final Testing and Evaluation

To judge the success of your product you could compare it with a similar bread product currently on sale. Comment on the taste, texture and appearance.

You will also need to say something about how well you have worked through the task. What have you learnt? What skills have you developed? Where have you made most progress?

Food Processes and Products (1)

Raw foods are processed to provide a range of ingredients which can be used in different ways. Food processing involves changing the raw food to a form suitable for eating.

Primary and Secondary Sources

The raw food material which will become the ingredient is known as the **primary source** (e.g. wheatgrain, milk). The processed ingredients are described as the **secondary source** (e.g. flour, cheese).

■ ACTIVITY

Study the chart below.
▶ Make a list of other raw foods which are processed to provide a wider range of ingredients or food products.
▶ Choose one food from your list. Research the stages of processing from its raw state to processed secondary source.
▶ Draw a flow chart to show the stages you have identified. You could use a word-processor or DTP program.
▶ Give examples of how the secondary source product would then be used.

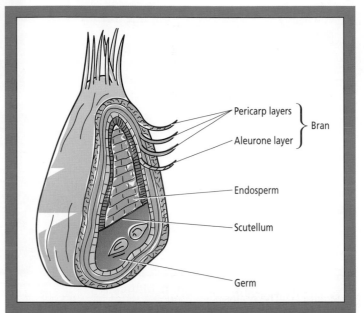

Wheat grains
The first farmers found that cereal crops stored fairly well. They could use these edible grains in many ways with some simple processing methods. The original way of grinding grains was between stones. Today the milling of cereals is a large-scale manufacturing process.

Collection/harvesting of raw food

Conversion of raw food into processed food ingredient

Combination of ingredients into manufactured food product

Raw foods		Food ingredients		Food products
Wheat grain	→	Flour	→	Pasta
Wheat grain	→	Flour	→	Bread/cakes
Sugar beet	→	Sugar	→	Caramel/toffees
Fruit	→	Jam	→	Jam tarts
Milk	→	Butter	→	Butter icing

The Milling Process

1 **Cleaning**: Wheat is sieved, scoured (rubbed clean) and passed through air currents to remove unwanted parts before washing in sterile water.

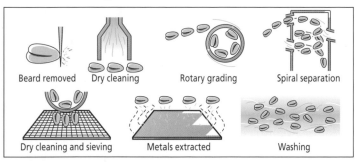

Beard removed   Dry cleaning   Rotary grading   Spiral separation

Dry cleaning and sieving   Metals extracted   Washing

2 **Conditioning**: Wheat is dried or moistened to make it just right for milling.

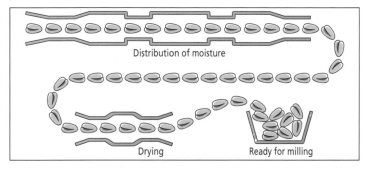

Distribution of moisture

Drying   Ready for milling

3 **Milling** (1): The grains pass through a series of rollers and sieves. The first are grooved rollers, called break rollers. They tear open the grain. The endosperm is then scraped from the bran and graded (sorted) by size.

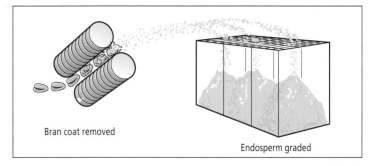

Bran coat removed

Endosperm graded

4 **Milling** (2): The graded endosperm is ground by 'reducing rollers' to make the particles smaller. Twelve sets of rollers may be needed to produce the fine white granular flour which accounts for about 75 per cent of all flour used.

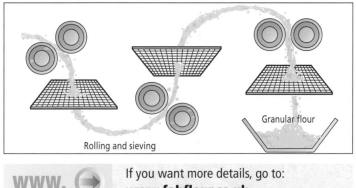

Rolling and sieving

Granular flour

WWW. ➡ If you want more details, go to:
www.fabflour.co.uk

5 **Mixing**: Computerised weighers deliver precise quantities of plain flour and ingredients to a mixer to make self-raising flour.

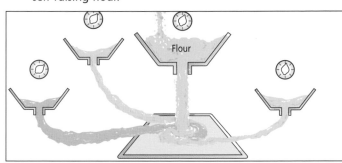

Flour

6 **Sterilising and packaging**: The flour is sieved again and sterilised before packing. Computerised control systems enable the bag to be opened, filled with the correct weight of flour, and be sealed automatically.

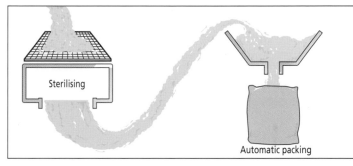

Sterilising

Automatic packing

7 **Delivery**: Milled flour is delivered to retailers to sell as flour, and to food manufacturers to make cakes, bread, biscuits, etc.

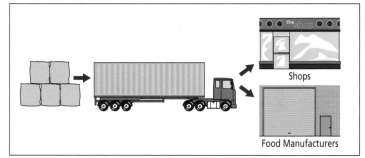

Shops

Food Manufacturers

IN YOUR PROJECT

- ▶ Are your ingredients primary or secondary source foods?
- ▶ Which primary foods have been used to produce the ingredients you will be using?
- ▶ Investigate the stages of processing one of your ingredients has been through.

KEY POINTS

- ● Raw food material is known as the primary source.
- ● Processed ingredients are known as the secondary source.
- ● Food processing leads to a wider range of food products being available to the consumer.

USE YOUR LOAF

manufacturing in quantity

31

Food Processes and Products (2)

Amazing Maize

Maize is a single raw food **commodity** which can be processed to make a wide range of different ingredients and food products. It is one of many cereals that are grown for their nutritious edible seeds.

Seventy per cent of the world's maize is grown in the USA, although it is also grown in South America and parts of Europe. Maize produces a bigger crop than wheat or rice. It can be transported cheaply and easily without going off, if it is kept in the right dry conditions.

From maize to corn oil

The maize seeds are cleaned to remove dirt and impurities. They are crushed between rollers, heated and then squeezed to release the oil. The oily mixture is filtered to remove the remains of the seeds. The oil is refined to remove acids, lighten the colour and improve the taste and smell.

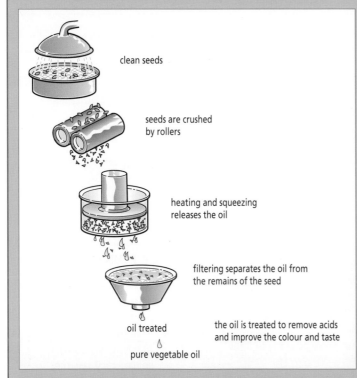

clean seeds

seeds are crushed by rollers

heating and squeezing releases the oil

filtering separates the oil from the remains of the seed

oil treated

the oil is treated to remove acids and improve the colour and taste

pure vegetable oil

Maize or corn oil is particularly suitable for frying as it can be heated to a high temperature before it starts to decompose (break down). It is cheap to produce and has a deep golden, yellow colour. It has quite a strong flavour, making it unsuitable for salad dressings or mayonnaise.

From maize to cornflour

Maize kernels are milled using the same process as the milling of wheat outlined on page 31. This produces a fine white powder which is almost 100 per cent starch.

Cornflour is used to thicken liquids such as sauces. It can also be added to recipes containing wheat flour, such as shortbread. It is not suitable to use when making cakes, biscuits or pastry because it doesn't contain enough of the sticky protein called gluten.

From maize to sweetcorn

Maize is eaten as a vegetable either as corn on the cob or as sweetcorn. It is high in carbohydrate, and contains some protein, dietary fibre, mineral elements, vitamins A, C and some of the B group vitamins.

From maize to popcorn

Popcorn is produced from a variety of maize which has small cobs of hard corn. The corn is placed in a covered pan and heated. The moisture and air inside the corn kernels expand as they are heated and steam is formed. This causes the kernel to explode and turn inside out, with the white starch part on the outside. It can have salt or sugar added or it can be rolled in butter or syrup. It is usually eaten as a snack.

From maize to corn syrup

This all-purpose syrup is produced from corn starch. It is available as light or dark syrup, the dark syrup having a stronger flavour. It can be used as a table syrup, or for baking.

Corn syrup is used commercially to sweeten frozen desserts and preserves. It gives ice cream a smooth texture and makes jam and jellies clear.

■ ACTIVITIES

1. Using food tables or a nutritional analysis program, compare the nutritional value of corn oil with other oils, such as olive oil and sunflower oil.

▶ What are its nutritional advantages and disadvantages?

2. Carry out an investigation to show the function or role of cornflour in a baked food product. Work in groups and use a biscuit recipe of your choice.

▶ Replace different amounts of wheat flour with cornflour, to achieve a crumblier consistency.

▶ Compare the taste, texture and appearance of the biscuits you produce, using a suitable sensory evaluation test (see page 114). Which ratio of cornflour to wheat flour produces the best results?

IN YOUR PROJECT

▶ What range of ingredients and products can be made from the main food commodity you are using?

KEY POINTS

● A wide range of ingredients and food products are made from maize.
● Maize is a single commodity and a primary source food.

From maize to breakfast cereals

Cornflakes were invented in 1894 by Dr John Harvey Kellogg and his brother. They were first produced and sold in 1906.

Cornflakes are made from maize and enriched with added minerals and vitamins. Find out more about the ingredients of cornflakes by reading the packaging. Find out which other breakfast cereals are made from maize.

From maize to cornmeal

Cornmeal is widely used as a staple food in parts of the USA. It is used to make cornbread, cornsticks and battercakes which are popular in the southern states of America.

From maize to polenta

This is the fine golden cornmeal which is popular in Italy. It is boiled to form a soft porridgey mass, (similar to semolina). It is served with fish, game or meat and can be cooled, sliced and then grilled or baked.

From maize to packet snacks

A number of packet snack products are produced from maize. For example, tortilla chips are currently a popular maize snack from Mexico.

Nutritious and Delicious

Different people have different dietary needs. It is helpful for them to know the nutritional profile of the food products they buy.

Food manufacturers aim to maintain or improve the nutritional content of their food products. The nutritional profile is an important part of the product specification.

Nutritional Profiles

The specification for a food product lists the energy and nutrients it should contain, not just the ingredients. This part of the specification is known as the nutritional profile.

The primary (raw) materials for the product may need to be adjusted or improved to meet the specification. If nutrients are added to a product it is said to be **fortified**. Some parts of the nutritional profile may need to meet legal requirements.

During manufacture the aim is to maintain nutritional content of the original ingredients. It may be necessary to guarantee the nutritional profile by changing the ratio and proportions of fat, **fibre** and sugar, or by fortifying with small amount of nutrients such as vitamins and minerals.

These food products have been fortified with vitamins and minerals

The proportions of fat, fibre and sugar have been adjusted in these products

Healthy Eating

A healthy diet is one of several factors that can contribute to good health. There is currently a great interest in healthy eating in the UK. The food industry has responded to this market opportunity by producing more ready-made meals with modified nutritional profiles which will appeal to consumers looking for healthy foods.

Special Diets

Other products have a nutritional profile which meets the needs of people with very specific diets. For example, coeliacs are people with an allergy to gluten in wheat. Diabetics need food with reduced sugar content. Some people have an allergy to dairy products. Examples of specific dietary food are gluten-free bread, low sugar jam and soya milk.

 **www.** If you want more details, go to:
www.nutrition.org.uk
www.coeliac.co.uk

The nutritional profile of bread products

Wholemeal, brown and white bread all contain different amounts of dietary fibre. The fibre content can be increased by adding different wholegrains or extra bran. White bread has a lower fibre content than wholemeal varieties, because the wheat has been refined to remove the bran. The fibre content may be increased by adding soft grains such as rye.

■ ACTIVITIES

1. You will need examples of wrappers from three different types of bread. Find your own or use the examples on this page. Look carefully at the nutrition information and ingredients.

Sample A   Brown bread with extra bran
Sample B   White bread
Sample C   White bread with soft grains

Create a table to show the nutritional content per 100g for energy, protein, fibre and sodium using a spreadsheet program. Highlight the highest and lowest values.

2. List the iron, calcium and vitamin B1 (thiamin) content for samples A and C. What do you notice? Draw a table to compare the content for 100g, using a spreadsheet program.

3. The contents for all the samples have carbohydrate stated as 'carbohydrate .....g of which sugars ..... g.'

Why do you think it is shown like this?

4. From the ingredients listed for each sample:

▶ name the two main ingredients (these are the first two on the list)
▶ list the ingredients which are the same for each bread
▶ explain why soya flour is used in these products
▶ give the percentage of bran in the brown bread with extra bran
▶ list which ingredients are added as grains in the white bread with soft grains.

A

NUTRITION INFORMATION

Typical Values	100g Provides	Per Slice (approx 38g)
Energy	928kJ/219kcals	353kJ/83kcals
Protein	12.6g	4.8g
Carbohydrate	35.0g	13.3g
of which: sugars	3.0g	1.1g
Fat	3.2g	1.2g
of which: saturates	0.8g	0.3g
Fibre	6.8g	2.6g
Sodium	0.4g	0.2g

Vitamins and Minerals		%RDA		%RDA
Thiamin (vitamin B1)	0.4 mg	28	0.15 mg	19
Niacin	9.9 mg	55	3.8 mg	21
Calcium	140 mg	17	53 mg	6
Iron	2.8 mg	20	1.0 mg	7

RDA = RECOMMENDED DAILY ALLOWANCE

INGREDIENTS: Water, Unbleached Wheat Flour, Wheat Bran (6.5%), Cracked Wheat, Cooked Wheatgerm, Wheat Protein, Yeast, Soya Flour, Salt, Sugar, Vinegar, Vegetable Fat, Emulsifier: E472(e); Flour Improver: Ascorbic Acid (Vitamin C).

B

NUTRITION INFORMATION

TYPICAL VALUES	per 100g of bread	per average slice (36.4g)
Energy	991 kJ (234 kcal)	361 kJ (85kcal)
Protein	10.1g	3.7g
Carbohydrate	44.7g	16.2g
of which are sugars	3.0g	1.1g
Fat	1.6g	0.6g
of which saturates	0.5g	0.2g
Fibre	2.7g	1.0g
Sodium	0.7g	0.3g

INGREDIENTS

Unbleached, Untreated Flour, Water, Yeast, Salt, Vegetable and Hydrogenated Vegetable Oils, Soya Flour, Preservative Calcium Propionate (added to inhibit mould growth), Emulsifier E472(e), Flour Improver Ascorbic Acid (Vitamin C).

C

NUTRITION INFORMATION

Typical Values	100g Provides	A daily serving of 200g (approx 5 slices) provides
Energy	951 kJ / 224 kcals	1902 kJ / 448 kcals
Protein	7.2g	14.4g
Carbohydrate	45.5g	91.0g
(of which sugars)	3.1g	6.2g
Fat	1.5g	3.0g
(of which saturates)	0.4g	0.8g
Fibre	3.7g	7.4g
Sodium	0.5g	1.0g
Vitamins and Minerals		
Thiamin	0.6mg	1.2mg
Niacin	7.1mg	14.2mg
Folic Acid	118.0μg	236.0μg
Vitamin B_{12}	1.0μg	2.0μg
Calcium	90.0mg	180.0mg
Iron	1.3mg	2.6mg

INGREDIENTS

Unbleached Wheat Flour, Water, Kibbled Rye, Kibbled Wheat, Yeast, Salt, Soya Flour, Vinegar, Wheat Protein, Emulsifiers: E471, E472(e), Vegetable Fat, Added vitamins: Niacin, Thiamin, Folic Acid, Vitamin B_{12}: Flour Improver: Ascorbic Acid (Vitamin C),

IN YOUR PROJECT

▶ Work out the nutritional profile of the food product you are developing.
▶ How could it be improved or adjusted to meet new or special consumer needs?
▶ Produce a nutritional information panel for your product.

KEY POINTS

● The nutritional profile is part of a product specification.
● Consumers have different nutritional requirements.
● Changing the proportions of ingredients affects the nutritional profile.
● Some foods are fortified with micronutrients.

Baking in Abundance

A good example of how manufacturing processes work is the making of bread. Large-scale production is used to make the wide variety of bread products the consumer wants. These need to be made available from different types of retail outlets.

Bread Products

Bread has been a staple food for thousands of years. Originally it was made from a variety of crushed grains such as rye and barley. These were more like savoury biscuits than the bread products made today.

Bread is now the main product made from wheat.

The range of breads available is vast. Most countries in the world produce some type of bread (e.g. pitta, chapattis, focaccia, parathas, rye and sweetened breads).

White sliced bread is still very popular. Other breads sold include wheatgerm, malted wheatgrain, soft grain white, bran enriched and multigrain. Morning goods are small bread items traditionally baked in the morning after the ovens are cooled, but are now produced throughout the day. These include muffins, crumpets, rolls and scones.

■ ACTIVITY

The following is a selection of breads traditionally associated with a country of origin. Name the countries.
- ▶ Baguette
- ▶ Cholla
- ▶ Croissant
- ▶ Muffin
- ▶ Pitta
- ▶ Soda bread
- ▶ Chapattis
- ▶ Bara brith
- ▶ Focaccia
- ▶ Naan
- ▶ Ciabatta
- ▶ Tortillas

Bread Production

At the beginning of the 20th century most bread was made and consumed at home. Today 20 000 independent bakers sell bread on a local basis. Large-scale production at plant bakeries became possible as production methods and mechanical slicing and wrapping methods developed. Plant bakeries now produce 78 per cent of all bread consumed. The manufacture of bread products is one of the largest sectors of the food industry, with sales of over £3 billion a year. Ten million large loaves of bread are consumed every day.

Independent bakers still have an important role but they have lost some trade to in-store bakeries. These use a technical development known as the bake-off system. Retailers buy in partially baked or unbaked frozen dough to finish on site. A supply of freshly baked products is available throughout the day, so less is wasted.

Market Share of UK Bread Production by Volume (%)		
	1984	2000
Plant bakeries	70	81
Master bakers	27	4
In-store bakeries	3	5
Total	100	100

Source: Federation of Bakers, London

WWW. ➡ If you want more details of the National Food Survey, go to: **www.maff.org.uk** click on '**statistics**'

Points of Sale

Bread can be purchased from a variety of retail outlets. Some shops are points of sale for bread made in large 'industrial plant bakeries'. Others sell bread at the point of manufacture, such as in-store bakeries and local bread and cake bakeries.

▷ Find out and list where bread is sold near you.
▷ Make a list of the different kinds of bread product available.

Consumption of Cereals and Bread

Information from a national food survey shows that cereals including bread are eaten in greater quantity than other foods.

▷ Study the information in the table below. This shows the average quantities of food eaten per person per week.
▷ List the foods and quantities consumed during 1993 in descending order. Cereals including bread will be near the top of your list.

Household consumption of bread has changed little since 1991. Standard white loaves still account for half the bread consumed in the UK. The consumption of wholemeal bread has increased but brown bread has decreased slightly.

Study the information in the consumption and expenditure table below.

▷ Why are standard white loaves popular with the consumer?
▷ Why are people eating more wholemeal bread?
▷ Purchases of other breads such as Vienna and French breads has increased. Suggest reasons for this.

per person per week	Consumption			Expenditure		
	1997	1998	1999	1997	1999	1999
	(grams)			(pence)		
Milk and cream (ml)	2108	2159	2064	139	134.3	131.9
Cheese	109	104	104	53	51.7	52.3
Meat and meat products	940	943	928	335.22	346.94	347.55
Fish	146	146	144	75	77.3	80.8
Eggs (no)	1.78	1.74	1.68	18	17	17
Fats and oils	64	65	67	15	15.1	13.3
Sugar and preserves	169	146	140	18	16.8	14.6
Vegetables	2061	2005	1966	59	67	67.2
Fruits	356	374	352	87	91.3	93.4
Cereals (incl. bread)	1518	1478	1464	197	195.7	199.5
Beverages	59	58	56	44.2	48.9	42.3
Other foods	444	433	435	80.2	81.7	82.3
Total food	–	–	–	£14.68	£14.80	£14.75

Consumption and expenditure for main food groups. MAFF National Food Survey 2000

per person per week	Consumption %				
	1995	1996	1997	1998	1999
CATEGORIES					
White bread (standard loaves)	53.1	43.5	37.4	37.1	40.5
White premium and softgrain bread	5.6	14.8	20.3	22.0	17.2
Brown bread	10.5	9.5	10.9	9.1	9.7
Wholemeal bread	12.4	13.2	12.2	10.9	12.3
Other bread (incl. rolls, sandwiches and speciality)	18.4	19.0	19.4	20.5	20.3
Total bread	100.0	100.0	100.0	100.0	100.0

Consumption of bread in the home per person per week. MAFF National Food Survey 2000

■ **ACTIVITIES**

1. Compare some bread products from different countries. Investigate the ingredients which influence their appearance and palatability.

2. Conduct a survey to find out what different types of bread people buy. You could present this information as a pie-chart using a spreadsheet.

3. List some of the different ways bread may be used as part of a staple diet.

USE YOUR LOAF

manufacturing in quantity

KEY POINTS

● Bread manufacture is an example of large-scale production.
● A range of bread products is needed to reflect current consumer trends.
● These products are available from a variety of retail outlets.
● Cereals (including bread) are eaten more than any other food commodity in the UK.

Going Up!

Consumers expect baked products such as bread and cakes to be light and airy. Raising agents are needed to produce the required open texture. These produce gases which expand on heating, causing the mixture to rise. Different types of raising agents are used for different food products.

Making Baked Products Rise

The first known breads were flat, with a heavy, close texture. They were described as unleavened, which means they had no **raising agent** added.

Consumers now prefer light, open-textured bread, cakes, pastries, batters, meringues and cold sweets. This is achieved by incorporating gas into the mixture. Raising agents work by releasing gas when the mixture is heated, causing it to rise.

There are three gases which make food mixture rise:

▷ air
▷ steam
▷ carbon dioxide.

The raising agents used to produce carbon dioxide may be chemical raising agents or yeast. Yeast is used to raise dough.

air beaten into fat and sugar

steam from liquid (egg)

carbon dioxide from baking powder

Baking Powder

CAKE

More than one type of raising agent may be used in a food product, e.g. a creamed cake product

Air

Air is incorporated into mixtures by mechanical methods:

▷ sieving flour (cakes, pastry, batters)
▷ creaming together fat and sugar (cakes, some biscuits)
▷ rubbing fat into flour (shortcrust pastry, scones)
▷ whisking egg white (meringue, whisked cake)
▷ beating mixtures (batters, choux pastry)
▷ rolling and folding (flaky pastry, rich yeast pastries).

Steam

For steam to make mixtures rise, two conditions are needed:

▷ a high proportion of liquid in the mixture
▷ a high baking temperature.

When the liquid content reaches boiling point steam is given off. This forces its way up through the mixture to stretch and raise it. The mixture cooks and sets in the risen shape, with large pockets of air left after the steam has escaped.

Food products which are raised mainly by steam have a very open and often uneven texture, (e.g. Yorkshire pudding and choux pastry).

Steam can also be combined with:

▷ air and carbon dioxide in cakes and bread
▷ air in shortcrust and flaky pastry.

Carbon dioxide

Carbon dioxide is produced in two ways:

▷ chemically from the action of bicarbonate of soda with an acid
▷ biologically from the **fermentation** process of yeast.

Chemical Raising Agents

These are powders which require liquid and heat to produce carbon dioxide gas. They are used in small quantities and must be measured accurately.

There are three types of chemical raising agents:

▷ bicarbonate of soda
▷ bicarbonate of soda plus acid (e.g. lactic acid in sour milk)
▷ baking powder or baking powder in self-raising flour.

Bicarbonate of soda
Bicarbonate of soda on its own leaves an unpleasant sharp taste and a dark yellow colour. It can be used successfully in recipes where other strong flavours disguise this (e.g. gingerbread, parkin, chocolate cake).

Bicarbonate of soda plus acid
Adding an acid prevents the undesirable taste and yellow colouring. The acid may be cream of tartar, sour milk or vinegar.

Baking powder
This is a commercial mix of bicarbonate of soda and an acid. Cornflour or rice flour is added to the mixture to prevent any reaction before use. Self-raising flour is plain flour with baking powder added by the manufacturer.

If you want more details, go to:

www.foodtech.org.uk
Click on '**food science**'

Biological Raising Agents

Yeast is a living organism which gives off carbon dioxide gas during fermentation. This **aerates** the dough. This only happens at certain temperatures, however, and takes more time than chemical raising agents. A liquid ingredient is also needed.

Warmth
Warm temperatures (25–35°C) are needed. Too much heat kills the yeast. Too cold a temperature will slow down the reaction.

Fresh yeast can be frozen until required.

Ingredients such as fat, sugar or flour slow down the time needed for the yeast to grow.

Moisture
Moisture is provided from liquid such as milk, water or egg added to the recipe. Dried yeast can't start to react without water.

Food
This is provided from the small amount of sugar in flour, or the sugar added to sweeter doughs.

Too much salt can prevent the yeast working well.

■ ACTIVITIES

1. Make up three small batches of scones using the same recipe for each. Change the type of raising agent for each batch. You could use ICT to scan a cross-section of each scone to assess the effect of the raising agent on volume, texture and density.

How can you make sure it is a fair test? Record and evaluate your results.

2. Dissolve 25g of fresh yeast in 150ml of warm water. Divide between four numbered test tubes:

Put number 1 in a warm place
Put number 2 in a warm place and add ¼ tsp sugar
Put number 3 in boiling water and add ¼ tsp sugar
Put number 4 in a refrigerator and add ¼ tsp sugar

Secure the open end of a balloon over each tube and leave for 15 minutes. Observe and record the results.

How much have the balloons expanded, and why?

IN YOUR PROJECT

▶ Will your food product require a raising agent? What type will you use, and why?

KEY POINTS

● Raising agents produce gases which expand on heating.
● Three types of gases make food rise – air, steam and carbon dioxide.
● Carbon dioxide can be produced chemically or biologically.

Making Bread

The different ingredients of a food product each have distinct characteristics. These influence the flavour, colour, texture, volume, shape and palatability of the product.

▷ *How do the ingredients of bread work together to produce the correct result?*
▷ *What processes are used to make bread?*

Bread has four essential ingredients: flour, yeast, liquid and salt. Other ingredients such as sugar and fat may be added to produce other types of bread. In the manufacturing industry flour treatment agents (such as vitamin C) are also added.

Flour
The type of flour used in the UK for making bread (at home or in industry) is 'strong' wheat flour. This flour is high in the protein called gluten which helps to produce a very elastic (stretchy) dough during bread production. It also helps the bread to be well risen with a light, open texture.

Wholemeal bread can have a closer (more dense) texture because the bran and wheatgerm it contains weakens the gluten and prevents it from working properly. To solve this problem wholemeal bread can be made using a mixture of white and wholemeal flour.

Liquid
The liquid used in bread is usually water. Milk or a mixture of milk and water may be used to improve the nutritional value or to give a softer texture and crust.

The temperature of the liquid should be luke warm (25–35°C) to encourage the yeast to ferment.

▶ Too high temperature will destroy the yeast.

▶ Too low temperature will slow down the action of the yeast.

Adding the correct amount of liquid is important.
▶ Strong flour absorbs more water than soft flour (flour with less gluten).
▶ Wholemeal flour absorbs more water than white flour.

Flour treatment agents
These are added to improve the texture of bread by making the gluten more elastic.

A commercial mix would include:
▶ an emulsifier
▶ soya flour
▶ ascorbic acid (vitamin C)
▶ preservative to stop mould growth.

Added nutrients
In the UK it is a legal requirement that every 100g of flour must have a minimum content of iron, calcium and B-vitamins.

Bleaching agents
Natural white flour looks slightly yellow, so a bleaching agent such as chlorine dioxide was added to produce a whiter product. Soya flour is a natural alternative bleaching agent now used.

Yeast
Yeast is used as the raising agent in bread production. Three types of yeast are available:

▶ Fresh yeast is blended with warm liquid just before adding it to the flour.
▶ Dried yeast has a long shelf-life and needs to be mixed with warm water and sugar to reactivate it. It then needs to stand for 10 minutes to produce a head of foam.
▶ Easy-blend yeast is dried yeast in a fine powdered form which is stirred directly into the flour before warm liquid is added. Ascorbic acid (vitamin C) is added to some easy-blend yeast to speed up the reaction of the yeast. The dough can then be made very quickly, requiring only one kneading and one proving.

Salt
Salt is an essential ingredient, added in the ratio of 2% of flour weight. Salt:
▶ strengthens the gluten
▶ controls the action of yeast
▶ gives flavour to the dough.

Sugar
Sugar can be added in bread making but it is not essential. The starch in flour is naturally converted into sugar by enzymes, so yeast can use this sugar during the fermentation process. Sugar is usually added to rich yeast doughs such as Chelsea Buns.

Fat
A small proportion of fat is usually added to bread. More is added to rich yeast mixtures. Margarine or butter in varying proportions can be used to:

▶ influence the texture and colour of the dough
▶ increase shelf-life by delaying the bread going stale.

Traditional Bread Making

In the traditional method of bread production there are three stages:

▷ mixing the dough
▷ fermentation
▷ baking.

Mixing

Flour, salt and sometimes fat are mixed with yeast and water. A small amount of sugar may be added to help the yeast start to ferment.

A fairly stiff but pliable (flexible) dough is formed. This is kneaded for about 10 minutes to make the gluten more elastic.

Fermentation

The dough is left to stand for one or two hours to allow the yeast to produce carbon dioxide gas. This is called proving. Carbon dioxide aerates, stretches and lightens the dough, giving it a sponge-like, cellular structure.

The dough is then thoroughly kneaded or 'knocked back' to release some of the gas. It is left again to ferment until it has doubled in size.

A ripe dough has the gluten distributed throughout: its spring and elasticity holds in the carbon dioxide bubbles.

▶ Under-ripe dough is tough: it will stretch but is not elastic.
▶ Over-ripe dough is soft but cannot be stretched without breaking.

Baking

Baking at the high temperature of 220°C allows the dough to rise a little more, to its final stage. The heat sets or coagulates the gluten. This establishes the final shape of the bread product.

Baking also gives colour by browning the crust and adding flavour to the bread.

Yeast cells are killed off and the enzymes responsible for fermentation are destroyed, so no more carbon dioxide is produced.

Commercial Bread Making

There are three main methods of commercially manufacturing dough:

▷ bulk fermentation
▷ activated dough development
▷ the Chorleywood bread process.

Bulk fermentation process

This is a traditional method. Ingredients are mixed together to form a dough and left to ferment for up to three hours.

During fermentation the dough changes from a dense mass into an elastic dough. The time taken to reach this state largely depends on the amount of yeast and the temperature of the dough.

Activated dough development

A bread improver is added to the dough. This produces bread quickly without any need to leave the dough to rise for long periods or to use high energy mixing.

Chorleywood bread process

This method was developed in 1961. The first fermentation stage is replaced with a few minutes of intense mechanical work in mixing the dough. The mixing machine does the job of carbon dioxide in traditional bread making. It rapidly stretches the gluten. Yeast is still required to produce carbon dioxide to aerate the bread.

New materials with modified properties and characteristics are now being used to increase the shelf-life of bread to up a week.

■ ACTIVITY

▶ Each member of the class could produce a batch of bread rolls using the same basic recipe, but some using dried yeast, some fresh and some easy-blend.
▶ Compare the appearance, taste and texture of the results.
▶ Which yeast would you recommend and why?
▶ Take a digital photograph of each sample.
▶ Display your results from a sensory test as a star diagram.

IN YOUR PROJECT

▶ Try out your chosen recipe using different types of the same ingredient (e.g. yeast) to find the best results.
▶ Find out how your product could be manufactured in the food industry.

KEY POINTS

● The four essential ingredients for making bread are flour, yeast, liquid and salt.
● Traditional bread making involves mixing the dough, fermentation and baking.
● The three main methods of commercial production are bulk fermentation, activated dough development and the Chorleywood bread process.

The Chorleywood Bread Process

Making bread today is largely done automatically. Many stages are monitored and controlled by computers. This all saves time and helps produce a consistent and cost-effective product.

 If you want more details, go to:
www.bakersfederation.org.uk

This bread process was developed by British Baking Industries Research Association at Chorleywood in 1961.

3 Kneading

The dough is kneaded continuously for about 2 minutes. It circles through a spiral shaped machine.

1 Delivery and storage

Flour is delivered to bakeries in road tankers and stored in silos. Salt and vinegar are stored in tanks. Yeast, flour treatment agents and vegetable fat are stored in cool conditions.

2 Mixing

All ingredients are directed by computer from the relevant areas into large mixing vats. A pre-determined weight of flour is pumped from silo to mixer. Flour treatment agents and yeast are weighed and added by hand. Chilled water is then added. The volume is automatically controlled according to the weight of flour in the mixer.

When all the ingredients are collected, a heavy metal lid slams down on the top of the bowl and the high-speed mixing starts. The bread recipe and its weight in the mixer determines the energy and time put into the mixing. The dough mixture is ready in less than 5 minutes, and the lids are removed.

Dividing
The mixture is transferred to a machine which divides the dough into pieces. The dough is divided by volume using a suction cutter.

Rounder
The dough is rolled into a manageable shape.

Proving
Pieces of dough are left to stand to:
▶ allow time for the yeast to produce carbon dioxide to make the dough rise
▶ increase the **plasticity** of the dough.

Ultra violet light kills organisms which could contaminate the dough.

5 Oven-baking

Tins of risen loaves pass on a conveyor belt into and through a huge oven about 20 metres long. The temperature is automatically set at 300°C. This creates 96°C at the middle of the bread to bake it.

The trays of bread move very slowly through the oven for about 22 minutes. Windows along the side of the oven enable staff to check what is happening.

Thermometers down the side of the oven show its exact temperature.

The size of a large-scale bakery is measured in sacks. A sack is equal to 216 large loaves. For example, a 30 sack bakery will produce 6480 loaves per hour.

KEY POINTS

The advantages of the Chorleywood bread process are that it:
- reduces factory space required for normal bulk fermentation
- does not require temperature and humidity control
- reduces production time
- lowers production costs
- produces higher yield of bread per unit of flour
- lowers the staling rate of bread
- produces a better quality bread in terms of volume, colour, keeping qualities and cost.

4 Filling tins

The dough is cut into four pieces. This makes the baked loaf firmer and more consistently coloured than if a single dough piece is used. They are put into pre-greased baking tins.

The dough passes along the conveyor belt until it is above the tins. These are lined up underneath on another conveyor belt. Tins are fixed fives (i.e. ☐☐☐☐☐), 13 of which fit across the conveyor.

If the bread is to be used for sliced sandwich loaves, lids are put on to keep the bread in a regular rectangular shape. Other bread has the more traditional rounded top.

Second proving
The tins pass into a warm area of 40°C with 85% humidity where the dough rises for a second time. The batch moves through in a fixed time according to the speed of the conveyor.

7 Slicing and bagging

Loaves pass through this stage very quickly. The conveyor belt stops if too many loaves line up at once. A system directs the bread down different channels so that the maximum amount of loaves can be sliced and bagged. Large blades slice the bread according to required thickness (thin, medium or thick).

An air machine inflates the plastic bags. The bread is carefully pushed into the bag and sealed. The seals are labelled with the price and the 'best before date' of the bread.

Bagged loaves are checked by a metal detector as they pass to large storage trays. Full trays are stacked by fork lift trucks ready for distribution.

6 Cooling

Baked bread moves from the oven to the cooling area. This is important. If the bread is not cooled for long enough it will not last as long once it is wrapped.

Lids are removed by large magnets and the bread is sucked out of the tins. The loaves cool for 2 hours at 20°C, 75% relative humidity.

8 Distribution

Bread is baked overnight and delivered fresh next morning to supermarkets, grocery shops and high street bakers who want to supplement their own products.

ICT →

This automatic bread manufacturing system can be emulated using a 'bread-maker'. It is pre-programable, allowing you to monitor and control the manufacture of a perfect loaf.

Unit Two: Introduction

Food production on a large scale is very different to making a single dish at home or in school. Manufacturers need to find out what people want and then develop a tasty, appetising product which is safe to eat. Then they must work out how to make it on a large scale.

Can you design and make a new cake or pastry product?

Inside a Test Kitchen (page 46)

Food Hygiene and Safety (page 62)

Introduction

When a new product appears on a supermarket shelf most consumers are unaware of all the work which has been done to get it there.

The ideas for the product have to be tested to see if people will want to buy it. Similar products will be tested and evaluated. Different ingredients and recipes will be considered. Many samples will be tried out until a final specification can be arrived at. It will be months before all the details of the new product are finally agreed.

The next stage is to 'scale up' the recipe so it can be made in quantity, and a production line designed. Everything needs to be in exactly the right place at the right time.

During production all the ingredients need to be measured accurately and mixed together. Regular checks are needed to ensure the product will be made to a consistent standard. Food **hygiene** is also extremely important.

Preparing for the Task

Read through the task outlined on this page. Before you can start to develop and finalise your ideas however, you will need to work through the rest of the sections which make up this unit. You may also want to review some of the sections from the Unit One. See the diagram above.

You will also need to refer to the Project Guide at the start of the book.

'As you know, our range of cakes and pastry products are selling well but we are facing tougher competition from the smaller, local bakeries.

We therefore need to expand the range of products we offer. Our market research department has discovered that young people are looking for alternatives to traditional cakes and pastries. At the same time, though, we need to continue to promote a 'home-made' image.

Of course the new product must be made efficiently and safely on a large scale so we can meet the demand.

I look forward to hearing your proposals, and sampling them, before you produce a final specification.'

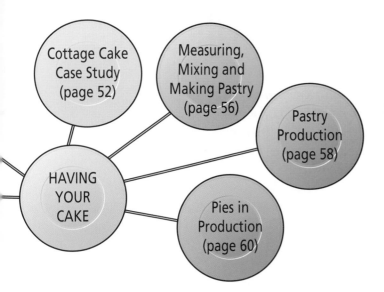

First Thoughts

▷ What sort of sweet or savoury baked products appeal to young people?

▷ How will the ideas be tested?

▷ How are recipes 'scaled up' for production in quantity?

▷ What information is needed in the final specification?

▷ In what order would the product be made?

▷ What checks could be made to ensure that every product will be safe to eat?

Getting Started

A great deal of the information you need to complete this task is provided in this unit. You will, however, need to do some research of your own to find out what sort of baked product to develop. What cakes and pastry products do young people buy? Where and when do they eat them? How much do they spend, and how often?

Research in local bakery shops would be most useful. You might decide to compete with an existing product, but to change and improve it. You might do this by using better ingredients or providing different fillings.

Identify a particular type of product to develop. For example, it might be a pastry case with a range of fillings, or cakes with unusual flavour combinations: how about chocolate with mint icing, or orange with chopped dried apricots?

Read through the pages on cakes, pastry and pies.

Developing your Ideas

As you develop your product you will need to follow the method used in a 'test kitchen'. This will involve thinking about the ingredients you are going to use: what purpose do they have in your product, and what quantities will be needed? Next consider what method will be used to combine the ingredients together.

You will need to test out some samples, to sort out what tastes and looks best. Then work out how the recipe will need to be adapted to make it suitable for large-scale production.

Planning and Making It

If you can arrange a visit to a local bakery you will learn a lot about how cakes and pastry products are made on a large scale. Study the Cottage Cake Case Study (pages 52 to 55) for more information on the processes of production. Check which processes need to be undertaken.

Make a small batch of your final product. Plan your use of time carefully.

Prepare a short illustrated report or display to explain how your product would be made in quantity.

Final Testing and Evaluation

As your product is specifically intended for young people, you will be able to test your products on each other. Prepare a product evaluation sheet for your testers to fill in. Include questions on things such as portion size, appearance, texture and taste.

Don't forget to write up a final evaluation. Comment on the success of your product, referring to the results of the final testing. How could you improve the specification?

How well did you carry out your research and development? Was the final making properly planned? How could you improve the way you worked?

Inside a Test Kitchen (1): Product Specification

In industry, food technologists work from an initial design brief towards a final product specification or profile – a precise description of its ingredients, their amounts and the method of mixing. This specification is developed and finalised in a test kitchen.

Ideas for new food products are found through market research. This involves questioning consumers about the foods they buy. This might be done by a food manufacturing company (e.g. Heinz), or a retailer (e.g. Sainsbury). A product may need to compete with other existing brands, be a variation of an existing product for a different market, or be something completely new.

The development of a new food product is carried out in a test kitchen. Here the food product development team work closely with the technical, production and purchasing departments. A set process is followed to ensure that all the relevant information is recorded.

Designing for large-scale production involves working out the **specification** for the:

▷ recipe ingredients
▷ ratio or proportion of ingredients
▷ methods of weighing and measuring
▷ mixing techniques
▷ heating or cooling methods.

If the product is to compete with similar brands, the first stage is to analyse the rival products. Food technologists focus on taste, texture and appearance. How could these be improved?

When a possible specification has been drawn up, samples are made for tasting using traditional small-scale equipment. The recipe, ingredients and production methods will then be adjusted as needed: many further samples may be made before the dish tastes and looks exactly right.

The final recipe is then tested on a wide range of consumers before it is finally approved.

The Product Specification

Finally the **product specification** is compiled. This is an official document which contains detailed and extensive information about all aspects of the product, its manufacture and packaging. It includes:

▷ ingredients
▷ recipe
▷ overall weight and volume
▷ manufacturing process
▷ quality standards
▷ food hygiene procedures
▷ packaging requirements
▷ product life (display until, use by and best before dates)
▷ distribution and display requirements.

No changes can be made to the product specification without approval from the company or retailer who produced the original design brief. Any alterations are made on a special form and included with the product specification.

The final stage is to manufacture the product, and launch it.

Pages 47–51 follow the basic process of recipe development used in a test kitchen, using a cake product as an example.

Choosing the Right Ingredients

Different ingredients serve different purposes. When a new product is being developed it is important to choose the right ones.

The main ingredients in cakes are fat, sugar, eggs, flour, a raising agent and sometimes a liquid. Flavourings may include dried fruit, spices, essences, chocolate, coffee and citrus fruits. Each ingredient performs an important function.

Fat
▶ holds tiny air bubbles which create texture and volume
▶ adds colour and flavour, particularly butter and margarine
▶ produces a cake with short crumb or rich texture
▶ helps increase shelf-life.

Sugar
▶ with fat, helps to hold air in the mixture
▶ increases the volume of the cake
▶ sweetens the mixture and adds flavour.

Eggs
▶ trap air, especially if they are beaten
▶ contain the protein albumen, which when beaten forms a foam, adding air into the mixture
▶ hold the fat in an **emulsion** once the mixture has been beaten
▶ contain lecithin (also a protein) in the egg yolk, which helps to keep the emulsion stable
▶ add colour and flavour.

Flour
▶ forms the main structure of most cakes
▶ soft flour has a low gluten content and gives a soft tender crumb
▶ with the correct amount of raising agent, it helps the product to rise.

Raising agent
▶ makes cakes light and airy
▶ needs to be measured accurately
▶ needs to be mixed evenly through the other ingredients.

Liquid
▶ usually milk or water, produces steam to help the mixture rise during baking
▶ combines with the protein in flour to form gluten.

It's a Piece of Cake!

A wide range of cakes is readily available, with a variety of flavours and finishes. Traditionally cakes are popular baked food products. Sometimes they are a local or regional speciality, such as Dundee cake, Dorset apple cake and Bakewell tart.

Cakes can be made at home or commercially manufactured and sold through retail outlets. The choice ranges from plain textured cakes to imaginatively iced and decorated special occasion cakes.

Most cakes are made from one of four basic recipes. These combine ingredients in different amounts (ratios) to obtain products with different textures and appearances.

IN YOUR PROJECT
▶ What is the purpose of each of the ingredients in your cake product?
▶ As you develop your ideas, work towards all the things which will be needed for the final detailed specification of your product.

KEY POINTS
● In industry, product development is carried out in a test kitchen.
● The product specification contains all the information about the development of the product. Each ingredient has a specific purpose in a recipe.

HAVING YOUR CAKE

manufacturing in quantity

Inside a Test Kitchen (2): Product Development

Cake Making Methods

Cakes are classified according to the method used for making them. The type and proportion of ingredients determine the method used. The four main cake making methods are:

▷ rubbing-in
▷ creaming
▷ melting
▷ whisking.

Look carefully at the four basic recipes given here. How does the ratio and type of ingredient alter for each recipe?

■ ACTIVITIES

1. Choose the basic recipe for either a rubbed-in cake or a creamed cake. Look up the method for making.

Carry out a fair test to find out what happens if the ingredients are changed in quantity or type. Using 50 g of creamed mixture each time, investigate:

▶ different sugars – caster, soft brown
▶ different flour – wholemeal, white
▶ different raising agents.

What is meant by the term 'fair test'?

2. Cakes are often decorated to make them look more attractive. Suggest a decorative finish for each of the following.

▶ carrot cake
▶ Victoria sandwich
▶ simnel cake
▶ novelty birthday cake.

3. Investigate ways in which you can test a cake to find out if it is ready to come out of the oven.

4. Find out what storage conditions are required to maintain cakes in good quality.

Rubbing-in method
used for farmhouse fruit cake, raspberry buns, rock buns.

Ingredients

200 g plain flour

10 ml baking powder

100 g margarine

100 g caster sugar

2 eggs

30 ml milk

flavouring ingredients:

175 g dried fruit or

75 g chocolate chips

- Mixing: fat rubbed into the flour.
- Ratio: half or less than half fat to flour. Higher proportion of liquid.
- Raising agent: chemical baking powder or self-raising flour.
- Texture: dry, open, crumb.

Creaming method
used for Victoria sandwich, Madeira cake, sponge buns, Dundee cake, etc.

Ingredients

100 g self-raising flour

100 g caster sugar

100 g soft margarine or butter

2 eggs

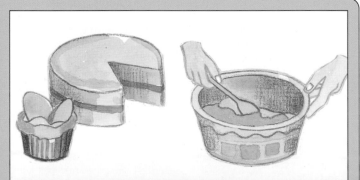

The **all-in-one creaming method** recipe is as above, plus 5 ml baking powder. All the ingredients are creamed together for 2–3 minutes by hand or mixer.
This saves time and effort.

- Mixing: fat and sugar creamed together.
- Ratio: half or more than half fat to flour.
- Raising agent: chemical self-raising flour. Air from creaming.
- Texture: fine, light, even.

A wide variety of flavourings may be added.
Equal quantities of all ingredients are usually used.

■ ACTIVITIES

1. Compare a home-made cake with a similar packet cake mix and a ready-made cake.

Compare the total cost, additional ingredients, time to make, time to bake, size, shape, colour, texture and taste to each cake in a chart.

2. Look at the range of packet cake mixes available in retail outlets.

▶ Is there a difference in price? Give examples and suggest reasons why this is so.
▶ Is it always necessary to add other ingredients?
▶ What ingredients are added? Give examples.
▶ What is the function of these ingredients?

3. Make a list of 10 types of ready-made cakes.

▶ Compare one type with a similar home-made cake.
▶ Comment on cost, size, colour, texture and flavour.

Compare the list of ingredients with the home-made recipe.

▶ What is the function of the ingredients in each recipe?
▶ What types of packaging are used for ready-made cakes?
▶ What is the function of the packaging materials?

Melting method
used for gingerbread, parkin, flap-jacks, brownies, etc.

Ingredients

200g plain flour
5ml bicarbonate of soda
10ml ground ginger
5ml mixed spice
50g soft brown sugar
100g margarine
150g black treacle
125ml milk
2 eggs
50g sultanas (optional)
50g golden syrup

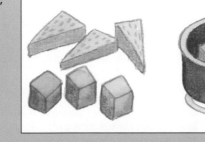

- Mixing: fat melted with treacle, syrup and sugar.
- Ratio: half or less fat to flour. High proportion of sugar ingredients.
- Raising agent: chemical – bicarbonate of soda.
- Spices mask the flavour.
- Texture: soft, moist, sticky.

These cakes have good keeping qualities.
Flavour develops and crust softens with time.

WWW.

Need help? Go to:
www.newfood.com
and search for '**cake mix**'.
Present the results from the three activities on a word-processor or spreadsheet program.

ICT ➡

Some cake manufactures use CAD to aid in the development of new products. These allow the baker to design and view the cake before baking.

Whisked method
used for Swiss roll, sponge sandwich cake, sponge drops, sponge flan case, etc.

Ingredients

50g caster sugar
50g plain flour
2 eggs

These sponges go stale very quickly because there is no fat in the mixture.

- Mixing: eggs and sugar whisked together.
- Ratio: equal proportions of sugar and flour to weight of eggs.
- Raising agent: air and steam from water in eggs.
- Texture: light, even, soft.

Inside a Test Kitchen (3): Small to Large-Scale Production

Developing the Recipe for Production

In the test kitchen a small-scale sample recipe is made. This needs to be scaled up for mass production. Added ingredients may be needed to maintain the flavour and texture or to increase the **shelf-life**. The method of production might also need to change.

Added Ingredients

The flavour and texture of a food product may change when made on a large scale. It also has to last longer. Unlike a recipe made at home, a factory-made cake may therefore need to include things like:

▷ glycerine, for added moisture during shelf-life
▷ salt, to bring out the flavour
▷ water, to create steam during baking which results in a more open texture
▷ **preservatives** to help the cake last longer
▷ **emulsifiers** to keep mixed fat and oil in water.

Different Methods

Study the two recipes below for creamed cake mixtures, to see the differences in the methods used in the home and the factory.

Victoria sandwich

Large-scale factory recipe
40 kg butter
47 kg granulated sugar
47 kg flour
47 kg whole egg
1 kg baking powder
glycerine
salt
water

Method
■ plasticise butter, 1 minute fast.
■ add sugar, mix 2 minutes fast.
■ add the egg in four stages, 30 seconds slow, 30 seconds fast.
■ add the flour and baking powder, mix 1 minute slow, 15 seconds fast.

Small-scale Standard recipe
100 g fat (butter or margarine)
100 g sugar
100 g flour
2 eggs
5 ml baking powder

Method
• Cream fat and sugar together.
• Gradually mix in egg.
• Gently fold in flour and baking powder.

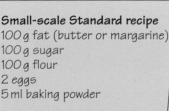

Use a spreadsheet to calculate the cost of your product for large scale production.

Scaling up a Cake Recipe

A standard batch size for a factory mixture is equivalent to 250 kg. On an initial trial to test out a test kitchen recipe, a half batch would be produced. This would be mixed and baked to the test kitchen specification.

When the results of this trial are known, changes can be made to the test kitchen ingredients, mixing method, baking time and temperature until a recipe is accepted.

Once in the factory, a couple of full batches are produced to judge and monitor any problems which could appear during production. Two batches mean the oven is full, so the bake can be assessed properly.

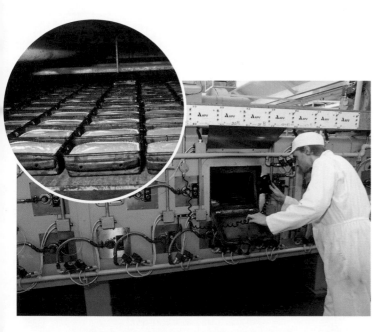

■ ACTIVITY

▶ Study a variety of cake packages. List the ingredients which would not normally be used in a home kitchen.
▶ Why do you think these extra ingredients have been added?

Manufacturers need to find out several things:

▷ Is the cake to be turned upside down or left the right way up for decorating?
▷ Will it be stored chilled or frozen?
▷ How much time can be allowed before the cake is decorated?
▷ What is its shelf-life (the time allowed at ambient temperature before the product starts to dry up)?
▷ What is the baked weight of the product (to establish the nutritional information, weights sheets and product costings)?
▷ How much mixture goes into each tin (deposit weights)?
▷ What oven temperature is required?
▷ What mixing methods are needed?
▷ What hazards may result in an unsafe product (see HACCP on page 134)?

From these factory trials, any adjustments can be made to the recipe (e.g. adding slightly more baking powder to aerate the cake a bit more and increase its volume).

The final product specification can now be used for production.

IN YOUR PROJECT

▶ Work out the quantities of ingredients needed for the large-scale production of your product.
▶ What extra ingredients might be needed if your product was scaled up for production?
▶ What methods of production might need to be changed?

KEY POINTS

● Recipes are tested on a small scale in a test kitchen.
● Recipes are scaled up for mass production.
● Extra ingredients are often added to maintain flavour and texture and to increase shelf-life.

HAVING YOUR CAKE

manufacturing guide

Cottage Cake Case Study (1)

At Cottage Cake Bakeries raw ingredients are turned into baked cakes.

Although their products have a 'home-baked' image they are made on a very large scale. This requires careful planning to ensure the final products are always of a high quality.

Planning for Production

Each step of the production process is identified and organised in detail, to ensure everything is in the right place at the right time.

Preparing the Raw Ingredients

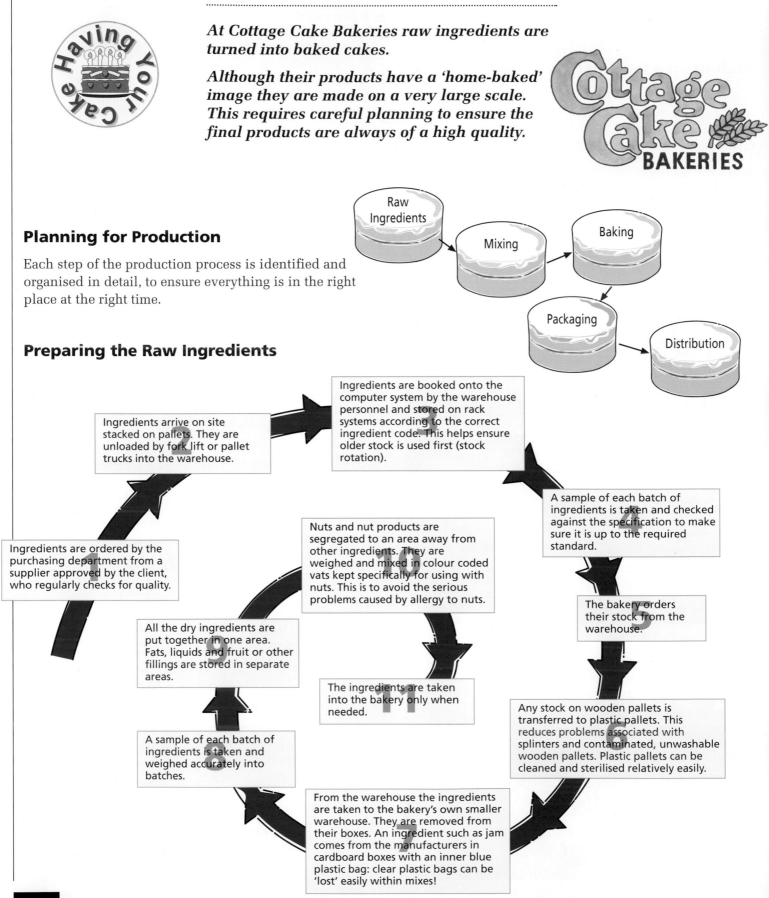

Raw Ingredients → Mixing → Baking → Packaging → Distribution

1 Ingredients are ordered by the purchasing department from a supplier approved by the client, who regularly checks for quality.

2 Ingredients arrive on site stacked on pallets. They are unloaded by fork lift or pallet trucks into the warehouse.

3 Ingredients are booked onto the computer system by the warehouse personnel and stored on rack systems according to the correct ingredient code. This helps ensure older stock is used first (stock rotation).

4 A sample of each batch of ingredients is taken and checked against the specification to make sure it is up to the required standard.

5 The bakery orders their stock from the warehouse.

6 Any stock on wooden pallets is transferred to plastic pallets. This reduces problems associated with splinters and contaminated, unwashable wooden pallets. Plastic pallets can be cleaned and sterilised relatively easily.

7 From the warehouse the ingredients are taken to the bakery's own smaller warehouse. They are removed from their boxes. An ingredient such as jam comes from the manufacturers in cardboard boxes with an inner blue plastic bag: clear plastic bags can be 'lost' easily within mixes!

8 A sample of each batch of ingredients is taken and weighed accurately into batches.

9 All the dry ingredients are put together in one area. Fats, liquids and fruit or other fillings are stored in separate areas.

10 Nuts and nut products are segregated to an area away from other ingredients. They are weighed and mixed in colour coded vats kept specifically for using with nuts. This is to avoid the serious problems caused by allergy to nuts.

11 The ingredients are taken into the bakery only when needed.

Mixing the Cake Batter

Cake batters are usually mixed in high-speed mixers. The method used depends upon the desired quality of the cake. All the methods used in a domestic kitchen can be used in a factory in the same way. A high-speed mixer is just a large Kenwood Chef. The mechanical action helps to produce a light open texture.

Consistent Cakes

It is important that each batch of a particular cake always comes out looking and tasting the same. The type and weight of raw materials used in each batch are recorded.

The mix is also recorded, (e.g. mix fats 30 seconds slow, 1 minute fast. Add egg mix 30 seconds slow, 1 minute fast.)

The weight of the product after mixing is monitored to check that the right amount of air has been added.

The standing time between the end of mixing and baking should be no more than 30 minutes. This is to prevent air being knocked out of the mix and the baking powder beginning to work too soon.

Cake batter should be covered to prevent **contamination**.

Baking the Final Product

Cakes are baked exactly to the specification to ensure they all turn out the same.

If any cakes are dipped, cracked or have crusty tops, the mixing method and weighing-up sheets will be checked and any oven faults examined.

Cakes are trayed up from the oven according to the desired finish. A domed cake with a sugar dusting (e.g. a Victoria sandwich) would be trayed the right way up to keep the domed appearance.

A cake which is to be frosted or requires a flat even surface on top would be trayed upside down. This limits the amount of cake needed to be trimmed to make a flat level surface.

Once the cake has been cooled, it is wrapped, coded, dated and then dispatched to the correct bakery to be processed further.

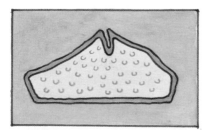

If the oven temperature is too high, the cake burns on top and rises unevenly.

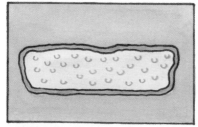

Flour beaten into the mixture (rather than folded) results in a heavy texture.

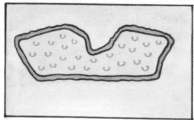

When a cake is taken out of the oven too soon, the centre sinks like this.

IN YOUR PROJECT

▶ How would you ensure that you could produce a consistent batch of your product each time?

▶ Could an electric mixer or processor be used to help make your product?

KEY POINTS

● In industry there are clearly defined procedures for ordering and handling raw ingredients.
● Each mix is carefully monitored to ensure consistency.
● High-speed mixers are used to mix ingredients together.

Cottage Cake Case Study (2)

Quality Assurance

It is essential for Cottage Cake Bakeries to maintain standards of safety and quality in their products. They aim to:

▷ provide the quality their customers expect
▷ comply with the Food Act 1990
▷ make all their employees aware of food safety
▷ work with their suppliers to ensure all the materials they use are safe.

Cottage Cake Bakeries maintain and improve standards of food safety in all areas of their business by closely monitoring the following:

▷ raw materials
▷ packaging
▷ process control checks
▷ foreign body controls
▷ final product checks
▷ calibration (weighing and measuring)
▷ traceability
▷ microbiological sampling.

Raw materials

Raw materials are bought to agreed specifications. These details are held by the technical department and contain the following information:

▶ raw material type
▶ supplier and percentage content
▶ quality assurance test limits
▶ nutritional information
▶ microbiological standards
▶ shelf-life and storage recommendations
▶ certification requirements.

On delivery, vehicles are inspected to ensure they are:

▶ checking off the goods
▶ dedicated to food use only
▶ free from contamination
▶ adequately protecting the goods
▶ at the correct temperature (if applicable).

Materials are checked for:

▶ correct type and quantity
▶ correct pallet and packaging
▶ special requirements (e.g. temperature).

They are either:

▶ accepted and passed to production using an 'oldest first' system, or
▶ put on hold, segregated and stored or rejected.

Cream Sponge Deluxe

Ingredients ordered

⬇

Inspect Ingredients using Quality Assurance

⬇

Ingredients released to Bakery

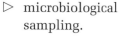

Packaging

Packaging is inspected by the site packaging technologist to make sure it is not damaged.

Process control checks

Process control checks are based on a HACCP Plan (see page 134) which accompanies each product. All quality control checks are done on a daily basis by the quality assurance supervisor. Copies are circulated to the bakery manager.

Foreign body control

Contamination by foreign bodies is prevented by:

▶ raw material inspections following delivery
▶ sieving ingredients and inspecting the sieve
▶ testing finished products for metals
▶ checks on hygiene, storage and handling of materials.

Final product checks

Random trays of each product are checked every day before they are sent out. Checks include:

▶ number in tray
▶ bar code
▶ date code
▶ seal.

Temperatures of cold products are also recorded to ensure they are within the specification before dispatch.

Calibration – weighing and measuring

Temperature probes are checked on a monthly basis in the bakery and on a weekly basis in cool areas. All weighing scales are checked on a three-monthly basis.

Refrigerator and freezer temperatures are continually monitored.

Traceability

Cottage Cake Bakeries operate a three-digit code system used each day. This gives a unique code to each raw material delivered. The code is transferred to bakery store records. This system allows everything in a finished product to be traced back to its raw materials.

Microbiological sampling

Sampling and analysis of finished product and raw materials are carried out according to the customers specification.

■ ACTIVITY

▶ Find out about another food production system. You could make a local visit, watch a video or research books and information leaflets.
▶ List the screening and checking procedures which ensure the product is safe and of a good quality from start to finish.
▶ Draw a flow chart or a block diagram to show the production stages and checking systems which take place. Use a DTP or graphics package.

IN YOUR PROJECT

▶ List the checks you would carry out when making your product.

ICT ➡

Identify the different points where ICT can be used to assess quality.

KEY POINTS

● Checks are made at each stage of production.

Measuring, Mixing and Making Pastry

Pastry can be made and used in a variety of ways in food production. It can be made from different ingredients using different methods. Each type of pastry has its own distinctive appearance, texture and flavour.

Making a Case for Pastry

Pastry is a very useful food product. It provides a contrast of texture, flavour and nutritional value to the fillings it is served with.

Pastry is used to form a case to hold sweet or savoury fillings such as fruit, vegetables, meat, fish, jam, cheese. The cases may be open to display the filling (e.g. flans, quiches, tarts) or closed (e.g. pasties, turnovers, pies).

There are three main types of pastry: shortcrust, flaky and choux. The texture, appearance and flavour of each is different. Other types of pastry include filo, hot-water crust and strudel.

The main ingredients of pastry are flour, fat, water and a little salt. Rich pastries may contain eggs, sugar, cheese or other flavourings. The type and proportion of ingredients determines the method used for making it.

Pastry may be made by combining basic ingredients or using a commercial packet mix. Alternatively it can be bought fresh or frozen, ready to use.

Shortcrust pastry is a popular and versatile pastry used for Cornish pasties, fruit pies, sponge tarts, etc.

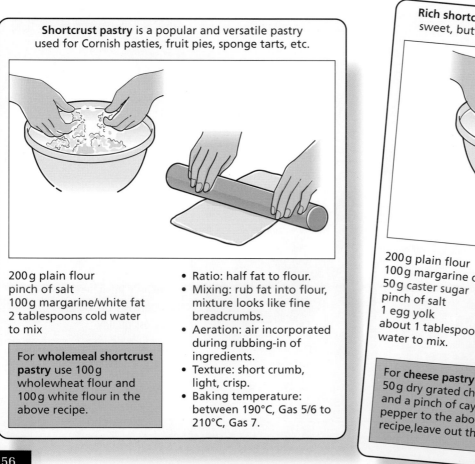

200 g plain flour
pinch of salt
100 g margarine/white fat
2 tablespoons cold water to mix

For **wholemeal shortcrust pastry** use 100 g wholewheat flour and 100 g white flour in the above recipe.

- Ratio: half fat to flour.
- Mixing: rub fat into flour, mixture looks like fine breadcrumbs.
- Aeration: air incorporated during rubbing-in of ingredients.
- Texture: short crumb, light, crisp.
- Baking temperature: between 190°C, Gas 5/6 to 210°C, Gas 7.

Rich shortcrust pastry is used for products needing a rich, sweet, buttery flavour (e.g. fruit flans, gateaux, tartlets).

200 g plain flour
100 g margarine or butter
50 g caster sugar
pinch of salt
1 egg yolk
about 1 tablespoon cold water to mix.

For **cheese pastry** add 50 g dry grated cheese and a pinch of cayenne pepper to the above recipe, leave out the sugar

- Ratio: half fat to flour.
- Mixing: rub fat into flour, mixture looks like fine breadcrumbs.
- Binding: use egg or water to bind; chill pastry before rolling out.
- Texture: short, sweet crumb, light, crisp.
- Baking temperature: 190°C, Gas 5/6. (Browns quickly because of high sugar content.)

■ ACTIVITIES

1. Study the recipes and information about these different pastries. Which would be most suitable for the following:
▶ a pastry high in dietary fibre
▶ a low fat pastry
▶ a pastry made in a saucepan
▶ a pastry suitable for a dessert.

2. Which ready-made pastry products would be suitable for serving on the following occasions? Try to use some different examples for each occasion.
▶ a children's picnic
▶ a packed lunch for a teenager attending a hockey tournament
▶ a buffet lunch for a charity fund-raising event
▶ desserts for a birthday party
▶ a lunch menu in a school cafeteria.

3. Use 50g plain white flour and 25g margarine to make some shortcrust pastry. Use this as a control.
Carry out a fair test and change
▶ the type of flour
▶ the type of fat

Evaluate and compare the results considering consistency during making, colour of baked product, surface appearance, texture and flavour. Record your results for future reference, a word-processor could be used if possible.

4. Look at the range of pastry mixes and frozen pastry available. List the types available and suggest uses for them. In what quantities can they be bought?

IN YOUR PROJECT

▶ If your product uses pastry, which type will you need?
▶ Could you extend the range of products by offering different pastry types (e.g. 'high in fibre')?

KEY POINTS

● Pastry is used for a wide range of sweet and savoury products.
● There is a range of types of pastry.
● Different ratios of ingredients are used.
● Different production methods produce different pastry textures.

Flaky pastry has a light texture. It is used for vol-au-vent, turnovers, cream horns, Eccles cakes, etc.

200g plain flour
pinch of salt
150g fat mixture – white fat with butter or margarine
2 teaspoons lemon juice
100ml cold water (approx.)

• Ratio: two-thirds/three-quarters fat to flour.
• Mixing: incorporate fat between thin layers of dough by rolling and folding.
• Aeration: air trapped between layers of dough expands during baking in a very hot oven and lifts each thin layer.
• Texture: short, crisp flakes.
• Baking temperature: 200°C, Gas 6.

Choux pastry is a light pastry ideal for filling It is used for eclairs, profiteroles, cheese aigrettes, etc.

75g plain flour
2 eggs
25g butter or margarine
125ml water.

The word 'choux' is French for cabbage. The pastry name comes from the way it trebles in size and bursts open like a cabbage.

• Ratio: third fat to flour – high proportion of water.
• Mixing: add flour to hot water and melted fat to make a thick sauce, then beat in the eggs.
• Raising agent: steam produced from high water content.
• Texture: light, airy, crisp, hollow pastry case.
• Baking temperature: 220°C, Gas 8.

Pastry Production

The main ingredients in pastry are flour, fat, water and a little salt. Sometimes cheese, egg, sugar or spices are added. Each ingredient has a particular purpose. Extra ingredients are needed for production on a large scale.

Different types of pastry contain similar ingredients, but the proportion of those ingredients and the techniques used in production make each pastry unique. The function or performance of each ingredient decides the end result of the pastry.

The purpose of each of the ingredients in three examples of pastry are explained below.

Function of Ingredients

Shortcrust pastry

Flour
- Soft plain flour contains less gluten.
- Sifting introduces air to give aerated texture.
- Wholewheat flour can be used for shortcrust, but because this flour is coarse-textured it can be heavy or difficult to roll. The proportion of half wholewheat flour to half white plain flour combines the flavour of wholewheat with the pliability of white flour.

Fat
- Fat shortens the mixture by coating the flour particles with fat, to produce a texture like breadcrumbs.
- Lard and white fat shorten the mixture well because they do not contain water. They help the pastry bake well at high temperatures.
- Hard margarine and butter add colour and flavour.
- A mixture of fats in shortcrust combines good texture, colour and flavour with ease of rubbing in and rolling out.

Salt
- Helps with flavour in the pastry.

Water
- Binds the ingredients together to ensure the pastry does not fall apart under manufacturing conditions.

Flaky pastry

Flour
- Strong plain flour is mixed with water to develop the gluten.
- Gluten is necessary for the dough to stretch and to give the pastry elasticity.

Fat
- Firm but not hard fat is used.
- A mixture of two fats may be used. They are blended together.
- Placed in small lumps on the dough, to trap air between layers of dough.

Water
- Develops the gluten to make the dough elastic.
- Lemon juice (citric acid) is added to the water. It strengthens the gluten.

Choux pastry

Flour
- Strong flour is mixed into boiling water.
- Some gelatinisation of starch occurs
- Beating in egg incorporates air in the mixture and develops the gluten in the flour.
- Baking produces steam bubbles inside the mixture, which stretch the elastic dough to produce crisp hollow shells when cooled.

Fat
- Butter or margarine melts, adding flavour and a smooth texture to thicken the mixture.

Eggs
- Help to hold in air when beaten into mixture.
- Form a smooth glossy mixture suitable for piping through a nozzle.

Water
- Must be boiling (100°C) before the flour is added (to ensure the starch is gelatinised).
- Develops the gluten in flour for elasticity.

Scaling up for Production

The choux pastry recipe on the right has been scaled up so that it can be mass produced for large-scale production.

Extra ingredients are often added to recipes when they are scaled up (see page 51). Notice the production recipe contains shortening (a type of fat) as well as butter. It also uses strong flour.

> ## CHOUX PASTRY PRODUCTION RECIPE
>
> | 14 kg | water |
> |---|---|
> | 4 kg | shortening |
> | 4 kg | butter |
> | 9 kg | strong flour |
> | 15 kg | egg |
> | optional | caster sugar |
> | optional | salt |

■ ACTIVITIES

1. Look at the choux pastry production recipe.
▶ Find out what is meant by 'shortening'. What is its purpose in the choux pastry recipe?
▶ Why might the production recipe for choux pastry require strong flour?

2. On two separate occasions a final baked batch of choux pastry eclairs were not of good quality.
▶ One batch was greasy and heavy.
▶ Another batch was soft instead of firm and crisp.
What might be the reasons for these faults?

3. Pastry often has a decorative finish. Investigate the different types of glaze and decorative finish used on pastry products. Test them out using small samples of shortcrust pastry. Record your results and suggest a suitable use for each finish.

4. Other types of pastry are available. Find out about one other pastry and the products made from it (e.g. hot-water crust, filo, strudel).

5. Find out what storage conditions are needed to maintain the following products in good quality:
▶ packet pastry mix
▶ frozen shortcrust pastry
▶ ready-made Cornish pastie.

IN YOUR PROJECT

▶ If you are using pastry in your product, you will need to carry out trials to discover the best type and ingredients.

KEY POINTS

● Ingredients have particular functions in pastry production.
● Extra ingredients are added to large-scale production recipes.

Pies in Production

This case study shows how Palethorpes produce a variety of pies using a production system known as the Rademaker twin-lane production line. The line is designed to produce large batches of high-quality pies.

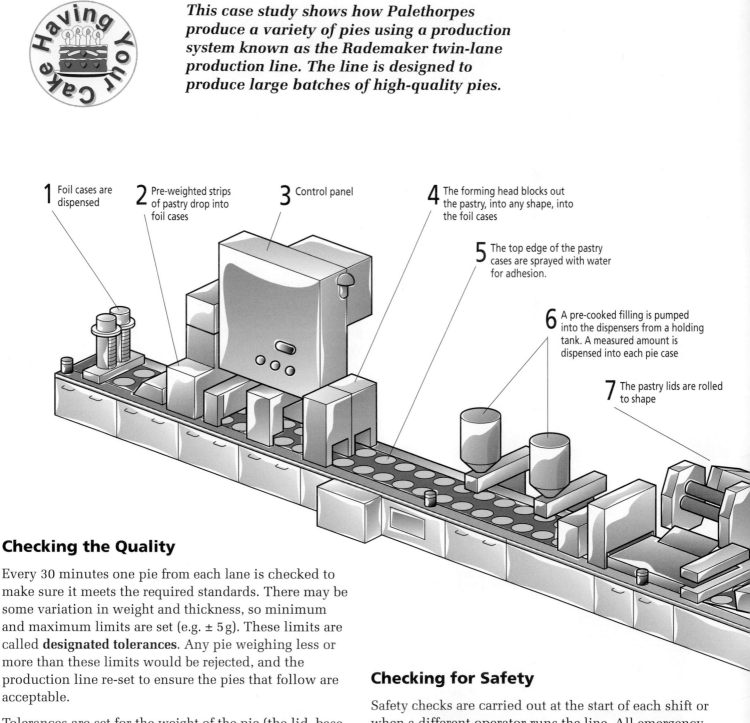

1 Foil cases are dispensed

2 Pre-weighted strips of pastry drop into foil cases

3 Control panel

4 The forming head blocks out the pastry, into any shape, into the foil cases

5 The top edge of the pastry cases are sprayed with water for adhesion.

6 A pre-cooked filling is pumped into the dispensers from a holding tank. A measured amount is dispensed into each pie case

7 The pastry lids are rolled to shape

Checking the Quality

Every 30 minutes one pie from each lane is checked to make sure it meets the required standards. There may be some variation in weight and thickness, so minimum and maximum limits are set (e.g. ± 5 g). These limits are called **designated tolerances**. Any pie weighing less or more than these limits would be rejected, and the production line re-set to ensure the pies that follow are acceptable.

Tolerances are set for the weight of the pie (the lid, base, filling and overall total) and thickness (of the lid and base). There are also checks to ensure that the pie walls are of even thickness.

Temperature is important during production. Lids must be cut at temperatures between 5 and 10 °C. Bases must be kept below 20 °C and the filling at less than 10 °C.

Checking for Safety

Safety checks are carried out at the start of each shift or when a different operator runs the line. All emergency stop buttons, safety switches and guards are checked.

Taking Action

Clear procedures are set down for what must be done if a product is not acceptable, or if there is a safety hazard.

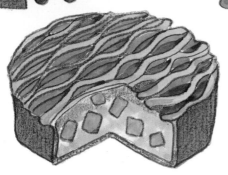

■ **ACTIVITY**

Study the process used by Palethorpes to make their pies.
Draw up a list of specific checks which would be needed during production.

8 The optional lattice former cuts the lids to create the lattice. Rollers stretch the tops to open out the lattice effect

Palethorpes
PIES
QUALITY CONTROL CHECKS

Q.C.C.	pass	fail	Procedure if fails
storage temp. of lid. 5-10°C	✓		Remove and dispose of lids. Fridge temp. to be checked

IN YOUR PROJECT

► Make a list of the designated tolerances your product would have to meet when being checked for quality and safety.
► What procedures would need to be followed if any of your products failed to meet the tolerance level?

9 The lids are placed on top of the pies, the pastry lid head presses the lid on and cuts off the excess pastry. The edges are crimped (pressed into waves) to give a good seal and decorative finish

10 The pies are lifted out onto the feed conveyor to be passed onto the oven line for cooking

ICT ●➜

Using ICT to monitor and control time, weight and temperature during production is crucial to the quality of the product.

KEY POINTS

● Checks must be carried out during and after production to ensure that products are of the necessary quality.
● A designated tolerance is the specific range within which the quality can vary.
● Designated tolerances are defined before production begins.

Food Hygiene and Safety (1)

Everybody in the food chain, from the farmer to the consumer, has a responsibility for the safety of food. A manufacturer producing large quantities of food quickly to meet demand must take particular precautions to make sure any infection does not spread.

Food Hygiene

Preparing and supplying food that is safe to eat involves careful food hygiene. Premises, staff and equipment must be kept clean. Food must be handled and stored safely. It must be prepared in safe surroundings to reduce the risk of serious illness.

Everybody involved in the production of food should receive training about safe practices and how to use them in the workplace.

Poor food hygiene can lead to outbreaks of food poisoning which can cause serious illness. Some groups of the population are particularly vulnerable, for example the elderly, the very young and people who are already ill.

Poor hygiene can also result in wastage of contaminated food, infestation by pests, time off from work because of illness, loss of customers and profits, as well as possible legal action.

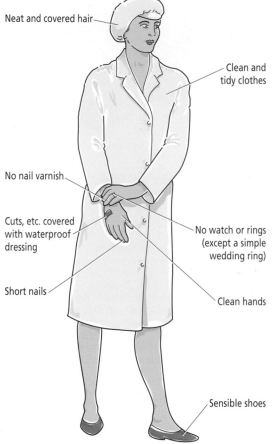

- Neat and covered hair
- Clean and tidy clothes
- No nail varnish
- Cuts, etc. covered with waterproof dressing
- No watch or rings (except a simple wedding ring)
- Short nails
- Clean hands
- Sensible shoes

Potential for cross-contamination in commercial food preparation

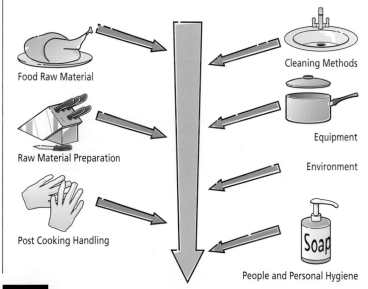

- Food Raw Material
- Raw Material Preparation
- Post Cooking Handling
- Cleaning Methods
- Equipment
- Environment
- Soap
- People and Personal Hygiene

The 1995 Food Safety Regulations

The aim is to make food hygiene rules standard across the European Union. The regulations concentrate on identifying and controlling food safety risks at each stage of producing and selling food. They are enforced by Environmental Health Officers employed by Local Authorities.

Food businesses must make sure that:

▷ food is supplied or sold in a hygienic way
▷ food safety hazards are identified
▷ critical stages in the production process are identified
▷ safety controls are maintained and reviewed.

See pages 134–136 for more information on food safety.

Types of Food Poisoning

Bacterial food poisoning is responsible for most food poisoning cases. The four types which are giving cause for concern in the UK are detailed on this page.

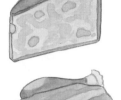
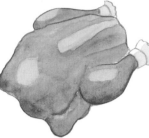

Campylobacter
This is the most commonly reported cause of food poisoning today. Most cases occur in young adults, particularly in the spring and autumn. The reasons for this are unclear.

Symptoms
These vary from mild diarrhoea to severe illness. They can take 1–10 days to appear but the average onset time is 2–5 days. Abdominal pain is usually accompanied by diarrhoea but there is very rarely any vomiting.

Sources
Poultry, meat, milk left on the door step that has been pecked by birds, untreated water, shellfish and non-food sources such as pets.

Temperature for growth
Above 30°C but most usually 42–45°C. It is destroyed by cooking.

Salmonella
These infections are the second most frequently reported type of food poisoning. There are several types, but *Salmonella enteriditis* is the most common followed by *Salmonella typhimurium*.

Salmonella enteriditis can be found in eggs. Advice from the Government is that raw eggs or foods that contain uncooked egg should not be eaten.

Symptoms
Diarrhoea, high fever, vomiting and severe abdominal pain. These usually appear 12–48 hours after eating the contaminated food. Illness can last for up to three weeks.

Sources
Meat, poultry, untreated milk, raw egg products, infected food handlers and pets.

Temperature for growth
This can be as low as 6–8°C. They are killed by heating to at least 70°C for 2 minutes.

Listeria
Certain groups of the population are at particular risk from food poisoning by *Listeria*. Pregnant women and those who are vulnerable to infection should not eat ripened soft cheese like brie, and meat-based patés.

Symptoms
These can range from those that resemble 'flu to meningitis. *Listeria* can cause miscarriages or premature labour in pregnant women. The onset time varies from 3–70 days.

Sources
Sheep and cattle, unpasteurised milk products including soft cheeses, meat-based patés, ready-to-eat poultry.Cook-chill meals may be a source, so these dishes should by eaten when they are piping hot.

Temperature for growth
Usually 30–37°C but they can grow at temperatures as low as –1°C.

VTEC (verocytotoxin)
These bacteria produce a powerful toxin. This type of food poisoning is not as common as the others, but it is more serious.

Symptoms
Vomiting, abdominal cramp and diarrhoea which can appear 12–60 hours after contact (but 48 hours is more typical).

Sources
Under-cooked minced beef including beefburgers, untreated cows milk and cheese, infected people and untreated water.

Temperature for growth
The optimum temperature is 37°C. Minced beef should be cooked until it is piping hot and the juices are clear. The pasteurisation of milk should kill VTEC.

IN YOUR PROJECT

▶ If the food product you have made was to be mass produced, which type of food poisoning could the food cause, if not made or stored correctly?

▶ Which are the critical temperatures you would have to be aware of, to prevent an outbreak of food poisoning?

KEY POINTS

- Everyone involved in the production and care of foods has a responsibility for its safety.
- Poor hygiene can lead to outbreaks of food poisoning.
- The 1995 Food Safety Regulations aim to identify and control food safety risks at every stage.
- There are four types of bacterial food poisoning causing most concern.

Food Hygiene and Safety (2)

Food poisoning is on the increase. It can be prevented by being very careful in the way food is prepared, stored and used. Cross-contamination may occur if raw and cooked foods are not kept separate.

Foods can be described as high, medium or low risk, depending on how easily they can cause food poisoning.

Food Safety

Food can make us ill in a number of ways. Food poisoning is caused mainly by pathogenic (disease-producing) bacteria, but also by chemicals, unwanted objects getting into food, and poisons.

The graph on the right shows that the incidence of food poisoning has increased steadily in recent years. (The increase is about 15% a year.)

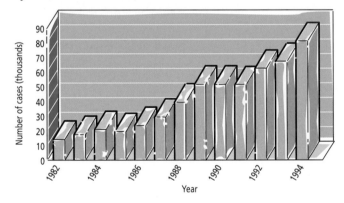

Food poisoning – England and Wales, 1982–94

Commercial premises 49%

Residential Institutions 9%

Other 16%

Hospitals and schools 9%

Private houses 17%

Locations of food poisoning outbreaks, England and Wales, 1992–93

Cross-contamination

This is when bacteria are transferred from raw to cooked food. It can be avoided by:

▷ preventing raw and cooked foods touching each other
▷ preventing blood and juices from raw foods dripping onto cooked foods
▷ preventing bacteria from being transferred on hands, knives, utensils, chopping boards or work surfaces.

■ ACTIVITY

Study carefully the graph and pie chart on the left.
▶ How would you account for the increase in the numbers of reported cases of food poisoning?
▶ Why do you think there were so many outbreaks in commercial premises?
▶ Why is the percentage of home-based outbreaks so low, given that the majority of meals are home prepared?

Food Risk Categories

High risk foods

Foods that are high in protein and are moist are most likely to cause food poisoning. They are classed as high risk and include:

▷ products containing fish, eggs, vegetables, cereals and dairy ingredients which need to be refrigerated
▷ raw meat, poultry, fish and dairy products
▷ liquid foods such as soups, stocks, sauces and gravy.

Medium risk foods

These are dried or frozen products containing fish, meat, poultry, eggs, vegetables or cereals and dairy ingredients, fresh sandwiches and meat pies, fat-based products such as chocolate, margarines, spreads, mayonnaise and dressings.

Low risk foods

These include pickles, fruit, fruit juices, unprocessed and unpacked raw vegetables, jams, marmalades and conserves, sugar-based confectionery products, edible oils and fats.

Avoiding Food Poisoning

Steps to avoid food poisoning can be taken at every stage of food preparation, storage and use.

Shops

Shops must have strict hygiene standards and efficient stock control systems. **Stock rotation** is important, with new stock placed at the back of shelves. Raw foods should be kept away from cooked foods. Freezers and refrigeration cabinets should be checked regularly.

Transport

Delivery vehicles are regularly inspected by Environmental Health Officers to make sure they are clean and, where necessary, at the right temperatures. Milk tankers must be cleaned between each delivery. Imported foods are examined to make sure they meet British food regulations.

Storage

Temperature control is vital. Harmful bacteria grow rapidly between 5 °C and 63 °C. Refrigeration slows down this growth and freezing suspends it. Freezer cabinets should be between −18 °C and −23 °C. They should be defrosted regularly and temperatures checked daily.

Colour identification on clothing indicates in which area the food handler is working

Food handlers

Staff who work in a food handling area of a factory, shop or restaurant should have good personal hygiene. Separate hand basins should be provided for regular hand washing. Suitable protective clothing, including hair covering, should be worn. Any illnesses should be reported, such as infected wounds, skin irritation, diarrhoea and vomiting.

Consumers

The consumer must take chilled and frozen foods home quickly using insulated bags, and place them in the freezer or refrigerator as soon as possible. A thermometer should be used to check the temperatures of freezers and refrigerators at home. Cooking instructions must be followed carefully. Reheated foods must be served piping hot: 70 °C is recommended.

■ ACTIVITY

Read the newspaper report below and answer the questions which follow.

> A popular and well known local restaurant served 800 Christmas meals over a period of five days. Almost 200 people became ill with *Salmonella* food poisoning. When investigations into the outbreak were carried out it was found that the turkeys were cooked and then sliced on wooden chopping boards where uncooked birds had been prepared for the oven. It was also found that the cooked turkeys had been left uncovered in the warm kitchen for several hours. Tests also showed that the temperature control in the refrigerator was poor and that raw and uncooked birds had been stored together.

▶ Why did the people who had eaten the Christmas meals become ill?
▶ Explain why turkey is classed as a high risk food.
▶ What type of surface should the turkeys have been prepared on?
▶ What should have been the correct procedure for storing the cooked turkey?
▶ What precautions should have been taken to ensure that cross-contamination between the raw and cooked food did not take place?

IN YOUR PROJECT

▶ Is the food product you have designed a high, medium or low risk food?
▶ What steps could be taken at each stage of production and sale to avoid food poisoning?

KEY POINTS

● Food poisoning can be avoided by hygienic handling of food at every stage of its production.
● Cross-contamination is when bacteria is transferred from raw to cooked foods.
● Foods can be classed as high, medium or low risk.

Examination Questions

Before spending between one and two hours answering the following questions you will need to have learnt about food processing and product manufacture. This has been covered in Units One and Two.

Write your answers on A4 paper. You are reminded of the need for good English and clear presentation in your answers.

1. This question is about research. *See pages 36–37.*

A food manufacturer wants to develop a new range of baked products.

Study the table on Bread consumption on page 37.

(a) Which two bread products were most popular during 1993?
(2 marks)

(b) Explain why sales of most bread products have decreased.
(3 marks)

(c) Give three multicultural bread products that may be included in 'other bread'. Name the country of origin of each. *(6 marks)*

2. This question is about Healthy Options. *See pages 34 and 64.*

Look at the labels below showing the nutritional profiles of white bread and wholemeal bread.

(a) How would the manufacturer use the information on these labels to help in the development of a new product? *(3 marks)*

(b) Explain how wholemeal bread fits the nutritional profile needed for a healthier option product.
(5 marks)

3. This question is about designing new products.
See pages 18–21 and 46–51.

The food manufacturer decides to develop a range of products suitable for packed meals.

The design team works to general design criteria:

● easy to package
● individual portion size
● suit a variety of dietary needs
● provides a healthy option.

(a) i) Use labelled sketches to show two design ideas for a new cake or pastry product that would meet this design criteria. *(6 marks)*

ii) Explain which is the best idea and why. *(2 marks)*

iii) Using notes and sketches describe your chosen idea in more detail.

Marks will be given for information on how the product meets the design criteria, quality of sketches and details of materials and processes used. *(10 marks)*

iv) Give a five-point product specification for the product you have designed. *(5 marks)*

NUTRITION INFORMATION – Cornflour			
		Typical Values	
		per 100g portion	per tblspn (25 grams)
Energy	KJ	2964	741
Energy	Kcal	708	177
Protein	g	1.20	0.30
Fat	g	1.40	0.35
Cholesterol	mg	0	0
Carbohydrate	g	184	46.0
Sugar	g	0	0
Fibre (NSP)	g	0.20	0.05
Sodium	mg	104	26.0
Calcium	mg	30.0	7.50
Iron	mg	2.80	0.70
Vitamin A	ug	0	0
Thiamine (B1)	mg	0	0
Riboflavin (B2)	mg	0	0
Niacin	mg	0	0
Vitamin C	mg	0	0
Vitamin D	ug	0	0

NUTRITION INFORMATION – Wheatflour			
		Typical Values	
		per 100g portion	per tblspn (25 grams)
Energy	KJ	1428	357
Energy	Kcal	341	85.2
Protein	g	9.40	2.35
Fat	g	1.28	0.32
Cholesterol	mg	0	0
Carbohydrate	g	77.6	19.4
Sugar	g	1.48	0.37
Fibre (NSP)	g	3.08	0.77
Sodium	mg	3.00	0.75
Calcium	mg	140	35.0
Iron	mg	2.00	0.50
Vitamin A	ug	0	0
Thiamine (B1)	mg	0.32	0.08
Riboflavin (B2)	mg	0	0
Niacin	mg	1.72	0.43
Vitamin C	mg	0	0
Vitamin D	ug	0	0

4. This question is about developing design ideas. *See pages 20–21, 46–51.*

The test kitchen is developing a sweet, fruity, crispy dessert for sale from a freezer cabinet.

Study the typical shortcrust pastry recipe below:

> 200g plain flour
> pinch of salt
> 100g fat
> 2 tablespoons of cold water

(a) Using the basic recipe above describe three ways of developing the recipe to produce three different products. *(6 marks)*

(b) Profiling is one method of sensory testing for new products.

Describe in detail one other method of fair testing that is used in industry. *(4 marks)*

(c) How can ICT be used to aid the communication of the results of fair testing? *(4 marks)*

5. This question is about materials and components. *See pages 58–59.*

A manufacturer buys in the main ingredients for the production of pastry products.

Explain why each of the following ingredients are important in the preparation and cooking of pastry products

(a) Strong plain flour in flaky pastry.

(b) A mixture of fats in shortcrust pastry

(c) Eggs in choux pastry.

(d) Lemon juice in flaky pastry.

(8 marks)

6. This question is about quality control and assurance. *See pages 60–61.*

Refer to the main illustration on pages 60–61.

In order to maintain quality control manufacturers work to 'designated tolerances'.

(a) What is meant by the term 'designated tolerances?' *(2 marks)*

(b) Describe four tolerances that must be met in the production of pies. *(4 marks)*

(c) Give three points where temperature control is carried out. *(3 marks)*

(d) Explain why temperature control is important. *(4 marks)*

7. This question is about production systems. *See pages 22–23, 50–55.*

Here is a list of the main stages in the production of a decorated cake product:

- baking
- packaging
- finishing
- distribution
- mixing
- storage of raw ingredients

(a) Produce a flow chart showing the correct order of these production stages. *(6 marks)*

(b) State three points where computers may be used within this production system, and describe how. *(6 marks)*

(c) Choose one area in the production flow chart. Describe how feedback may be used to ensure that poor quality products are identified and removed.

(3 marks)

8. This question is about Health and safety. *See pages 62–65.*

Manufacturers are responsible for ensuring the health and safety of employees.

(a) Describe how a food production worker should be prepared for work on a food production line. *(4 marks)*

(b) Describe how the development of technological equipment such as refrigerators and freezers has helped the retailer and the consumer to ensure safe food storage? *(4 marks)*

Bread rolls on a packaging production line.

Total marks = 100

Unit Three: Introduction

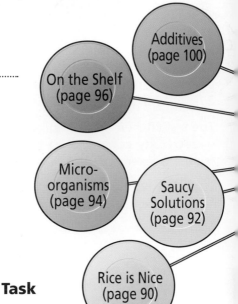

Additives (page 100)

On the Shelf (page 96)

Micro-organisms (page 94)

Saucy Solutions (page 92)

Rice is Nice (page 90)

Most food products can now be chilled rapidly after being cooked. This means they can be stored safely for a limited time until needed by the consumer. These new 'cook-chill' convenience products have become extremely popular.

Introduction

Cook-chill meals can contain a wide variety of ingredients. Fish, meat and meat substitutes, poultry and vegetables can be combined with pasta, rice and a range of sauces to produce popular dishes such as cottage pie, chilli con carne, lasagne, chicken and rice, sweet and sour pork, toad in the hole, sausage with onion gravy, chicken tikka marsala, lamb passanda and steak pie.

Meat is a popular, tasty and nutritious food item, but can be expensive. Manufacturers continue to explore ways of including meat in a more cost-effective way, while ensuring they produce a nutritious and tasty meal.

To develop a successful cook-chill product, food technologists need to have a good knowledge of the raw ingredients. They must know about:

▷ their nutritional value
▷ how they are stored when raw
▷ different ways in which they can be cooked
▷ how their texture, flavour and appearance will change during cooking and chilling
▷ how well they can be reheated
▷ which other ingredients will combine well with them.

They will also need a good understanding of the cook-chill process.

Food manufacturers and retailers are always looking for new ideas for cook-chill products which will appeal to consumers in a highly competitive market. They are mainly bought by working adults with little time to cook, but who can afford convenience foods. Successful dishes need to taste and look good, and offer good value for money. Satisfied customers will not only continue to buy a product they like, but will try others made by the same manufacturer, and tell their friends about them.

Preparing for the Task

Read through the product brief below. Before you can start to develop and finalise your ideas for a new cook-chill product however, you will need to work through the rest of the sections which make up this unit. Look through the sections on packaging and labelling at the end of the book. See the diagram above.

You will need to refer to the Project Guide at the start of the book. You may also want to review some of the sections from the previous units.

COOK-CHILL PRODUCT BRIEF

We wish to extend our range of cook-chill ready meals and need a specification for something that:

- is a savoury meal, suitable for a special occasion
- serves two adults.

The product should contain three of the following:

- at least one protein food (e.g. meat, fish) or protein substitute ingredient (e.g. TVP, Quorn)
- at least one vegetable
- at least one carbohydrate food (e.g. rice, pasta)
- a sauce.

These will need to combine together to produce a distinctive variety of textures, colours and flavours.

The product ingredients must continue to reflect our 'healthy meals' brand image. This will need to be emphasised in its name and packaging.

First Thoughts

▷ What is involved in the cook-chill process?
▷ How long can cook-chill products be stored safely?
▷ How are cook-chill products packaged?
▷ What is the nutritional importance of protein and carbohydrate foods?
▷ How are sauces made?
▷ What makes a product a 'healthy' item?

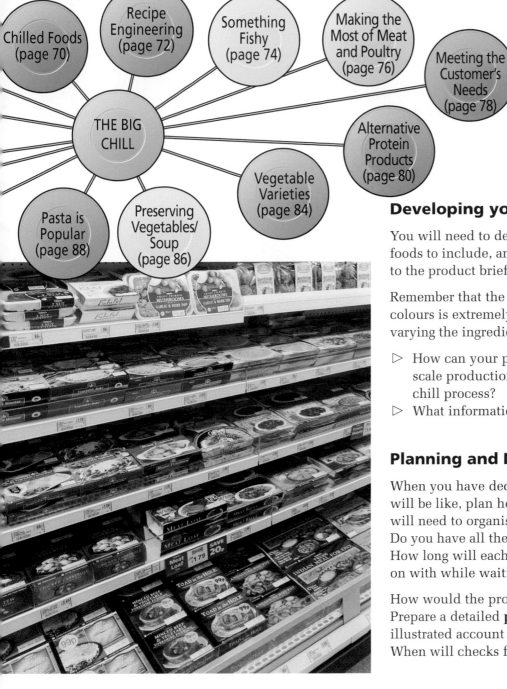

- Chilled Foods (page 70)
- Recipe Engineering (page 72)
- Something Fishy (page 74)
- Making the Most of Meat and Poultry (page 76)
- Meeting the Customer's Needs (page 78)
- THE BIG CHILL
- Alternative Protein Products (page 80)
- Vegetable Varieties (page 84)
- Pasta is Popular (page 88)
- Preserving Vegetables/Soup (page 86)

Developing your Ideas

You will need to decide which protein and carbohydrate foods to include, and which sauce. Keep referring back to the product brief.

Remember that the combination of tastes, textures and colours is extremely important. Make up some samples, varying the ingredients. Record the results of your tests.

▷ How can your product be made suitable for large-scale production? Will it be suitable for the cook-chill process?
▷ What information will be needed on the packaging?

Planning and Making It!

When you have decided what your final cook-chill meal will be like, plan how to make the final product. You will need to organise everything carefully beforehand. Do you have all the necessary ingredients and utensils? How long will each stage take? What can you be getting on with while waiting for something else to cook?

How would the product be made on a large scale? Prepare a detailed **product specification**, and an illustrated account of the main stages of manufacture. When will checks for quality and safety be made?

Getting Started

You will need to find out all you can about cook-chill products. Most of the information is on the following pages, but you will also need to visit some supermarkets to look at the range of existing products.

As you work through the unit you will learn about the preparation, storage, cooking, uses and nutritional values of a range of foods. These include fish, meat, poultry, TVP (textured vegetable protein), Quorn, Tofu, vegetables, pasta, rice and sauces.

Food safety and **preservation** is extremely important. You will need to know how food that is cooked and chilled can be made safe to store, reheat and eat.

Final Testing and Evaluation

Set up and carry out a test of the taste, flavour, texture and appearance of your product. As well as obtaining test data (such as scores out of 10), record the comments and suggestions made by your testers.

Write up a final evaluation report. Compare your product with the product brief. If it does not meet all the requirements, explain why. Refer to the product test, and the things your testers said. What ideas have you got for improving the product?

Remember also to evaluate the process of investigation and design development. What were your strengths and weaknesses?

Chilled Foods

Chilling is a short-term way of preserving fresh food. Chilled foods can be a single food or a mixture of foods which the consumer can use with little or no additional preparation.

Preservation

Without preservation, food decays or 'goes off' naturally by the action of micro-organisms such as bacteria, yeasts and moulds and by enzymes. Preserving food means we can extend the length of time before it must be eaten.

Reducing the temperature slows down the rate of decay. Temperature-controlled refrigerated lorries can transport frozen and chilled food over great distances without it going off.

Cook-Chill Products

Cook-chill products are often thought to be of a better quality than frozen products. They have a shorter shelf-life (usually a few days) but do not need to be defrosted first. Frozen products can be stored for much longer (usually several months), but often need to be thawed fully before being cooked.

Cook-chill products are prepared, cooked and chilled rapidly. They are stored at a temperature just above 0°C. This slows down:

▷ the rate at which micro-organisms multiply
▷ the rate of any chemical reactions which could affect the quality of the food.

They need to stay at or below this temperature until they are used. For this reason they are always sold from the chiller cabinets in shops.

Chilling Decisions

Most foods are suitable for chilling. The main advantages are:

▷ there is very little change in flavour, colour, texture or shape
▷ fresh foods can be kept at maximum quality for a longer time
▷ the consumer can be offered a much larger range of fresh and convenience foods
▷ nutrients are not destroyed.

Chilled food products can be:

▷ a single raw food (e.g. meat, fish)
▷ made from a mixture of raw foods (e.g. coleslaw, stir-fry vegetables, mixed lettuce leaves)
▷ made from cooked ingredients (e.g. recipe meals such as lasagne)
▷ a mixture of both raw and cooked foods (e.g. potato salad).

There are other methods which will preserve foods for longer than chilling: freezing, canning, drying, salting, pickling, chemical preservation and irradiation. Nevertheless, chilling is extremely popular. Why do you think this is so?

WWW. ◉ If you want more details, go to:
www.chilledfood.org

■ ACTIVITIES

1. Here is a list of popular chilled foods:

▶ coleslaw, chicken curry, stir-fry, spring rolls, yoghurt, chocolate mousse, trifle, lasagne, potato salad, pizza, chicken Kiev, salads, dips, breaded fish, stewing steak.

Draw up a table like the one below. Place each of these foods in the correct column.

Raw ingredients only	Cooked ingredients only	Mixture of raw and cooked

IN YOUR PROJECT

▶ Does your food product need to be preserved in some way?
▶ Would chilling be a suitable method?
▶ What temperature would be needed?
▶ How should your food product be packaged?

■ ACTIVITY

Visit a local supermarket.
▶ Are all the different types of chilled foods stored at exactly the same temperature?
▶ What special packaging materials are used?

2. There is a wide range of prepared, washed and ready-to-use vegetables available in single or mixed variety packs, for example:

▶ mixed lettuce containing iceberg, lollo rosso, frisée and little gem
▶ stir-fry vegetables containing mushrooms, carrots, beansprouts and water-chestnuts.

Buying vegetables in this way saves preparation time and avoids waste, although they can be quite expensive. Carry out the following investigation in order to find out how useful chilling can be for these products:

▶ Select four vegetables and prepare them in the usual way (wash, peel, etc.).
▶ Weigh three 25g portions of vegetable.
▶ Place one sample of each on a plate and leave, uncovered on a shelf **(Test 1)**.
▶ Place one sample of each in a plastic bag, remove the air and secure the top, put in the fridge **(Test 2)**.
▶ Place one sample of each plate, uncovered and put in the fridge **(Test 3)**.
▶ Leave for up to one week.
▶ Observe any changes in the colour, texture, shape, size and acceptability.
▶ Produce a table to record the results. The table shown here could be used as a guide.

Observations: colour/texture/shape/size/acceptability			
Sample	Test 1	Test2	Test 3
carrot			
lettuce			
mushroom			
celery			

KEY POINTS

● Chilling is a method of preserving food temporarily.
● Many different foods and mixtures of foods can be chilled.
● Some foods which cannot be preserved by other methods can be chilled.
● There is little loss or change of flavour, colour, texture, shape or nutritional value.

Recipe Engineering

Manufacturers can use standard recipes for food products. They may change the ingredients in standard recipes for various reasons. This is known as recipe engineering. New ingredients may be substituted, or proportions of ingredients changed. Whatever, manufacturers try to make sure the finished product keeps its characteristic taste, texture and appearance.

Recipe engineering is carried out by manufacturers during research and product development. There are several reasons:

▷ to change the nutritional profile of a product (e.g. high-fibre bread)
▷ to alter the amounts of **additives** and seasonings used to develop flavour, texture and colour
▷ to make the recipe suitable for large-scale production (e.g. using vegetable oil instead of solid fat in biscuits)
▷ to use cheaper ingredients (e.g. soya in beefburgers).

Manufacturers must take care when changing recipes to ensure consumers will still like the finished product.

It is important to understand the purpose of each ingredient. For example, sugar is needed to preserve the fruit in jam-making, so the amount of sugar can only be reduced to a certain level.

Jam is also a good example of where cheaper ingredients are used to produce a lower-priced product.

■ ACTIVITIES

1. Compare the ingredients listed on these two jam labels.
► Explain how the manufacturer of the economy jam has changed the recipe to reduce costs.
► Find out the prices of 454g jars of these products.
► Carry out a suitable sensory evaluation test to rate the two products (see page 114). If possible present your results using a spreadsheet.

2. Look at the ingredients of some other food products. Find examples where:
► cheaper ingredients have been used to produce a lower-priced product
► vegetable oil has been used in place of solid fat to help large-scale production
► the amount of seasonings has been reduced.

Fat
Fat gives flavour to cooked food. Reducing the amount of fat in a standard recipe has to be controlled carefully to avoid loss of flavour.

Fibre
The amount of fibre in cakes can be increased by replacing white flour with wholemeal flour. This makes a big difference to the texture and flavour of the finished cake, which is unacceptable to some people. One way to overcome this is to replace half of the white flour with wholemeal flour.

Gluten
Gluten-free flour gives an entirely different texture and taste to a finished bread product.

Sugar
Care is needed when reducing the sugar content of recipes because of the functions of sugar in cooking. Some preserves are made without any added sugar, but they must be stored in the refrigerator once they are opened.

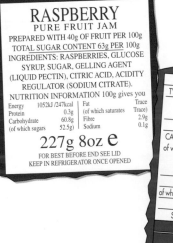

RASPBERRY
PURE FRUIT JAM
PREPARED WITH 40g OF FRUIT PER 100g
TOTAL SUGAR CONTENT 63g PER 100g
INGREDIENTS: RASPBERRIES, GLUCOSE SYRUP, SUGAR, GELLING AGENT (LIQUID PECTIN), CITRIC ACID, ACIDITY REGULATOR (SODIUM CITRATE).
NUTRITION INFORMATION 100g gives you

Energy	1052kJ /247kcal	Fat	Trace
Protein	0.3g	(of which saturates	Trace)
Carbohydrate	60.8g	Fibre	2.9g
(of which sugars	52.5g)	Sodium	0.1g

227g 8oz ℮
FOR BEST BEFORE END SEE LID
KEEP IN REFRIGERATOR ONCE OPENED

NUTRITION INFORMATION		
TYPICAL VALUES	PER 100g (3.5oz)	PER 15g Teaspoon
ENERGY	254 k cal	38 k cal
	1080 kJ	163 kJ
PROTEIN	0.2g	less than 0.1g
CARBOHYDRATE	63.0g	9.5g
of which-SUGARS	55.2g	8.3g
POLYOLS	0.2g	less than 0.1g
STARCH	0.0g	0.0g
FAT	less than 0.1g	less than 0.1g
of which-SATURATES	less than 0.1g	less than 0.1g
FIBRE	0.9g	0.1g
SODIUM	less than 0.1g	less than 0.1g
PER 15g TEASPOON		
38 CALORIES less than 0.1g FAT		

INGREDIENTS
GLUCOSE SYRUP, SUGAR, APPLES (WITH PRESERVATIVE: SULPHUR DIOXIDE), RHUBARB (WITH PRESERVATIVE: SULPHUR DIOXIDE), PLUMS (WITH PRESERVATIVE: SULPHUR DIOXIDE), GELLING AGENT: PECTIN; CITRIC ACID, ACIDITY REGULATOR: SODIUM CITRATE; COLOURS: CARMOISINE, PONCEAU 4R.

Engineering a Lasagne Recipe

Lasagne is a popular dish with many people. But to meet a specific dietary need, it may be necessary to adapt the recipe. For example, a person suffering from coronary heart disease would need a lasagne with a lower fat content.

Study this recipe for a lasagne. Suggestions for changes to lower its fat content are shown on the right.

Lasagne Recipe
olive oil for frying
1 large onion peeled and chopped
1 clove of garlic
100g streaky bacon
500g minced beef
1 can of tomatoes
1 teaspoon of sugar
mixed herbs
175g lasagne verdi
50g parmesan cheese to finish

For the sauce
25g butter
50g flour
600ml milk
200g cheddar cheese
seasoning

either omit or use vegetable oil

use lean back bacon

use extra-lean minced beef

use low-fat cheddar cheese

use polyunsaturated margarine

use skimmed or semi-skimmed milk

use cottage cheese

■ ACTIVITY

Look at the nutrition information for the three different types of lasagne on this page. Answer the following questions:

▶ How would you account for the difference in the energy values (kilojoules or calories) of the three products?

▶ Why is the protein content similar?

▶ You will notice that the fibre content of the three products is relatively low. How could you increase the fibre content of these lasagnes?

▶ How can you account for the high carbohydrate content of the vegetable lasagne?

▶ Which of the three products do you think could be cheapest and most expensive to manufacture?

HEAT THEN SERVE
Lasagne

INGREDIENTS
WATER, TOMATOES, BEEF, COOKED PASTA (WATER, WHEATFLOUR, EGG WHITE, DURUM WHEAT SEMOLINA, VEGETABLE OIL, DRIED EGG YOLK), CHEDDAR CHEESE (WITH COLOUR: ANNATTO), VEGETABLE OIL, SKIMMED MILK POWDER, WHEATFLOUR, ONIONS, TOMATO PUREE, MARGARINE (WITH COLOURS: ANNATTO, CURCUMIN), MUSHROOMS, STARCH, SUGAR, SALT, DIJON MUSTARD, GELATINE, BEEF BOUILLON (WITH FLAVOURINGS, ANTIOXIDANT: BUTYLATED HYDROXYANISOLE), GARLIC, PEPPER, OREGANO, BASIL
(MINIMUM 10% MEAT)

NUTRITION INFORMATION
TYPICAL VALUES (COOKED AS PER INSTRUCTIONS)

	PER 100g (3.5oz)	PER PACK
ENERGY	729 kJ	2187 kJ
	175 k cal	524 k cal
PROTEIN	7.8g	23.4g
CARBOHYDRATE	11.8g	35.4g
of which SUGARS	3.0g	9.0g
STARCH	8.6g	25.8g
FAT	10.7g	32.1g
of which SATURATES	3.5g	10.5g
MONO-UNSATURATES	4.7g	14.1g
POLYUNSATURATES	2.0g	6.0g
FIBRE	0.6g	1.8g
SODIUM	0.4g	1.2g

STAY TRIM
Beef Lasagne

INGREDIENTS
Skimmed Milk, Water, Beef, Cooked Pasta (made from Wheat and Egg White), Onions, Concentrated Tomato Puree, Mushrooms, Tomatoes, Modified Cornflour, Vegetable Bouillon, Cheese, Flour, Garlic Powder, Flavouring, Herbs, Spices, Onion Powder
Minimum 15% Beef

NUTRITION INFORMATION

Typical Values	Amount per 100g	Amount per Serving (295g)
Energy	397 kJ/94 kcal	1196 kJ/284 kcal
Protein	6.0g	18.0g
Carbohydrate	10.4g	31.2g
(of which sugars)	(2.7g)	(8.2g)
Fat	3.2g	9.7g
(of which saturates)	(1.5g)	(4.5g)
Fibre	0.6g	1.7g
Sodium	0.3g	0.8g

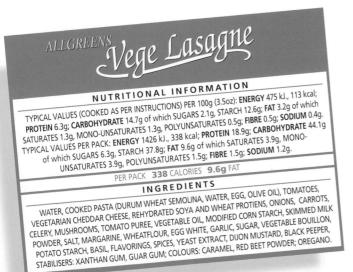

ALLGREENS Vege Lasagne

NUTRITIONAL INFORMATION
TYPICAL VALUES (COOKED AS PER INSTRUCTIONS) PER 100g (3.5oz): **ENERGY** 475 kJ., 113 kcal; **PROTEIN** 6.3g; **CARBOHYDRATE** 14.7g of which SUGARS 2.1g, STARCH 12.6g; **FAT** 3.2g of which SATURATES 1.3g, MONO-UNSATURATES 1.3g, POLYUNSATURATES 0.5g; **FIBRE** 0.5g; **SODIUM** 0.4g.
TYPICAL VALUES PER PACK: **ENERGY** 1426 kJ., 338 kcal; **PROTEIN** 18.9g; **CARBOHYDRATE** 44.1g of which SUGARS 6.3g, STARCH 37.8g; **FAT** 9.6g of which SATURATES 3.9g, MONO-UNSATURATES 3.9g, POLYUNSATURATES 1.5g; **FIBRE** 1.5g; **SODIUM** 1.2g.

PER PACK **338** CALORIES **9.6g** FAT

INGREDIENTS
WATER, COOKED PASTA (DURUM WHEAT SEMOLINA, WATER, EGG, OLIVE OIL), TOMATOES, VEGETARIAN CHEDDAR CHEESE, REHYDRATED SOYA AND WHEAT PROTIENS, ONIONS, CARROTS, CELERY, MUSHROOMS, TOMATO PUREE, VEGETABLE OIL, MODIFIED CORN STARCH, SKIMMED MILK POWDER, SALT, MARGARINE, WHEATFLOUR, EGG WHITE, GARLIC, SUGAR, VEGETABLE BOUILLON, POTATO STARCH, BASIL, FLAVORINGS, SPICES, YEAST EXTRACT, DIJON MUSTARD, BLACK PEEPER, STABILISERS: XANTHAN GUM, GUAR GUM; COLOURS: CARAMEL, RED BEET POWDER; OREGANO.

IN YOUR PROJECT

▶ Explain how you have used recipe engineering during the development of your product.

▶ What changes were needed to make it suitable for large-scale production?

KEY POINTS

Recipe engineering involves adapting recipes to make them:
● suitable for people with special dietary needs
● cheaper to make in large quantities.

Something Fishy

Fish is a versatile food which can be used fresh, frozen or canned. There are many different types of fish, and a variety of ways in which they can be processed to prolong shelf-life.

A Fishy Business

Fish is a popular food for people wishing to cut down on saturated fats. It is also quick to prepare and helps provide greater variety in the diet.

The number of fish products on the market has therefore shown a steady increase in recent years.

Fish can be classified as white fish, oily fish or shell fish.

White fish

Cod, haddock, plaice, halibut and whiting are known as white fish because of the colour of their flesh and not their skin.

Oily fish

In herrings, mackerel, salmon, pilchards and tuna the fat is distributed throughout the flesh and is found in the muscle fibres. This means that the flesh will be darker in colour than white fish. The amount of fat present is approximately 10%.

Shell fish

There are two types within this group:

▷ Crustacea (e.g. crabs, prawns and shrimps). These have legs and a hard outer shell. They are quite often sold ready-cooked.
▷ Molluscs (e.g. cockles, whelks and winkles). These also have a hard outer shell but no legs.

Shell fish goes off very quickly and so should only be eaten when absolutely fresh.

The Nutritional Value of Fish

Fish is good to eat from a nutritional point of view. All fish contains good quality protein (high biological value) which can be used easily by the body. It is a good source of vitamins A and D, but contains only small amounts of B vitamins and hardly any vitamin C.

White fish contains a very small amount of fat. It is suitable for people on calorie controlled diets, or for those recovering from an illness. The fat is stored in the liver, where the fat-soluble vitamins A and D are found. Oily fish contains polyunsaturated oil, distributed throughout the flesh. Vitamins A and D are therefore present in the whole fish, not just the liver.

Fish is a source of calcium and phosphorus, if the bones are eaten (e.g. canned tuna and salmon). It does not contain carbohydrate.

The Structure of Fish

The flesh of fish is made up of bundles of short muscle fibres held together by connective tissue. This is mostly made of the protein collagen which is easily converted to gelatine during cooking. There is no elastin, which holds meat tissue together. This is why fish is much easier for the body to digest than meat.

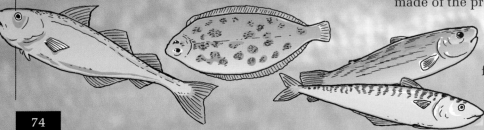

Preserving Fish

There are three main ways in which fish can be kept fresh.

Freezing

Most of the fish sold in the UK is frozen. Fresh fish is prepared, cleaned and frozen. It can then be cooked without any further preparation.

Most frozen fish has been filleted, cut into steaks, or trimmed. It can be coated in batter or breadcrumbs, as with fishfingers, and cooked in any of the ways used for fresh fish. Alternatively, it can be packed in a 'boil in the bag' form with a sauce.

Canning

Canning is used a great deal for sardines, mackerel, pilchards, salmon, tuna and shrimps. The fish are packed in brine, oil or tomato sauce. These products are particularly useful as snacks, as a topping for pizzas and in sandwiches.

Smoking

The UK exports large amounts of smoked fish to other countries, for example kippers and smoked salmon. The fish has to be salted before it is smoked. It is then put in a kiln. Smoke is blown over the fish for varying lengths of time. The fish can either be cold or hot smoked.

Storing fish at home

Fish should be used as quickly as possible. This is because the enzymes present in fish that cause it to deteriorate are active at low temperatures. Re-wrap fish in clean paper and place it in a polythene bag in the refrigerator soon after purchase. Store it away from other foods that could absorb the flavour.

IN YOUR PROJECT

▶ Would fish be a useful main ingredient for your food product?
▶ What particular advantages would it have for the consumer and the manufacturer?

KEY POINTS

● Fish can be classified as white, oily or shell fish.
● Fish requires a short cooking time.
● Fish can be processed by canning, freezing or smoking.

■ ACTIVITIES

1. Use a nutritional analysis program to compare 100 g of baked white fish, oily fish, stewed mince beef and grilled steak. Present your results as a table. What do your results tell you?

Food (100 g)	Protein	Fat	Carbohydrates	Vitamin A
baked white fish				
oily fish				
minced beef				
grilled steak				

2. Look at the range of processed fish products on the market. Select one type of fish that has been processed by more that two methods.

Find out how the processing has been carried out, and compare the methods. For example, which method will keep the greatest proportion of the nutrients in the fish after processing?

3. Visit a retail outlet that sells frozen fish. Survey the range of frozen fish products on offer. Put your findings into a table, using the four headings:

Frozen fillets/ steaks, Fish in batter, Fish in breadcrumbs, Fish in Sauce.

▶ How does the cost differ for each of these types of fish?
▶ List the fish products which particularly appeal to children.
▶ List the fish products which are suitable for people concerned about their health.
  ▶ List the products which are sold in individual portions.
    ▶ Which products are sold in economy packs?

4. A food manufacturer wishes to inform customers about the way tuna fish can be used. A promotional pack in the form of five recipe cards will be given to customers buying 400 g or 200 g cans of tuna steaks, chunks or flakes packed in either brine or vegetable oil.

Some suggestions for the recipe cards include new main course dishes, sandwich fillings and salad combinations. Generate and develop a range of ideas for the recipe cards. Remember the card has two sides and is likely to be no larger than A5 size.

Give details of a recipe and method, and other information which could be included on the card to inform customers of the value and safe use of tuna fish.

WWW. For further details go to:
www.seafish.co.uk
and use the fish database.

Making the Most of Meat and Poultry

A wide range of meats and poultry can be served as a main course. They are available fresh or in cook-chill, frozen or part-prepared food products. Meat and poultry form an important part of the diet in the UK. They can be cooked in many ways and are a valuable source of protein and other nutrients.

What are Meat and Poultry?

Meat and poultry are the muscle tissue of animals and birds. The internal organs such as liver, kidney and heart are known as offal. The muscle tissue contains protein, water, vitamins and minerals. The fibres are held together in bundles by connective tissue.

There are two types of connective tissue:

▷ collagen: surrounds the bundles of muscle fibres
▷ elastin: makes up the wall of the muscle fibre.

Collagen and elastin are proteins. Proteins coagulate (set) when they are heated. Collagen is converted into gelatin which helps to moisten the meat. Elastin does not soften. It is found mainly in the muscles (like the leg) of animals that have had to work hard, or in older animals.

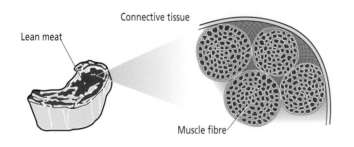

Lean meat
Connective tissue
Muscle fibre

When choosing which meat is most suitable for a meal or product, it is important to know how its structure will be affected by the cooking.

The length and size of muscle fibres decides how tender or tough meat will be. Short, thin fibres in a quality steak, for example, will mean the meat will be tender. The long, fat fibres of a leg of lamb mean the meat will be tougher and will need a longer cooking time. Moist methods of cooking are usually chosen for tougher cuts of meat. Why do you think this is?

Types of Meat and Poultry

Below are some examples of different types of meat and poultry.

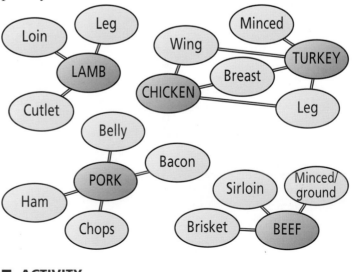

Loin — Leg — LAMB — Cutlet
Wing — Minced — Breast — TURKEY — Leg — CHICKEN
Belly — Bacon — PORK — Ham — Chops
Sirloin — Minced/ground — Brisket — BEEF

■ ACTIVITY

Produce a table to show how each type of meat might be used as part of a main meal.

Nutritional Value

Both meat and poultry are highly nutritious products. These tables show their nutritional value.

Meat	Nutritional value
Protein	high biological value approx. 20 g per 100 g
Fat	amounts vary according to the type
Minerals	rich source of iron small amount sulphur/phosphorus
Vitamins	B1 (niacin), B2 (riboflavin), B12

Poultry	Nutritional value
Protein	high biological value approx. 18 g per 100 g
Fat	white (breast) meat is lowest
Minerals	less iron than red meat some potassium
Vitamins	B1 (niacin), B2 (riboflavin)

To produce healthy meals and products, lean cuts of meat and poultry such as chicken or turkey are chosen. Alternatively, all visible fat could be removed during preparation (e.g. cutting the fat off bacon). Fat can also be removed during cooking, for example, by grilling rather than frying.

Meat

Minced or ground beef is beef which has been passed through the mincer once or twice. Pale mince usually has quite a lot of fat in it; darker mince will be leaner (contain less fat). Mince is usually used for making cottage pie, lasagne, chilli con carne and beefburgers.

Sirloin, fillet and rump steak come from parts of the animal where there is little muscular movement, and so the meat is very tender. These cuts are used extensively in cook-chill products, often accompanied by a sauce. They are suitable for use in stir-fry dishes, which is a popular method of cooking.

Chuck/stewing steak is not as tender as sirloin or fillet and requires long, slow cooking. It produces an excellent flavour when used in casseroles and meat pies.

Fillet or tenderloin of pork is very tender and is used for stir-fry dishes and in a variety of oriental dishes.

Lamb is a red meat which can be used for grilling, roasting or stewing, but is not widely used in cook-chill products.

Ham and bacon have many uses in cook-chill products (e.g. in patés, pizzas, salads).

Poultry

Chicken is by far the most popular type of poultry. Chicken breast and joints are used in a wide range of products. They can be cooked by a variety of methods (e.g. grilling, frying and barbecuing). Marinades and other cook-in sauces enhance their flavour.

Turkey and chicken are frozen by being immersed in a water chiller. The weight of the frozen bird will include a quantity of water, which will drain off when it is thawed.

Offal

Offal is the edible internal parts of animals: liver, kidneys, heart, tongue. It should be bought and used when it is very fresh because it does not keep well.

Offal contains protein of high biological value and very little fat. Liver and kidneys are excellent sources of iron, vitamin B2 (riboflavin) and vitamin A.

The method of cooking which is chosen will depend on the type, tenderness and texture of the offal.

Meat and Poultry in other Cultures

Some religious faiths have very strict beliefs about the way meat and poultry can be prepared and eaten.

For example, Halal meat is meat slaughtered according to strict Muslim ritual. It is eaten by Muslims and includes all meats except pork.

Meat prepared and eaten by followers of the Jewish faith is described as kosher. Animals are slaughtered in a particular way and supervised by the Rabbi. Before use the meat must be:

▷ immersed in cold water for 30 minutes, then drained
▷ sprinkled with salt and left for 1 hour
▷ washed in cold water three times.

Both halal and kosher meals are readily available in most of the large cities in Britain.

■ ACTIVITY

1. Find out about other examples of ways in which foods are prepared and served according to different religious beliefs.

2. A manufacturer of cook-chill main course meals has the following product lines: Eastern, Oriental, Mediterranean, Traditional British, and New World.

Research and list dishes which could be included in each product range. Try to include dishes using beef, chicken, lamb or pork. Present your findings in a table.

 Want want more details? Go to:
www.bmesonline.org.uk
or **www.meatmatters.com**

IN YOUR PROJECT

▶ What type of meat of poultry could you use?
▶ Which method of cooking would be the most appropriate, and why?

KEY POINTS

● Meat and poultry are versatile food products.
● The structure of the muscle fibre affects the choice of method of cooking.

Meeting the Customer's Needs

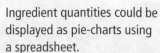

Ingredient quantities could be displayed as pie-charts using a spreadsheet.

Preparing cuts of meat for sale requires craft skill. Careful marketing is also needed to keep up customer enthusiasm for meat.

Marketing Meat Products

Meat is tasty and nutritious, but it is expensive. Also, more people are now becoming vegetarian or reducing their intake of meat for health reasons. Marketing meat products has therefore become essential.

Advances in technology have allowed food manufacturers to produce many new and interesting products using meat.

Taking shape

Processing and production techniques mean that meat can be cut up, shaped and formed into nuggets, goujons, boneless chops or cutlets, and even animal shapes.

Enrobing

Many new shaped products are covered in a type of breadcrumb – a process known as 'enrobing'. They are convenient for consumers because they are either ready to eat, or are part-cooked so they can be finished quickly in the oven, microwave, grill or by frying, to bring them to the correct, safe temperature.

A cut above the rest

New cutting techniques encourage customers to try different recipes and ways of cooking. These may be influenced by methods used in other parts of the world.

Marinating meat

Other developments in food technology include the use of marinades. These are usually in the form of a powder which is put on the meat during processing to draw out moisture and form a liquid flavouring. Examples are sweet-and-sour or with pork, beef and lamb, and lemon and coriander with chicken.

Marinades are also sold separately as sauces, pastes and powders.

Seasonal Trends

Traditional joints of meat, steaks and lamb's liver and kidney continue to sell all the year round. There are, however, seasonal trends for some cuts of meat. In the summer, for example, barbecuing is very popular. A wide range of meat cuts and manufactured raw meat products have been developed especially for this market.

Barbecue products

A range of products has been specially developed for cooking on barbecues:

▷ sausages varieties: e.g. pork and apple, tomato, Lincolnshire, sage, pork and leek, pork and beef
▷ burgers: beef, lamb and pork, with flavours and mixes such as stroganoff, and continental
▷ kebabs: turkey, lamb, pork and a mixture of all three.
▷ coated: chicken and lamb grill sticks – minced meat shaped and flavoured with spice then skewered
▷ steaks: various cuts and weights
▷ chops and cutlets: pork and lamb

Different shaped presses are used to shape burgers into triangles and ovals as well as the familiar round ones.

Meeting the Regulations

All recipes for manufactured raw meat products must comply with the 1984 Meat Products Regulations, which include:

▷ stating the minimum meat content at point of sale
▷ stating the lean meat-to-fat ratio.

This is written as a percentage of visual lean meat. For example, 60:40VL is beef with a lean content of 60% and fat content of 40%.

The tables on the right show the different lean/fat contents of some burgers.

Beefburgers (minimum 80% meat)	
Lean beef (90:10VL)	22.5%
Beef flank (70:30VL)	60.0%
Burger seasoning	7.5%
Water/ice	10.0%

Economy burgers (minimum 60% meat)	
Beef flank (60:40VL)	62.5%
Textured dried soya mince	6.25%
Water to hydrate soya	13.75%
Burger seasoning	10.0%
Water/ice	7.5%

Food safety: handle with care!

Food manufacturers and retailers have a responsibility to ensure that food is safe to eat. This is particularly important when dealing with 'high risk' foods such as meat and poultry.

Raw meat and poultry are high risk foods because some of the bacteria they contain can cause food poisoning if not prepared properly. Bacteria multiply rapidly at room temperature so all meat and poultry should be kept covered and at a temperature of 4°C or below. This will slow the growth of the bacteria. If frozen, the growth of the bacteria will be suspended until the food is thawed out.

Frozen meat and poultry must be thawed properly before cooking, otherwise the centre of the food may not get sufficiently heated during cooking to kill the bacteria. This can occur particularly in poultry, which carries the risk of *Salmonella* poisoning.

Cooking

Meat or poultry must be cooked thoroughly to kill all bacteria, whether it has been frozen first or not. The centre is furthest away from the heat source, so a temperature probe is placed into the thickest part to check it has reached the correct temperature of 70°C.

Once cooked, all meat and poultry must be cooled rapidly to prevent the growth of bacteria in the warm temperatures after cooking. It is packaged and stored in either a refrigerator or freezer.

There must be no cross-contamination between raw and cooked meat or poultry. Manufacturers must prepare raw food in a different area from cooked food. Equipment such as chopping boards will be colour-coded to show which type of food they are to be used with. All work-surfaces will be stainless steel. Non-porous plastics are used for chopping boards.

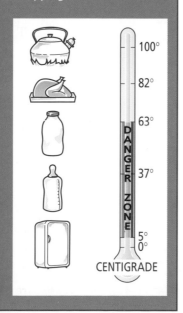

100°
82°
63°
37°
5°
0°

DANGER ZONE

CENTIGRADE

■ ACTIVITIES

1. Carry out some research in your local supermarket to find out the following information about 'enrobed' products:

▶ the different types of fillings used
▶ the different type of crumb used
▶ how, if at all, they need to be cooked
▶ where they should be stored at home.

2. Produce a simple flow chart to show how you would hygienically prepare, cook and store a frozen chicken which is to be sold as a whole, cooked chicken in a supermarket. If possible, use ICT to draw the flow chart.

IN YOUR PROJECT

▶ How will your product help maintain the consumer's desire to buy meat?
▶ At what stages in the production and storage of your food product are spoilage or cross-contamination most likely to occur?

KEY POINTS

● Meat can be prepared and sold in a variety of new ways.
● Food safety is particularly important when preparing meat.

Alternative Protein Products (1)

As more people become vegetarian, food manufacturers respond by producing a greater variety of non-meat foods. Textured Vegetable Protein (TVP), Quorn and Tofu are some of the 'new' protein foods.

Just for Vegetarians?

Alternative protein products are widely used in vegetarian foods, both commercially and in the home. However, non-vegetarians will almost certainly have eaten some of these alternative protein foods as well. Textured Vegetable Protein (TVP) is often used in catering as a meat extender, to bulk out the meat content of some foods and keep the cost low. It is also added to many of the dehydrated foods we buy in supermarkets.

Soya Bean Products

Soya beans have been eaten as the main protein food in most parts of the Eastern world for thousands of years. Today 70% of the world crop is grown in the USA and is now widely used in Western countries. Soya beans were first grown as an oil seed to produce soya oil. Although the oil crop is still important, the rest is now used to produce soya products such as TVP.

Soya protein products are found in a wide range of processed foods. Soya flour was first added to bread in the UK in the 1920s. It helps to produce a whiter loaf with improved keeping qualities.

Soya concentrates are used in some infant foods, where the level and type of protein is important. Soya lecithin (protein) is used as an emulsifier in a wide range of products to prevent separation of ingredients (e.g. low fat spreads).

■ ACTIVITIES

1. Make a list of ten foods containing soya products.

2. Find out what forms of TVP are available in your local health food store and supermarket.

3. List the advantages and disadvantages of TVP to:

▶ the caterer
▶ the food manufacturer
▶ the consumer.

Soya bean production

The soya bean is a member of the legume family – a relative of peas and French beans. The plant grows best in a warm damp climate. It produces a crop of hairy pods, each containing 2 to 5 smooth, oval, green or yellow beans.

These hard beans are squeezed or pressed in large industrial machines to extract the oil. The oil content is relatively low (15 to 20%) but because they are grown in such large quantities, soya beans are an important source of vegetable oil.

After the oil is extracted the remains of the beans are ground down into fat-free soya flour. This contains 50% protein. The flour is mixed with water to form a dough. Colourings and flavourings can be added at this stage.

The dough is heated, then extruded (forced through a nozzle). As it comes into contact with air it expands and forms a spongy, textured mass. It is usually dehydrated for retailing, giving it a shelf-life of about a year.

This process can be varied to produce chunks, flakes or granules.

Other soya protein products are soya flour, soya protein concentrate, and soya protein isolate.

Soya beans

Soya flour

Soya protein

Beef flavoured chunks

TVP

Textured Vegetable Protein is produced from soya beans to give a cheap high quality protein food. Although naturally it does not look or taste like meat, it can be processed to resemble it in both flavour and texture.

The nutritional content of TVP is similar to that of meat. All the essential aminoacid are present, making it a high biological value food. However, the essential amino acids methionine and tryptophan are sometimes added during processing to increase the amount present. TVP is also fortified with thiamin (B1), riboflavin (B2), vitamin B12 and iron.

TVP has a low fat content. This makes it useful for low calorie products. However, fat is sometimes added to improve the flavour. It is low in cholesterol and high in dietary fibre.

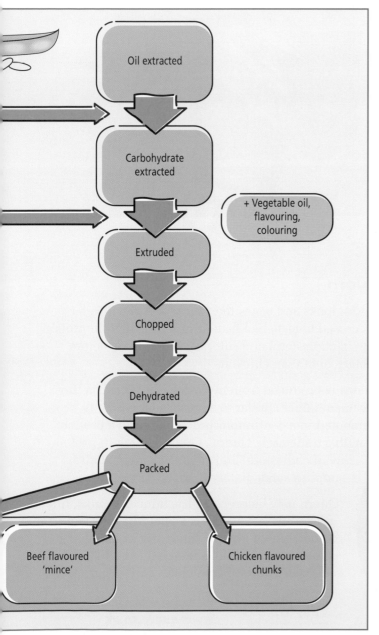

Oil extracted

Carbohydrate extracted

+ Vegetable oil, flavouring, colouring

Extruded

Chopped

Dehydrated

Packed

Beef flavoured 'mince'

Chicken flavoured chunks

Uses of TVP

TVP is found in many canned, **dehydrated** or frozen convenience foods such as ready meals or snack meals (e.g. Pot Noodles). It is widely used in vegetarian foods to imitate meat products such as mince, sausages or burgers. These are now available in all the large supermarkets as well as health food stores.

TVP is often used by the catering industry as an extender in foods such as burgers, sausages, curries and pies, to reduce the cost. It is also sold in packets to use at home in vegetarian dishes or as an extender with meat.

Dehydrated TVP has to be rehydrated with 2 to 3 times its own weight of liquid. Stock is often used, because TVP absorbs flavours well. If cooked with meat, it will take on the flavour of the meat. It only needs a few minutes cooking time if used alone, but it will not lose texture or shrink with longer cooking. It really is a useful product!

THE BIG CHILL

developing a quality product

Alternative Protein Products (2)

Tofu

Tofu, also known as soya bean curd, is becoming more popular. It was discovered more than 2000 years ago in China and is an important food in many parts of Eastern Asia. It has little flavour of its own, but takes on the flavour of the ingredients with which it is mixed. Tofu looks like a smooth textured light cheese. It can be made commercially or at home. Tofu is widely used in oriental dishes, soups, casseroles, salads and desserts. It contains 8% protein.

Tofu Production

Soya beans are soaked in water at 25°C for 5 to 6 hours. The beans are then ground and pressed through cheese-cloth. The milk which this produces is first boiled and then cooled to 50°C

The protein is separated from the liquid (precipitated) by adding calcium or magnesium compounds. The mixture is then strained through cheese-cloth and pressed to remove the excess moisture.

Quorn

Quorn looks and tastes like chicken. It can also be processed to taste like ham or veal. It is high in protein, low in cholesterol and calories, and contains more dietary fibre than chicken.

Quorn is produced from myco protein. This is a tiny organism rather similar to a mushroom which is fermented in a continuous process to form a product with a trademark 'Quorn'. Quorn is high in protein, low in cholesterol and yet unlike meat, it also supplies some dietary fibre.

Quorn may be processed as mince, chunks, fillets or in ready-meals. It has a bland flavour and pale colour, which gives it versatility as flavours and colours can be easily added using herbs, spices, sauces and other ingredients.

WWW. ➔ For further details go to:
www.quorn.co.uk

Mild vegetarian curry
For four servings

Ingredients

155 g beef/brown chunks
of TVP
170 g finely chopped onion
4 cloves garlic, crushed
2 cardamons
3 whole cloves
30 ml oil
5 ml ground cinnamon
¼ teaspoon ground turmeric
½ teaspoon ground ginger
2 teaspoons ground
coriander
½ teaspoon ground cumin
½ teaspoon ground chilli
salt to taste
ground black pepper
600 ml water or stock

Method

- Simmer TVP in plenty of water or stock for 20 minutes. Strain.

- Fry onion, garlic, cardamons and whole cloves in oil until onions are brown. Add remaining spices and seasonings. Mix in well and cook over a low heat for 5 minutes.

- Add TVP and fry in the mixture for 5 minutes.

- Add water or stock and cover. Simmer until a thick sauce has formed.

- Serve with rice, chappattis and raita – chopped cucumber mixed with yoghurt and a little salt and pepper.

Chinese Quorn stir-fry
For two servings

Ingredients

1 tablespoon vegetable oil
175 g Quorn pieces
1 clove garlic, finely chopped
1 red pepper, sliced
4 spring onions, chopped
100 g beansprouts
75 g broccoli florets,
blanched

For the sauce:
2 teaspoon cornflour
100 ml vegetable stock
2 tablespoons dark soy sauce
1 tablespoon hoisin sauce

Method

- Heat the oil in a wok or large pan. Fry the Quorn until golden brown. Add the garlic, red pepper and spring onions. Stir-fry for 5 minutes.

- Add the beansprouts and broccoli and stir through.

- Mix the cornflour, vegetable stock, soy sauce and hoisin sauce together and add to the wok. Stir until thickened and cook for a further 4-5 minutes.

- Serve with fried rice or noodles. Not suitable for freezing.

Mass production of Quorn

Quorn is produced commercially in fermenters. The ingredients are nitrogen, oxygen, glucose and minerals – supplied in controlled temperature conditions to produce rapid growth. Quorn grows as fibres. It doubles approximately every 5 hours.

After a few days the Quorn is heat-treated to stop further growth, and is pasteurised. It is then harvested into thin moist, fibrous sheets with a natural wheaty flavour. Egg white is added to bind the protein fibres together, so the Quorn can be chopped.

Texture can be altered by varying the length to which the fibres grow, and by grouping the fibres together to give the texture of meat. Flavours and colours are mixed into the Quorn.

Quorn is sold fresh or frozen, or used to make ready meals.

■ ACTIVITY

Working in pairs, compare two alternative proteins used with meat in a main course dish. Choose either the curry or stir-fry recipe above.

One of you should make the dish using the recipe, which includes either TVP or Quorn.

The other should replace the alternative protein with meat (e.g. beef or lamb) in place of TVP, or chicken in place of Quorn.

- ▶ Use a suitable sensory evaluation test to compare your results (see page 114). Present the results as a star diagram.
- ▶ Compare the energy and nutrients provided by the two recipies using a nutritional analysis program. Are there any noticeable differences?
- ▶ Compare the costs of using TVP, Quorn and chicken.

KEY POINTS

- ● TVP is produced from soya beans.
- ● Tofu is soya bean curd.
- ● Quorn is a protein produced from a fungus.
- ● Alternative protein products are cheap, low in cholesterol and calories, and high in fibre.

IN YOUR PROJECT

- ▶ Could the meat or fish in your product be substituted with a suitable alternative protein?
- ▶ What adjustments would be needed to the flavourings?
- ▶ What difference would be made to the cost of your product?

Vegetable Variety

The variety of vegetables available has never been greater. Vegetables are important because they provide:

▷ *many different textures and colours which make meals more appetising*
▷ *almost 90% of our vitamin C intake*
▷ *dietary fibre, and therefore add bulk to the diet.*

Vegetables may be sold washed and ready to use from chilled cabinets.

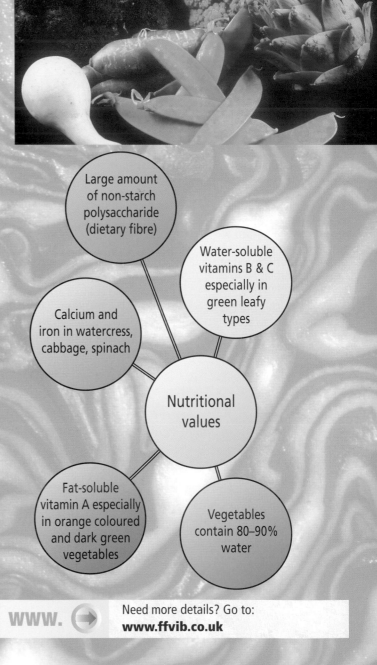

Types of Vegetable

Roots	carrots, swedes, turnips, parsnips, radishes, celerics, beetroot, cassava
Bulbs	onions, shallots, leeks, spring onions, fennel, garlic
Tubers	potatoes, yams, artichokes, sweet potato
Leaves	sprouts, spinach, cabbage, watercress, kale, Brussels sprouts, Chinese cabbage
Fruits	tomatoes, marrows, courgettes, cucumbers, peppers, aubergines, avocados, chillies
Pods and seeds	peas, beans, mangetout, sweetcorn, okra
Flowers	broccoli, cauliflower
Stems	celery, asparagus.

New vegetables

New varieties of vegetables are often introduced in a wide range of shapes, colours and sizes, including baby vegetables. Organic vegetables which are grown without any chemical aids are also more widely available. They are becoming increasingly popular, even though they are more expensive to produce.

Preparation and Cooking

In the home vegetables need to be prepared and cooked carefully to retain as many of the nutrients as possible. In industry vitamins can be added synthetically to vegetables to boost their nutritional value.

Large amount of non-starch polysaccharide (dietary fibre)

Water-soluble vitamins B & C especially in green leafy types

Calcium and iron in watercress, cabbage, spinach

Nutritional values

Fat-soluble vitamin A especially in orange coloured and dark green vegetables

Vegetables contain 80–90% water

WWW. ➔ Need more details? Go to:
www.ffvib.co.uk

IN YOUR PROJECT

► What types of vegetables could you use in your product?
► Which nutrients do they contribute?
► Could their preparation and cooking methods be adapted to help retain more of the nutrients?

KEY POINTS

● Vegetables add colour and texture to the diet.
● They provide most of our vitamin C and dietary fibre.
● Vegetables should be prepared and cooked quickly to minimise the loss of vitamin C.

■ ACTIVITIES

1. Compare the cost per 100 g of a fresh vegetable with its frozen and canned equivalent. Consider the appearance, flavour, texture and difference in price.

Vegetable (100 g)	Price	Appearance	Flavour	Texture
Fresh carrots				
Frozen sliced carrots				
Canned carrots				

2. Vegetables sold in chilled cabinets are often washed and ready to use. Suggest the types and amounts of each vegetable which could be included in the following ready-prepared packs:

► 500 g pack Chinese-style stir-fry vegetables
► 350 g pack mixed salad vegetables
► 400 g pack root vegetables for casseroles
► 500 g pack mix of three vegetables for serving hot – microwaved or boiled
► 400 g pack mixed vegetables for serving with savoury dips
► 220 g pack mixed lettuces.

Choose one of these packs and develop the information which would need to be on the label to inform the consumer about the product. Include information such as: list of ingredients, nutrition information, preparation guidelines, weight, shelf-life details and dates. (See pages 162 to 165.)

3. The following activity asks you to study the effect that adding various substances to the cooking water has on the texture and colour of vegetables.

You can use any green vegetable which is in season. Prepare the vegetables in the usual way. Use small quantities – no more than 50 grams.

Place 150 ml of water in each of 5 small pans. Heat to boiling point.

► **Sample A**: add nothing – this is your control.
► **Sample B**: add a small amount of salt.
► **Sample C**: add a pinch of sodium bicarbonate.
► **Sample D**: add one teaspoon of vinegar – use white vinegar, if possible.
► **Sample E**: add nothing as this will have a different cooking time.

Now add the measured amounts of vegetable to each pan.

Boil sample A, B, C, and D for 10–12 minutes and remove from the heat.

Boil sample E for 1 minute and remove from the heat.

Drain the water from the vegetables into separate beakers.

Evaluate the samples by performing a sensory evaluation test. Note any differences in appearance, odour, flavour and texture. A digital camera could be used.

Record the results as a table, using a word-processor, or as a star diagram using a spreadsheet program.

Devise a test sheet using a DTP program.

You could extend your investigation in the following ways:

► microwaving a sample
► soaking the vegetables in water before cooking them
► putting the vegetables in cold water and bringing them to the boil
► cutting up some of the vegetables and leaving others whole
► cooking the vegetables in a pan with and without a lid
► using a different type of vegetable, e.g. carrots, cauliflower.

Preserving Vegetables/Super Soups

Manufacturers use a variety of ways to process vegetables to keep them fresh. There are many ways in which vegetables can be preserved. They are also used in a range of food products, from soup to main-course dishes.

Preserving Vegetables

Modern methods of processing vegetables are very quick and efficient. This means the preserved vegetable will retain more vitamins and minerals than the fresh equivalent. Preserving also means that a large variety of vegetables is available to consumers when traditionally out of season.

Freezing

Freezing has many advantages. It retains the original flavour, shape, texture, colour and vitamin content of the vegetables. The vegetables are picked, prepared and blanched very quickly. This helps to retain vitamin C. Frozen vegetables often cost more than fresh vegetables, but there is no preparation or wastage and the cooking time is usually shorter.

Drying

Drying is one of the oldest methods known. It is not as popular today, but is used for pulse vegetables (e.g. lentils). Food used to be left to dry in the sun. Now vegetables are air-dried in a warm oven. Vitamin B is lost during the process, and the vitamin C content is destroyed completely.

Freeze-drying

Freeze-drying is a modern method where the food is first frozen and then dried under high pressure. The ice is converted to water vapour and this leaves the food dehydrated. The advantages are that the products are easy to store, they are light in weight, do not require refrigeration and there is very little loss of nutritive value. Freeze-dried foods are easily reconstituted by adding cold water.

Canning

Canning is still a popular method of processing vegetables. Canned or tinned vegetables are quick and easy to use, because the food has already been cooked so it just requires reheating. It is now possible to buy canned foods that have been processed with no additional salt.

Irradiation

Irradiation is a completely new technology. It involves the use of X-rays to preserve food. Vegetables such as potatoes are given very low doses of radiation to prevent them from sprouting during storage. The use of irradiation as a method of preservation is strictly controlled, although it has been allowed in the UK since 1991.

Weighing powdered spices on a computerised scale for a commercial recipe

Super Soups

Soups are popular as an inexpensive starter, a snack or for lunch accompanied by crispbread or rolls. Most soups are quick and easy to prepare. They can be made in advance of serving and frozen.

There are many flavours of soups, some traditional and some new, with interesting combinations of ingredients and flavours. The basis of a good soup is the stock. This can be home-made or, more often, a commercially prepared stock cube is used.

Wheeled bins of portioned ingredients for soup and sauces

A boiling vat

■ ACTIVITIES

1. Find out about some soups made from vegetables. Make a series of lists to show which:
▶ have one main ingredient
▶ have two or more main ingredients
▶ are linked to a specific country of origin
▶ can be served cold or chilled
▶ vegetables are often used for creamed soups.

Compare a home-made soup with a commercially prepared equivalent of the same flavour (e.g. canned, packet, cook-chilled). Compare factors such as cost per 250 ml, colour, texture, flavour, ease of preparation and shelf-life.

2. A food manufacturer wishes to extend its product range of soups to increase consumer interest and boost falling sales.

Carry out research and generate some ideas for a new product range of vegetable soups. They should be suitable for serving hot or cold.

You may wish to base your ideas on a theme such as 'Country style' or 'Continental', emphasising the use of unusual vegetables or herbs.
▶ Work out the total cost of the ingredients needed to make the soup using a spread. How much would each individual serving cost? What is the effect of changing portion size?
▶ Calculate the energy and nutrients provided by the soup.
▶ The manufacturer would make the soup in large quantities. Use a spreadsheet to work out the quantities required to make 20 portions, 50 portions and 100 portions.

IN YOUR PROJECT

▶ What methods would be used to preserve and process the vegetables in your product?
▶ Remember to scale up quantities of ingredients to make them suitable for large-scale manufacture.
▶ Would a theme help make your product more appealing?

KEY POINTS

● Vegetables are used in a wide range of commercial products.
● They are sold ready to use from chilled cabinets.
● Vegetables can be preserved by freezing, drying, freeze-drying, canning or irradiation.

THE BIG CHILL

developing a quality product

87

Pasta is Popular

You only have to look at the number and range of pasta and rice products available in the supermarkets to see how popular they are. Tastes have changed and food manufacturers realise that many people now want alternatives to the traditional British accompaniment of potato to a meal.

Pasta is becoming more popular because it is quick to cook, cheap to buy and combines well with many other foods. In Italy it is a staple food and is often made at home. Pasta is also used in the Far East where it is made from rice flour or cornflour, giving it a different texture and appearance.

Types of Pasta

In the UK we usually buy commercially prepared dried pasta, although fresh pasta is also available and increasingly popular.

▷ Wholewheat pasta contains 9.8 g of dietary fibre per 100 g dried pasta. This compares with 3.0 g dietary fibre in the same weight of white pasta. It has a nutty flavour and needs a longer cooking time than white pasta.

▷ Spaghetti are long rods of pasta usually served with a tomato or meat sauce.

▷ Macaroni are small tubes of pasta cut into short lengths and usually served with a cheese sauce.

▷ Cannelloni are wide tubes which are stuffed with a meat or vegetable sauce and covered with a cheese or tomato sauce before cooking.

▷ Tagliatelle are flat narrow ribbons of pasta served with a sauce or as an accompaniment to meals.

▷ Lasagne are flat wide sheets which are layered alternately with a meat or vegetable sauce and a cheese or white sauce.

▷ Ravioli are little pockets of pasta stuffed with meat and served with a tomato-based sauce.

Developments in the range include flavoured varieties such as garlic, chilli, mushroom and truffle tagliatelle.

Production
Pasta is made from durum wheat, which is grown in Italy, parts of the USA and Canada. Durum wheat is the hardest of all wheats grown and contains the most gluten.

The wheat grains are milled to produce semolina.

A dough is made by adding water to the semolina. Eggs, salt and vegetable oil may be added. Spinach and tomato purée can be added, to give flavour, colour and increase the nutritive value.

The dough is kneaded for 10 to 20 minutes. It is then rolled thinly and cut into strips, or extruded into a variety of shapes.

The pasta may be sold fresh at this stage of processing, or dried to give it a much longer shelf-life.

Cooking
Pasta is usually boiled in water. It absorbs the water, expands and the starch gelatinises.

■ ACTIVITY

Compare the following for rice, pasta and potatoes:
▶ nutritional values
▶ cost of 100 g
▶ preparation and cooking times.

Present your results in a suitable way (e.g. table, graph, pie chart).

Pasta Sauces

A wide range of ingredients can be used to create interesting sauces as a part of cook-chill products (see page 70). Pasta with a sauce is a very good example.

The shape of the pasta and the method by which it is cooked will be the deciding factors in the type of sauce that is chosen.

For example, spaghetti lends itself to a tomato sauce or a dressing made from olive oil, because it is smooth and slender so will not hold a very thick sauce well. Penne and shell-shaped pasta are suited to a coating roux sauce. This is because the pasta is thicker and the sauce can be folded into it. Pasta shapes with wavy edges and flat sheets of lasagne also hold sauces extremely well.

Some popular sauces are:

▷ alla carbonara: a sauce made with eggs, ham and cream, flavoured with black pepper
▷ con ragu: a meat sauce which we often call Bolognese sauce
▷ alla Napoletana: a sauce made from fresh tomatoes, onion, olive oil and garlic
▷ al pesto: a rich sauce made using olive oil, basil, nuts, garlic and Parmesan cheese.

IN YOUR PROJECT

► Which type of pasta (if appropriate) could you use in your food product?
► How will it affect the nutritional profile?
► What type of sauce would be best?
► What are the advantages and disadvantages of providing ready-made sauces?

KEY POINTS

● Pasta can be rolled or extruded into a wide variety of shapes.
● It is sold fresh or dried.
● Pasta is high in carbohydrate but low in fat.
● A wide range of ingredients can be used to create interesting sauces.
● Ready-made sauces are also available.

■ ACTIVITY

Working in groups of four, carry out an investigation into the various types of convenience sauces that are available. Some of the sauces you could include are:

► packet sauces
► cook-in sauces in cans
► cook-in sauces in jars
► stir-fry sauces.

Carry out product evaluation and record details in a table.

Then carry out a sensory evaluation exercise on the sauce you have made (see page 114).

Put all your results together and produce a fact sheet. This could form part of a product development pack.

	Packet sauce	Cook-in sauce (can)	Cook-in sauce (jar)	Stir-fry sauce
Price				
Possible use				
Energy value per 100 g				
Added ingredients for flavour				
Thickener				
Additives or preservatives				
Taste				
Texture				
Appearance				

THE BIG CHILL

developing a quality product

Rice is Nice

Rice is the staple food for over a third of the world's population. It is a good source of energy and contains a small amount of protein. It is available in a range of shapes and sizes and in a number of forms.

Rice produces the best crops when grown in water. It needs high temperatures and a high rainfall during the growing season.

Ninety per cent of the world's rice is grown and eaten in Asia. The UK imports rice from the USA, Italy, China and Australia.

Types of rice

Rice is classified according to the size and shape of the grain.

▷ Long grain rice: Patna rice is named after the district in India from where it came. It has long grains and is served with savoury dishes. Basmati rice has thin delicate long grains and is more expensive than Patna rice. It has a nutty aroma and distinctive flavour which goes well with Indian food.

▷ Medium grain rice: This is rounder and shorter. It can be used in sweet or savoury dishes, but is best known as risotto rice.

▷ Short grain rice: Carolina rice is named after the region of North America where it was first grown. It is traditionally used in puddings with milk.

Production

The grain is enclosed in a thick husk when harvested. This is removed, leaving a brown seed which is the brown rice we buy. It is usually more expensive than white rice, but contains more nutrients, particularly the B vitamins and fibre.

It has a nutty flavour and needs longer cooking.

The grains are milled to remove the germ and bran, leaving whole white grains of rice. Half the B vitamins, dietary fibre and some protein are lost in this process. In countries where rice is the staple food, the loss of B vitamins during processing can cause the deficiency disease beri-beri.

Cooking

Rice is usually cooked in boiling water so that the starch absorbs the water. The grain swells and the starch begins to **gelatinise**.

If it is over-cooked, the starch will gelatinise completely. This causes the grains to stick together in a mass.

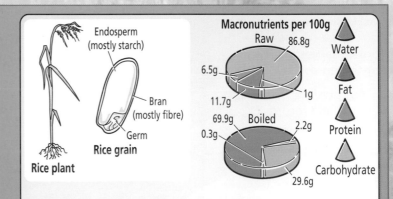

Energy value per 100g: Raw grain 361 kcal, 1536 kJ, Boiled 123 kcal, 522 kJ

Rice can be bought in a variety of forms:

▷ Easy-cook: This is long grain rice which has been treated with steam or boiling water before milling to help retain the B vitamins. The starch is partly gelatinised as a result of the process. Cooking time is therefore reduced and the grains are fluffy, plump and separate.

▷ Pre-cooked: After milling, the rice is completely cooked and then dehydrated (the moisture content is removed by drying). This rice only needs reheating in water before serving. Pre-cooked rice can also be bought canned or frozen.

▷ Boil-in-the-bag rice: This is pre-cooked rice which is sold and reheated in a heat-resistant bag. It is more expensive than uncooked rice.

▷ Ground rice: Small broken grains of rice are ground into a rice flour which can be used for thickening soups, in puddings and cakes, and in biscuits to make them shorter in texture.

▷ Flaked rice: This is used for puddings.

Rice is also used to make some breakfast cereals, and is found in a wide range of ready meals.

Basic rice salad recipe
75 g long grain white, brown or easy-cook rice
50 g frozen peas
50 g sweetcorn, canned or frozen
1 large tomato

- Cook rice according to packet instructions.
- Add peas and sweetcorn during last 5 minutes of cooking time.
- Drain and cool.
- Add chopped tomato. Season.

■ ACTIVITIES

1. Experiment with different ways of cooking rice. Try altering the amount of water used and time left to boil or stand. Try cooking it in the oven, microwave or pressure cooker. Present your results and conclusions clearly.

2. Work in groups of three to compare white, brown and easy-cook rice. Prepare a rice salad for each type, using the same recipe. Set up a taste panel to compare the results. You could also compare the cost and the cooking time. Present your results in a clear table.

3. A Bistro wishes to attract more vegetarian customers. Use your knowledge of alternative proteins (e.g. nuts, Quorn, soya, pulses) to make suggestions for a range of rice-based main course dishes.

▶ What market research might you carry out to identify consumer needs?
▶ Generate a range of ideas and develop a product specification.
▶ Consider the viability in terms of costs, batch production, nutrition, safety, etc.

ICT ➡
Sensory evaluation results and costs can be presented using a spreadsheet.

IN YOUR PROJECT
▶ What type of rice (if appropriate) would be most suitable for your product?
▶ How will it be cooked?

KEY POINTS
- Rice is a staple food in many countries.
- There are several varieties, each with their own flavour and use.
- Rice contributes carbohydrate to the diet.
- Rice is used in a variety of sweet and savoury dishes.

THE BIG CHILL

developing a quality product

91

Saucy Solutions

Sauces are used to add colour, flavour, moisture and nutritive value to food. There are many different flavours and types, such as cook-in and pour-over. The properties and characteristics of sauces are influenced by the way they are made and the proportion of ingredients.

Many traditional sauces are made by adding starch to liquid. Sauces can be thickened in one of the following ways, by using:

▷ starch present in either wheat flour (e.g. white sauce), or cornflour (e.g. custard) or arrowroot (e.g. glaze for desserts)
▷ a purée of either fruit (e.g. strawberry sauce) or vegetables (e.g. Napoletana)
▷ an emulsion of oil and water (e.g. mayonnaise)
▷ the coagulating properties of eggs (e.g. egg custard).

Starch-based Sauces

Cornflour and arrowroot are pure starch. Wheat flour contains a very high percentage of starch. When mixtures of starch and liquid are heated they will thicken. This is known as **gelatinisation**.

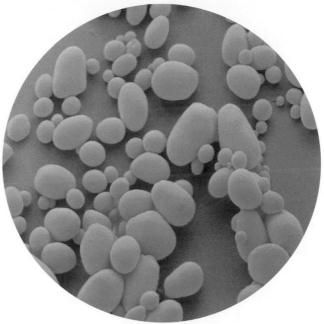

Highly magnified starch granules (magnification x 200)

Critical points in the production of starch-based sauces

Starch consists of tiny granules. They do not dissolve when mixed with a liquid, but are suspended in the liquid.

Stirring the sauce throughout the cooking process ensures the liquid will be heated throughout. If not stirred the starch granules clump together as lumps in the liquid.

When heated to about 60°C the starch granules begin to absorb water from the liquid and swell. Most starch mixtures will start to thicken at between 75 and 86°C. But gelatinisation is not complete until boiling point is reached.

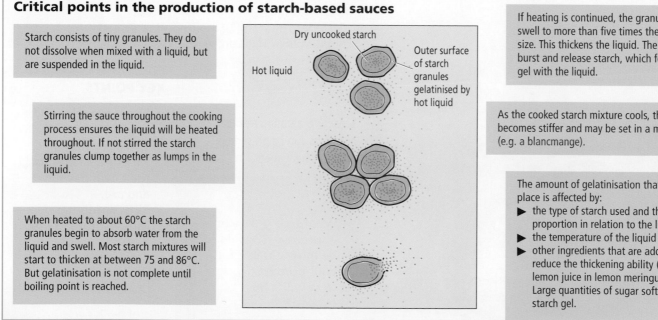

Dry uncooked starch
Hot liquid
Outer surface of starch granules gelatinised by hot liquid

If heating is continued, the granules will swell to more than five times their normal size. This thickens the liquid. The granules burst and release starch, which forms a gel with the liquid.

As the cooked starch mixture cools, the gel becomes stiffer and may be set in a mould (e.g. a blancmange).

The amount of gelatinisation that takes place is affected by:
► the type of starch used and the proportion in relation to the liquid
► the temperature of the liquid
► other ingredients that are added. Acids reduce the thickening ability (e.g. lemon juice in lemon meringue pie). Large quantities of sugar soften the starch gel.

Making Sauces

Starch-based sauces can be made by the blended method, the roux method or the all-in-one method.

The Appearance and Texture of Sauces

When new products are being designed, the effects of cooling, freezing and re-heating may be important in deciding the best ingredients to use. Many cook-chill dishes produced by manufacturers contain a basic white, starch-thickened sauce.

Modified Starches

New technology has brought about the development of modified starches. For example, some modified starches can be whisked into a cold liquid and will thicken without any heating. Others can be sprinkled onto very hot liquids and will thicken without clumping.

Blended sauces

The simplest sauce to prepare is made from cornflour or arrowroot with milk or liquid. It does not contain any fat. It has a pouring consistency and is used to make custard, gravy and arrowroot glaze for flans.

▶ Measure out 14g of starch and 275ml of liquid.

▶ Blend the starch with a small amount of the liquid. This separates the starch grains.

▶ Heat the rest of the liquid until it is almost at boiling point.

▶ Pour this onto the blended liquid, stirring all the time.

▶ Return the mixture to the heat and keep stirring until boiling point is reached and the starch has gelatinised.

▶ Cook the mixture for about 2 minutes, to make sure all the starch has gelatinised.

The roux method

This type of sauce is made from flour or cornflour, butter or margarine and either milk, vegetable liquid or fish stock.

The proportion of flour and margarine used in relation to the amount of liquid will determine the consistency or thickness of the sauce. The roux is made from equal proportions of fat and flour.

Sauce	Flour	Fat	Liquid
pouring	15g	15g	250ml
coating	25g	25g	250ml
binding	50g	50g	250ml

▶ Melt the fat and stir in the flour. The starch grains will become coated with flour.

▶ Add the liquid gradually, stirring well after each addition.

▶ When all the liquid has been added, return the pan to the heat and slowly bring the contents to boiling point.

The starch will gelatinise and thicken the sauce.

The all-in-one method

This is a quick and easy way of making a white sauce. The ingredients and proportions are the same as for a roux sauce.

▶ Put the flour, liquid and fat altogether in a pan. The large amount of cold liquid will separate the starch grains.

▶ Put the pan on the heat and bring the contents to the boil, stirring or whisking all the time. The starch will gelatinise in exactly the same way as in a roux sauce.

■ ACTIVITY

Make up the following sauces, using 275ml of milk or water and the starches and methods listed below. Label the samples **A** to **D**.

▶ **Sample A**: 25g cornflour / blended method
▶ **Sample B**: 25g wheatflour, 25g margarine / roux method
▶ **Sample C**: 25g wheatflour, 25g margarine / all-in-one method
▶ **Sample D**: 25g arrowroot/blended method

Describe the results of their appearance using a table with the following headings:

Extend the table by experimenting with other combinations of quantities, starches and methods.

Sample
Hot
Cool
Re-heated
Frozen and thawed
Thawed and re-heated

Which sauce would you recommend to use as part of a vegetable lasagne to be sold frozen and then reheated?

ICT ➔ Datalogging devices can be used to ensure that temperature is constant for all samples. Results can be easily recorded on a spreadsheet in a word-processor.

KEY POINTS

● Sauces are used to add colour, flavour, moisture and nutritive value to food.
● Sauces can be starch-based using wheatflour, cornflour or arrowroot.
● There are three methods of making sauces.

IN YOUR PROJECT

▶ Which of the three methods will you use to make your sauce?
▶ If you chill or freeze the sauce, how can you ensure the desired outcome on re-heating?

Micro-organisms

Micro-organisms can spoil food. Food preservation is about making conditions difficult for micro-organisms to grow and multiply.

There are three main types: moulds, yeasts and bacteria. Some are harmless, others can make you ill, and a few are used to create certain flavours and textures in processed food.

Individual **micro-organisms** are visible only under a microscope. However, they can multiply very rapidly. Some form colonies which can be seen by the naked eye. The conditions for this growth are:

▷ food
▷ moisture
▷ correct temperature
▷ time.

Moulds

Moulds are minute plants which can just be seen with the naked eye. They grow from special cells called spores that are found in the air. These settle and multiply on any suitable food, forming a fluffy mass. Moulds grow best in moist conditions and temperatures of between 20 and 40°C.

Moulds grow on many different types of food but particularly bread, fruit, meat and cheese. In the manufacture of certain types of cheeses (e.g. Stilton, Danish Blue and Gorgonzola) moulds are used to give the cheese its characteristic flavour and texture. This is done by injecting harmless moulds into the cheese using copper wires. The cheeses are only lightly pressed so that the moulds have a greater chance to develop.

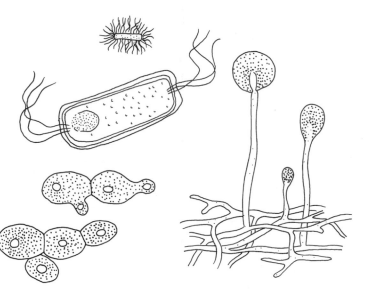

Yeasts

Yeasts are found in the air and on the skin of some fruits, for example grapes. They multiply by 'budding', (dividing in two). They only grow on foods which contain sugar and do not need oxygen to reproduce. Yeasts will reproduce most rapidly at temperatures between 20 and 40°C.

Yeasts can spoil fruits and jam by bringing about fermentation of the sugar, so producing carbon dioxide and alcohol. This can also happen in yoghurts that contain fruit.

Yeasts can, however, be effectively used for fermentation and as a raising agent for bread (see page 39).

Bacteria

Bacteria are single-cell organisms. They are found nearly everywhere – in the air, in water, in animals and in plants. Many of them are completely harmless to us.

If bacteria are given the right conditions they will multiply extremely rapidly, by splitting into two every 20 minutes.

This means that millions of bacteria may develop in food in a very short space of time. This will contaminate the food. What makes bacteria so dangerous is that food can be infected but look, taste and smell quite normal. Those bacteria that can cause disease are described as pathogenic. It is therefore essential to deprive pathogenic bacteria of the conditions which allow them to grow and multiply.

Bacteria are active over a wide temperature range, from 75°C to as low as –5°C. So particular care has to be taken when storing and preparing food. Some bacteria can form spores even if the conditions for growth are not favourable, for example if moisture is not present. These spores remain dormant until the right conditions become available again, when they will germinate and divide. Spore-forming bacteria are very resistant to heat and difficult to kill during normal cooking methods, so great care is needed.

Dead Bacteria

63°C

Active Bacteria

5°C

Passive Bacteria

Making Yoghurt

Bacteria are put to good use for making yoghurt. A culture of lactic acid bacteria is added to either pasteurised or skimmed milk. At 43°C the bacteria clot or set the milk into a cream which resembles custard. After treatment the yoghurt must be cooled to 5°C and stored at this temperature. The organisms which cause the souring are still active at this temperature and this means that the yoghurt will slowly become more acidic. This limits its storage life.

Cream cheese and soured cream are produced in a similar way, using cultures of lactic acid bacteria to bring about the souring process.

www. ➡ For more detaila go to:
www.milk.co.uk

THE BIG CHILL

developing a quality product

■ ACTIVITIES

1. When foods are stored incorrectly or for too long and the datemark is passed, which micro-organisms would cause the following visible signs, and why?
▶ pot of yoghurt with a bulging lid
▶ bread which is dried, cracked and with a blue tinge
▶ milk with an unpleasant smell.

2. Research and list cheeses which have a characteristic flavour, texture and/or colour introduced by moulds.

3. Find out more how yoghurt is made on a large scale. Yoghurts are available in a wide range of types and flavours.
Make a table to show the types and range available in a supermarket chilled cabinet.

IN YOUR PROJECT

What conditions would stop micro-organisms multiplying in the food product you are making?
Produce guidelines for the safe storage and shelf-life of your food product.

KEY POINTS

● Micro-organisms can bring about the spoilage of foods and food poisoning.
● There are three types: yeasts, moulds and bacteria.
● Some micro-organisms can be used in the production of food products such as yoghurt and bread.

On the Shelf (1)

No food will keep fresh and safe to eat indefinitely. The length of time it can be kept safely is known as its shelf-life. Food processing techniques can increase the shelf-life of many foods.

Preservation

Bacteria is present in or on all foods. Some bacteria will spoil food and may lead to illness if allowed to grow.

Preservation techniques aim to do the following:

▷ destroy micro-organisms completely
▷ prevent the growth of micro-organisms
▷ prevent the action of enzymes.

There are a number of ways in which food can be preserved:

▷ using heat
▷ using chemicals
▷ removing moisture
▷ using low temperatures
▷ using X-rays
▷ using modified atmosphere packaging.

Use of Heat

Canning

Canning is still one of the most widely used methods of preserving food. This involves the use of heat sterilisation to kill micro-organisms and destroy harmful enzymes. The food is sealed under pressure to prevent contamination during storage.

Fruit is canned at a temperature of 100°C and the cans are sterilised for 10 minutes. The processing time is short and the temperature low because:

▷ if a higher temperature were used the fruit would be over-cooked
▷ fruit is acidic and so harmful spore-forming bacteria cannot grow and germinate in it.

Vegetables, meat and fish are canned at a higher temperature of 121°C, and the sterilisation process is longer at 15 minutes. This is because:

▷ these foods require a longer cooking time than fruit
▷ vegetables, fish and meat are not acidic, so spore-forming bacteria could germinate and grow if lower temperatures were used.

Pasteurisation

Milk is the most familiar pasteurised product. It is rapidly heated to 72.2°C and kept at that temperature for 15 seconds, before being cooled rapidly. This destroys many of the bacteria.

Sterilisation

Sterilised milk has a longer shelf-life because the processing effectively kills all the bacteria. The bottled milk is heated to 104°C for 40 minutes, or 113°C for 15 minutes.

UHT

This uses ultra high temperatures which destroy all bacteria. The milk is heated to 132–140°C for 5 seconds then cooled quickly.

Use of Chemicals

Sugar, salt and vinegar are the most common chemicals used to preserve food. Strong solutions are necessary. Water from the cells of micro-organisms is removed by a natural process known as osmosis (see page 98).

Sugar

Sugar is used in large quantities in the jam-making process, in order to act as a preservative.

Bacteria cannot survive if the sugar concentration is between 40–50%, but yeasts and moulds are still able to develop. Therefore a concentration of 60% sugar is required. This means that in a finished jam 60% of it must be sugar in order for it to keep well.

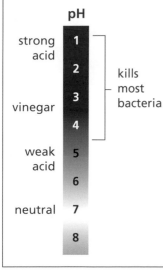

Acidity is measured on a pH scale

Salt

Salt was used a great deal for preserving meat, fish and vegetables. With the introduction of freezing to preserve these foods, salting is far less popular today. However, salt can add flavour to foods such as cheese, sausages, and vegetables canned in brine.

Vinegar

Vinegar contains acetic acid and most micro-organisms do not like acidic surroundings.

The acidity of a substance is measured in terms of its pH value. The pH value of pickles is usually about 3.5 and most bacteria cannot survive below pH 4.5.

Other methods of preservation may use a combination of sugar, salt and vinegar (e.g. chutney).

WWW.

The pH of different products can be measured using a datalogging device. This is useful for product analysis and quality control.

Curing

Curing agents such as salt, sugar and sodium nitrate discourage microbial growth. They are added to meat and meat products such as sausages. Curing agents also add flavour.

Smoking

Meats, fish, sausage and cheese can all be preserved by smoking (see page 75). Smoking adds flavour and prevents bacterial growth, but is less effective against moulds.

Additives

Preservatives such as ascorbic acid can be added to food to extend the shelf-life (e.g. orange squash). These must be listed on the label.

KEY POINTS

- Preservation techniques extend the shelf-life of many foods.
- Preservation destroys micro-organisms or prevents them from growing.
- An increasing number of techniques is used to preserve food today.

THE BIG CHILL

developing a quality product

On the Shelf (2)

Removal of Moisture

Drying is one of the oldest methods of preservation. Micro-organisms cannot grow and reproduce without moisture. Removing water from food means the concentration of salt and sugar increases. This causes water to be withdrawn from the cells of micro-organisms through the natural process of osmosis. Their cells are destroyed and so they die.

One way of drying food is to spread it out in the sun to dry. In industry, mechanical drying methods are used. The food is put on trays and passed through a tunnel where hot air is blown over it until the moisture content is reduced to 25%.

The most modern method of commercial drying is AFD (accelerated freeze-drying). The food is frozen and the moisture is then removed from it. Products processed in this way have an open texture and are easy to reconstitute. The colour and flavour of the food is much improved from conventional drying methods, but the products are fragile and need to be handled with care.

Use of Low Temperatures

Chilling

Refrigerators are used for short-term storage of perishable foods and ready meals that have been prepared by the cook-chill process.

The temperature inside a refrigerator should be kept at 1-4°C. At this temperature most bacteria are dormant and cannot multiply to dangerous levels, although food spoilage can still take place.

By law, certain foods made and kept commercially must be stored below 5°C (e.g. cooked ready-to-eat foods that contain meat, fish, eggs, cheese, ripened soft cheeses, cured meats, and prepared sandwiches).

Freezing

In the freezing process a temperature of −10°C must be reached so that the dissolved solids in food will be frozen as well as the liquid. At this temperature micro-organisms are unable to grow. But not all the bacteria will be killed and some will remain dormant until the food is thawed out. Although the action of their enzymes is slowed down considerably in freezing, they are not destroyed.

For this reason a temperature of −18°C is recommended for domestic freezers.

Blast freezing

Fresh food should be frozen quickly so that very small ice crystals are formed within the cells of the food. This causes much less damage to the food when it is thawed out. In commercial freezing a temperature of −30°C is used and the process is carried out in blast freezers.

THE BIG CHILL

developing a quality product

Irradiation

This involves the use of X-rays to preserve food. For information on this process see page 86.

Modified Atmosphere Packaging

Air inside packages is replaced with gases which help prevent food going off (e.g. crisps, prepared salads). See page 157.

Examples of Preservation Techniques

Principle	Preservation Method	Examples
Using heat	canning and bottling	meat, fish, fruit and vegetables
	sterilisation	milk
	pasteurisation	milk
	UHT	milk
Using chemicals		
• sugar	jam making	soft fruit
• acids	pickling	onions, cabbage, fish
• salt	canning in brine	sausages, bacon, fish
• sodium nitrate	curing	meat, sausages
• smoking		meat, fish, sausages, cheese
• additives – preservatives		
Removing moisture	dehydration accelerated freeze-drying	coffee, milk, herbs and vegetables
Using low temperatures	freezing –18°C min chilling 3–4°C	most vegetables and fruit, meat, fish, ready-prepared meals
Irradiation	use of X-rays	fruit, vegetables, fish
Fermentation	use of helpful bacteria	sauerkraut, Tofu, cheese, yoghurt, bread, beer, wine
Modified atmosphere packaging	gas(es) added to food package just before it is sealed	meat, vegetables, crisps

■ ACTIVITIES

1. Many foods are processed in a number of ways. Choose one food which can be bought processed in at least three ways (e.g. mushrooms which are available canned, frozen and dried). Compare the products' shelf-life, price, taste, texture and nutritional value.

2. Preservation techniques can increase the diversity of foods. Look at the product range within one canned commodity. Fish is a good example, with canned tuna, mackerel, salmon, pilchards, etc. List all the products available within the range you have chosen.

IN YOUR PROJECT

► What preservation method could you use on your food product?
► Will this influence the type of packaging you will choose?
► What will the shelf-life be after preservation?

KEY POINTS

Food decay can be prevented by:
● heating
● removal of moisture
● removal of air
● reduction of temperature
● addition of chemical preservatives.

Additives

Additives are substances added to food during processing. Food manufacturers and consumers need to understand the purpose of additives in order to make informed decisions regarding their use.

Foods which contain anti-oxidants

For thousands of years we have been adding chemicals to our foods to preserve, colour and enhance its flavour. As food science and technology has developed, a much wider range of chemicals has been used in foods during their processing. Many of the foods we buy would not be available without them.

Additives are used to give some additional quality to processed food. They are added in very small quantities. Some are synthetic (created in a laboratory), making it easier to control their purity. Others are natural (extracted from plants or animals). For example the chemical E300 (L-ascorbic acid) used as an anti-oxidant is in fact vitamin C, which is found naturally in many fresh fruits and vegetables.

Foods which contain preservatives

The Advantages and Disadvantages of Additives

Advantages
▶ help the processing and preparation of foods
▶ prevent food spoilage and prolong shelf-life
▶ improve or enhance the flavour or appearance of foods
▶ maintain or increase the nutritional value of foods
▶ produce food of a reliable and consistent quality.

Many food products would not exist without additives. This would reduce consumer choice.

Disadvantages
▶ A number of people may be sensitive to some additives.
▶ Although they are tested before being approved, it is not always possible to forecast the long-term effects of their consumption.
▶ They could be used to mask inferior ingredients.
▶ Some colours and flavours are believed to be unnecessary.
▶ Some people object to chemicals being added to their food.

Foods which contain colouring

Examples of additives people might be sensitive to are:
▶ E101 tartrazine affects some children and asthmatics.
▶ E110 sunset yellow can cause a skin rash and stomach upset.
▶ E211 sodium benzoate can affect asthmatics and cause skin rashes.

'E' Numbers

All additives go through long and strict safety tests to obtain and then keep approval from the Government's Food Advisory Committee.

When an additive is approved it is given a number as a means of identification. If it is accepted for use in the European Union it is given an 'E' prefix to the number.

Additives are constantly reviewed. An additive could be withdrawn if it is thought to be a risk to health.

For example, in 1990 potassium bromate (used to treat flour), was withdrawn because it was found to cause nausea, vomiting, severe abdominal pain and convulsions in some people.

Foods which contain emulsifiers and stabilisers

Type	Numbers	Purpose	Examples (N) Natural (S) Synthetic	Found in
Colours	E100–199	restore colour lost during processing or make food more colourful	(N) E160	margarine, pre-packed Cheshire cheese
			(S) E132	sponge pudding, biscuits, sweets
Preservatives	E200–299	increase storage life by preventing the growth of microbes	(S) E227	soft drinks, fruit yogurt, processed cheese slices, dried fruit, dehydrated vegetables, cider, beer and wine
Anti-oxidants	E300–321	prevent food containing fat from going rancid	(N) E306	packet dessert toppings, vegetable oils
			(S) E321	soft margarine, gravy granules
Emulsifiers and stabilisers	E322–499	enable oil and water to form an emulsion and stop them separating	(N) E322	chocolate, powdered milk, dessert mixes
			(S) E450	cheese, condensed milk, dried milk products

Numbers above 500 are given to acids, anti-caking agents, anti-foaming agents, bases, buffers, bulking agents, firming agents, flavour modifiers, flour improvers, glazing agents, humectants, liquid freezants, packaging gases, propellants, release agents, sequestrants and solvents.

■ ACTIVITIES

1. Look carefully at the ingredients listed on a range of low fat products.
▶ What additives have been used in the product?
▶ What is their purpose?

2. Select five products which make claims about additives on their labels (e.g. do not contain artificial additives, free from colours).

Check the ingredients listed. Are there any other additives included in the list? Do you think the claims are in any way misleading?

WWW. ⊙

If you want more details go to:
www.faia.org.uk
www.ifst.org

IN YOUR PROJECT

▶ Is there a need to use additives in the mass production of your food product?
▶ If so, why?

KEY POINTS

● Additives are synthetic or natural substances added to foods during processing.
● They can prolong shelf-life, improve flavour and appearance and maintain or increase nutritional value.
● The use of additives is strictly controlled by law.
● Additives must be listed on food labels.

THE BIG CHILL

electronic components

Examination Questions

Before spending between one and two hours answering the following questions you will need to have learnt about cook-chill products, pasta, fish, meat, alternative proteins, milk products and food spoilage. This has been covered in Unit Three.

Write your answers on A4 paper. You are reminded of the need for good English and clear presentation in your answers.

1. **This question is about market influences.** *See pages 68–73.*

(a)   Give three reasons why cook-chill products have become more popular in recent years.   *(6 marks)*

(b)   A food manufacturer carries out a survey on cook-chill products and obtains the following information.

The product must be:

● healthy
● give value for money
● includes rice or pasta
● provide variety
● give clear consumer information
● be appealing and interesting.

Taking into account the results of the survey produce a design specification for a vegetarian cook-chill product.   *(6 marks)*

(c)   Name two tests that may be carried out in the test kitchen to ensure the product is suitable for chilling.   *(2 marks)*

2. **This question is about product development.** *See pages 80–85.*

The recipe shown below is a pasta sauce already used by a manufacturer.

(a)   Alternative proteins have been manufactured to take the place of meat. Name three alternative manufactured proteins that could be used to replace the meat in this recipe. Explain what each is made from.   *(6 marks)*

(b)   Explain how the use of alternative manufactured proteins change the nutritional profile of the recipe.   *(4 marks)*

(c)   The test kitchen has found that the pasta sauce product is lacking in flavour and texture. Give two ways of developing this recipe to make it more interesting and appealing to vegetarians.   *(4 marks)*

(d)   Explain why manufacturers are increasing the range of vegetarian products on sale.   *(6 marks)*

3. **This question is about materials and components.** *See pages 92–93.*

Fish is considered a healthy alternative to meat but is often thought to be bland. As a result a manufacturer wishes to develop a range of sauce based fish dishes.

(a)   Give two reasons for the use of each of the following ingredients in preparing and cooking a basic white sauce:
   i)   plain flour
   ii) milk
   iii) butter   *(6 marks)*

(b)   The manufacturer often buys in ready prepared sauce mixes. A list of ingredients is printed on the packaging. Give two reasons for this.   *(2 marks)*

(c)   Instructions for the preparation of the sauce includes 'stir vigorously to aid gelatinisation'.
   i)   Explain why the sauce must be stirred vigorously.   *(3 marks)*
   ii) Explain what is meant by the term gelatinisation?   *(3 marks)*

Pasta Sauce Ingredients
● 500 g red meat   ● 500 g fresh tomatoes
● 50 g butter   ● 250 ml meat stock
● 1 onion   ● 125 ml double cream
● 50 g mushrooms

Method
● Fry meat in butter
● Add chopped onion and mushrooms
● Fry until soft
● Add skinned tomatoes and meat stock
● Simmer
● Add cream just before serving
Serve with buttered tagliatelle.

---

4. **This question is about product manufacture.** *See page 79.*

(a) Explain the meaning of 'high risk foods'. *(2 marks)*

(b) Produce a list of instructions which the meat manufacturer could supply with raw barbecue chicken to ensure it will be safe to eat. *(5 marks)*

(c) How are manufacturers engineering meat based recipes to ensure they meet consumer demands for healthier options? *(4 marks)*

5. **This question is about quality control and assurance.** *See pages 86–87, 95 and 99.*

(a) How could computers be used to ensure efficient quality control and assurance in the following:
   i) production of fruit yoghurt
   ii) use of modified atmosphere packaging for meat products
   iii) preparation of vegetables for soup. *(6 marks)*

6. **This question is about a manufacturer's responsibility.** *See pages 100–101.*

Recent trends have shown an increase in the numbers of products that are labelled 'Additive free'.

(a) Food additives are often shown by an E number on the list of ingredients. What does the 'E' mean? *(2 marks)*

(b) Give reasons for the recent increase in the manufacture of 'additive free' foods and their value to the consumer. *(8 marks)*

Total marks = 75

Quality control checks are carried out on apples before packing them.

Unit Four: Introduction

Making desserts at home can be complicated and time-consuming. They used to be luxuries that were only eaten at weekends or on special occasions. Today, modern food processing technology means that many mouth-watering desserts are sold ready-to-eat from the cook-chill cabinet or freezer.

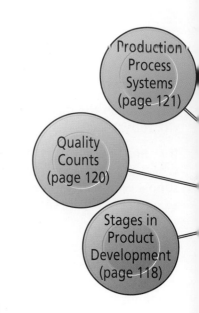

Production Process Systems (page 121)

Quality Counts (page 120)

Stages in Product Development (page 118)

Introduction

Eggs, chocolate, cream, butter, soft cheese and fruit are some of the main ingredients used to create many different types of desserts. Their particular properties or characteristics produce the range of interesting flavours, textures and colours we look for in a dessert.

Most desserts are time-consuming to prepare, however, and often require hours of practice to perfect. Food manufacturers now make a wide range of products to satisfy our needs: we can be easily tempted!

Preparing for the Task

Read through the task below. Before you can start to develop and finalise your ideas for a range of desserts you will need to work through the sections which make up this unit. See the diagram above.

You should also refer to the sections on packaging and labelling at the end of the book, and to the Project Guide at the start of the book. You may also want to review some of the sections from the previous units.

The Brief: Just Desserts

Just Desserts is a small family-owned company. It specialises in providing a range of unusual and visually-striking dessert dishes for local functions.

Just Desserts has decided to expand its business and launch a number of ready-to-eat chilled or frozen desserts, which it intends to supply to specialist retail outlets in its region.

Each dessert needs to be aimed at a specific target group of customers.

The company has asked you to design and make some possible chilled or frozen desserts for its new range.

▷ Which food products would you recommend?
▷ Will they be sold in individual portions, or as 2, 4 or 6 portion products?
▷ What target market should they be aimed at?
▷ What advice can you give Just Desserts on how to make its business a success in terms of setting up a production system?
▷ Many of the ingredients used in the desserts are 'high risk'. What steps will the company need to take to ensure that its products are safe to eat?

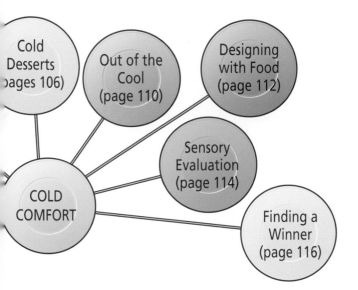

Cold Desserts (pages 106)

Out of the Cool (page 110)

Designing with Food (page 112)

Sensory Evaluation (page 114)

COLD COMFORT

Finding a Winner (page 116)

First Thoughts

▷ What sort of cold desserts are currently on sale?
▷ What ingredients and recipes are involved in making desserts?
▷ How are desserts made and chilled or frozen?
▷ How can sensory evaluation be used?
▷ What are the main stages involved in developing successful new products?
▷ How is production planned?
▷ What safety and hygiene procedures need to be followed?
▷ What type of packaging could be used?
▷ Under what conditions can the product be stored?

Getting Started

First you will need to learn more about the way in which desserts are made. You will need to examine existing products carefully, and find out what people really look for when choosing what to buy. Identifying a specific market is important at this stage: different people buy different desserts for different occasions.

As you work through the unit you will learn about how high and low temperatures are used to process a variety of ingredients commonly used in making desserts. There is also information about the way in which new markets are developed and production processes organised.

Developing your Ideas

Generate your own range of ideas for a suitable cold dessert. Remember that it must be suitable for your target market. You are not expected to come up with a completely new idea, so start with some existing desserts and think how they might be adapted. Experiment by changing things like their ingredients, texture, appearance, size and shape.

Make sure you test some samples using sensory evaluation techniques (see page 114), and record the results.

Work towards writing a final product specification.

Planning and Making it!

Plan the making of your final solution to present to Just Desserts for approval.

Produce a series of display panels to explain the overall process of product development to the company.

Prepare an illustrated report to explain how your product would be manufactured in quantity, and what safety procedures would need to be followed.

Final Testing and Evaluation

Set up further sensory evaluation tests to evaluate your final product. The tests will need to be done by people who represent your target market.

In your final evaluation, refer to the results of your tests and discuss the success of your product in terms of taste, texture and appearance.

Cold Desserts (1)

Food technologists often analyse existing products when searching for new products.

▷ *What do they taste and look like?*
▷ *What ingredients have been used?*
▷ *How have they been made?*

Product Evaluation

■ ACTIVITY

Select a chilled or frozen dessert such as mousse (chocolate or fruit), cheesecake, trifle, crème caramel, or something pastry based (e.g. fruit pie, custard tart, profiteroles, eclairs).

Study the product, the information on the label, the packaging and the price.

Evaluate some of the features of the product such as taste, texture, appearance, portion, size, cost, ingredients, content, etc. Use some sensory evaluation techniques (see page 114).

► What type of ingredients are used in the cold dessert?
► Are additives used? If so, for what purpose?
► Is the dessert eaten straight from the container?
► What is its shelf-life?
► How long can it be stored and under what conditions?
► What is its nutritional value?
► What is the cost of an individual portion or individual serving?

what type of ingredients are used in the cold dessert?

Are additives used, and if so for what purpose?

what is the cost of an individual portion?

Is the dessert eaten straight from the container?

what is its shelf life?

How long can it be stored and under what conditions?

what is its nutritional value?

■ ACTIVITY

Make this recipe for a cold mousse. Try to identify some of the main stages in its production.

▶ What are the correct proportions of ingredients?
▶ How are they added?

Lemon mousse
Ingredients
3 large eggs or 3 medium eggs
Grated rind of 3 lemons
90 ml lemon juice
100 g caster sugar
15 ml gelatine
300 ml double cream

Method
▶ In a deep bowl, whisk the lemon rind, juice, sugar and egg yolks together over a pan of hot water until thick.

▶ Sprinkle the gelatine into 45 ml of cold water in a small bowl and leave to soak. Place over a pan of simmering water and stir until dissolved.

▶ Stir into mousse mixture and chill.

▶ Lightly whip the cream until it just holds its shape.

▶ Whisk the egg whites until stiff.

▶ Fold half the cream into the mousse, then the egg whites until evenly blended.

▶ Pour into a dish and level the surface. Chill in the refrigerator for at least 4 hours until set.

▶ Decorate the mousse with the remaining cream.

Partial coagulation of the yolks will take place by whisking with the sugar over heat. This will make the mixture more stable.

The gelatine should be transparent.

The gelatine must be distributed evenly throughout the mousse. The temperature of both must be the same, otherwise the mixture will separate.

If the cream is over-whipped, a smooth texture will not be obtained.

Eggs should be at room temperature. Any grease in the bowl will reduce the amount of foam formed.

This is so that the mousse will have an even texture.

Length of time for setting is important to achieve a successful result.

■ ACTIVITY

On the right are a recipe and a nutritional analysis of profiteroles. Study them and answer the questions which follow.

1. Choose another cold sweet recipe. Carry out a nutritional analysis of it. Set out your work out in exactly the same way as for the profiteroles.

2. Are the energy value and fibre content of the recipes different? Why is this so?

3. Which recipe would you recommend for a person who was anxious to lower their intake of fat? Give some reasons for your choice.

4. The profiteroles contain very little of the B group of vitamins and no vitamin C. Make some suggestions as to how these could be increased without altering the balance of the recipe.

PROFITEROLES
Serves 4
85 g strong plain flour
50 g butter or block margarine
150 ml water
2 eggs
150 ml whipping or double cream
175 g plain chocolate
50 g soft brown sugar

Energy	8858 kJ	Iron	8 mg
Protein	29.87 g	Vitamin A	865 µg
Total fat	129.6 g	Vitamin B1	0.46 mg
Carbohydrate	230.6 g	Vitamin B2	0.77 mg
Fibre	2.6 g	Niacin	2 mg
Sodium	597.5 mg	Vitamin C	0 mg
Calcium	198.5 mg	Vitamin D	2.425 µg

IN YOUR PROJECT
▶ Evaluate some of the features of a product similar to the one you are designing.
▶ Write an initial product specification for the product you are going to develop and make.

KEY POINTS
● Product evaluation is a way of gaining information about existing products.
● A nutritional analysis of the ingredients of existing products will reveal their nutritional profile.

Cold Desserts (2)

Food technologists trying to create new desserts need to know about the types of raw ingredients available, and how each will react when processed.

Eggs

Eggs are one of the main ingredients of cold desserts, sauces, hot puddings and many different types of cake mixture. They are convenient to use and extremely versatile.

Eggs are graded and sold according to their weight. Sizes 2 and 3 are the most popular for cooking.

The proteins in eggs have three properties which make them useful in cooking:

▷ The protein sets or coagulates when it is heated.
▷ When eggs are beaten the protein stretches and holds air.
▷ The protein in the yolk is a good emulsifying agent.

A *Salmonella* scare in 1989 led the Government to advise not giving raw or partially cooked eggs to babies, the elderly, pregnant or frail people. Some recipes for icings, soufflé toppings and mousses contain raw eggs.

Size of egg

X = 73g+

L = 63-73g

M = 53-63g

S = below 53g

The nutritional value of eggs
▶ protein of high biological value (ovalbumin)
▶ vitamins A, D and B2 (riboflavin)
▶ yolk of the egg contains fat and iron.

How is air introduced into the mixture?
Eggs have the ability to form a foam which can be used to aerate a mixture. The whole egg can be whisked up to hold air and therefore act as a raising agent in, for example, Swiss rolls, sponge flans and hot soufflés.

When egg whites are whisked on their own they can hold much more air and can be folded into cold desserts (e.g. mousse, soufflés).

Egg whites are also used to make meringues or a topping for a cold dessert.

What makes the mixture set?
Eggs set or coagulate when they are heated. The yolk takes longer to set than the white.

▶ Egg white will start to set at 62°C and is completed by the time 70°C is reached.
▶ Egg yolk starts to set at 65°C and becomes firm at 70°C
▶ When the white and yolk are mixed together the coagulation process starts at between 63–65°C .

Meringues
The aerating and coagulation properties of eggs are important in meringues.

Meringues are made from sugar and egg white. Whisking makes it possible to create a stable egg white foam into which sugar can be incorporated.

When it is heated, the mixture coagulates to form a crisp light texture. For the meringue to 'dry out', long slow cooking at a low oven temperature is needed.

■ ACTIVITY

Work individually or in a group to investigate whisking egg whites. Test out:

▶ the use of different equipment
▶ whisking at different temperatures
▶ adding sugar at different times during whisking.

Cream

Cream is one of the main ingredients of cold desserts. It contains all the main constituents of milk but the quantity of water is lower and the fat content is higher.

It is important to use cream with the correct fat content for a particular recipe.

▷ Double cream has a fat content of 48% and whipping cream 35%. They can both be whipped up until they are stiff, and used in cheesecakes and mousses.
▷ Crème fraiche has a fat content of 35%. This means that it cannot be whipped. The cream has a bacterial culture added to it which makes it slightly acid but not sour. It can be used instead of cream as an accompaniment to many desserts.
▷ Yoghurt and fromage frais are low fat alternatives to cream.

Cheese

Cheese is a preserved form of milk. It is a very concentrated food and has a high energy value. It is an excellent source of protein, calcium, vitamins A and B2 (riboflavin).

There are many different types used in the making of cold desserts. For example:

▷ Cream cheese: made from single or double cream. It has a smooth texture, rich butter-like taste and can be bought plain or flavoured. A lower fat version is also available.
▷ Curd cheese: made by allowing the milk to go sour naturally. It has a refreshing, slightly tart flavour.
▷ Cottage cheese: a type of curd cheese made from skimmed milk. It has a very low fat content, and is available either plain or with other ingredients added (e.g. prawn, chives or pineapple).
▷ Quark: fresh curd cheese which comes from Germany. It is made from whole or skimmed milk and sometimes has cream added. It has a slightly sour but rather delicate flavour.

 For more details go to:
www.britegg.co.uk
www.milk.co.uk

Butter

Butter is produced from the cream of milk. It gives a very good flavour to many desserts, and can be used in home-made ice cream, in sauces and as part of the base in cheesecakes. Margarine is a cheaper alternative, but the flavour is not as good.

Gelatine

Gelatine is a protein substance which is extracted from animals when they are slaughtered. It is used as a setting agent in many desserts because it is colourless and almost tasteless. It is used in ice cream, and to set jellies, mousses and cheesecakes. For vegetarian products, agar can be used instead of gelatine. This is made from seaweed.

Fruit

Today a huge variety of fruit is available from all over the world. There is a wide range of textures and different flavours.

The nutrient content of fruits varies a great deal, but they are an important source of vitamin C and dietary fibre.

IN YOUR PROJECT

▶ If the mixture in your product has to set, which ingredients will you use?
▶ If your product needs to have a light, aerated texture, how will it be achieved?

KEY POINTS

● Different textures and flavours are created by using different ingredients.
● When new products are designed, the working characteristics of the ingredients are used to create the desired outcome.

Out of the Cool

Milk is a versatile food ingredient, but it needs heat treatment before it can be sold. The following case study of a small family business shows how low temperature treatment of milk can produce a range of ice creams.

Ice cream is another milk product. This time, however, lower temperatures have been used to change its properties. Low temperatures slow down or even stop bacteria from spoiling foods.

A family firm has managed to combine a raw product (i.e. milk) with other ingredients to make a highly successful range of ice cream products.

'The company started in 1986 on a very small scale making ice cream in the farmhouse kitchen. We now make it on a commercial basis in premises designed to meet the current Food Safety regulations.

The ice cream is sold from the farm shop and retail outlets including a supermarket, museums, tourist centres and garden centres.

Winning several small business awards for developing an innovative product helped us to finance study of ice cream making, setting up a small business and working out practical issues for a commercial ice cream industry.

Small-scale development to supply local retail outlets was chosen in preference to supplying a major supermarket chain, which would have meant investing £750 000 in manufacturing plant and equipment.

Our main raw ingredient is milk from 96 Jersey cows, which in total produce around 3000 litres per day. The jersey milk has a 6% fat content and 3.8% protein content. It is this characteristic feature that makes this ice cream product very distinctive.

The company makes 300 litres of ice cream per hour in 15 litre batches. The mixture is gradually frozen and stirred intensely using a special beater fitted with scraper knives. These stop the ice cream freezing onto the sides of the barrel. The ice cream is then stored at −30°C until it is dispatched to the retail outlets.'

Ice Cream Ingredients

The ingredients used in the production of ice cream are:

▷ milk: with high fat, protein and lactose content
▷ cream for palatability: alternatives are butter and vegetable fat, but these do not carry the flavour as well as cream
▷ sugar: cane sugar as a sweetener
▷ dextrose: to make ice cream better to handle for scooping
▷ stabiliser: to increase shelf-life
▷ emulsifier: to make the ice cream more tolerant to temperature change and to enable the structure of the mixture to hold air properly
▷ flavours: a wide variety to stimulate appeal.

Product lines

Flavours

'The business makes 30 varieties of ice cream. They range from firm favourites, such as vanilla and strawberry, through to the unusual. The best selling line is Clotted Cream Ice Cream.

Flavours include:

▶ 'Ginger and Honey' with ginger from Australia and acacia honey from China
▶ 'Yum Yum' which contains chocolate, pecan nuts, toffee pieces, biscuits, toffee sauce and vanilla mainly imported from Canada
▶ 'Mint Chocolate Chip' with mint flavouring, green colouring and chocolate chips from Italy.

Blackcurrant is only popular in summer, and the chocolate and orange failed to gain customer approval.

The ice creams are sold in single or double sugar cones, with additional toppings of fresh clotted cream, nuts and rainbow strands.

The company is always looking for new ideas to develop, such as low calorie ice cream and frozen yoghurt.

Low calorie

Research and product development led to the successful launch of a low calorie Vanilla Dairy Ice. This tastes like ice cream but has a low fat and low sugar content, which makes the product suitable for diabetics and other specific low calorie or low fat diets. This

nutritional profile is achieved by using:

▶ skimmed milk
▶ fat replacer in place of milk fat
▶ artificial sweetener in place of cane sugar.

Frozen yoghurt

Skimmed milk is the base ingredient of frozen yoghurt. Dried skimmed milk is used to increase the solids content. Yoghurt culture is mixed in and left for 12 hours. This makes a light ice cream mix, with a low fat and higher sugar content.

Frozen yoghurt forms 50% of the iced dessert market in the USA, but is less than 5% in the UK. It is thought that the market share may increase in the future.

■ ACTIVITIES

1. Obtain some wrappers and cartons of ice cream products and list each ingredient and its purpose. Use a computer to make a spreadsheet to record your findings.
2. Find out the temperature of the freezer cabinet from which ice cream is sold. Suggest reasons for this.
3. Research the differences between evaporated milk and condensed milk.

Milk is a very versatile food. It is relatively cheap and has many uses in food product development. It has a high nutritional value and therefore provides a breeding ground for micro-organisms. By law, all milk sold in the UK has to undergo some form of heat treatment to kill harmful bacteria. This also helps the keeping quality of the milk.

Methods of Heat Treatment

The main methods of heat treatment are:

▷ Pasteurisation: milk is heated to 72°C for 15 seconds and then cooled rapidly to below 10°C. This does not change the flavour of the milk and the cream line can still be seen. Fat contents – whole milk 3.9%, semi-skimmed 1.6%, skimmed 0.1%, Channel Island 5.1%.
▷ Homogenisation: milk is warmed and forced through tiny holes. The cream does not rise to the top but is evenly distributed through the milk in the form of very small drops. The homogenised milk is then pasteurised.
▷ Sterilisation: milk is homogenised, put into bottles and sealed with a metal top. It is heated to 112°C for 15 minutes. Sterilised milk will keep for several months if it is not opened.
▷ UHT: milk is homogenised and heated to an 'ultra high temperature' of 132°C for 1 second. It will keep for over 6 months if it is not opened.

The nutritive value of milk

Milk contains:
▶ protein content of high biological value
▶ fat content at least 3%
▶ sugar in the form of lactose
▶ calcium and phosphorus
▶ vitamin A and vitamin D
▶ vitamins B1 (thiamin) and B2 (riboflavin)
▶ little vitamin C.

The effect of heat processing on the nutrient content of milk is that:
▶ vitamin C is destroyed during processing
▶ vitamin A is removed during production of skimmed milk
▶ the fat content varies according to the type of milk.

IN YOUR PROJECT

▶ Should any of the ingredients in your product be kept at a low temperature to prolong storage life?
▶ Would it be beneficial to freeze your product?
▶ How might the product line be developed further?

KEY POINTS

● Low temperatures are used to preserve a variety of foods.
● New product lines are developed through the use of popular and unusual flavours, textures and altered nutritional profiles.

Designing with Food

Our choice of food is strongly influenced by our senses. We look at food and smell it before we choose to eat it. Taste and texture are important qualities. Even the sense of sound plays a part. These experiences do not happen by chance – they are all carefully designed.

Food manufacturers aim to get us to choose to buy their products. If we don't, they will go out of business.

Making Sense of it All

We use all five senses to evaluate food: taste, texture, appearance, smell and sound. Together these shape the way we experience the product.

To begin with, the appearance, smell and sound of the food influence our expectation.

Making your mouth water
We see our food before we eat it. What it looks like raises our expectations of what it will taste like. Food needs to look appetising: its shape, colour and texture need to make us want to eat it. A colourful and attractively garnished meal will lead us to expect it to be tasty.

The food container will also contribute to our anticipation and enjoyment – anything from a highly decorative delicate bone-china plate and lead-crystal glass goblet, to a plastic dish and paper cup.

Snap, crackle and pop
Sounds can increase our expectations of some foods: for example, the sizzle of a steak cooking or the fizz of a soft drink.

Smelling delicious
Smell is sensed in the upper cavity of the nose, which can distinguish up to 10000 different odours. Smell is very important in the anticipation of flavour. Smell in combination with taste gives the full sensation of the flavour.

Repeating the experience
If the experience of eating a particular food product has been enjoyable and satisfying, you are more likely to do two things. One is to recommend your friends to try the product, and the other is to decide to buy the product again. These are both essential outcomes for the manufacturer, because:
▶ potential customers are much more likely to try something new if it has been recommended to them
▶ strong sales depend on the habit of repeated purchases.

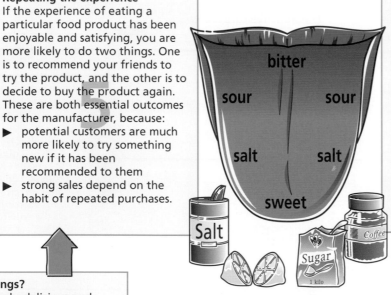

Sticky fingers
The next stage is to begin to transfer the food to our mouths. We may use knifes, forks or spoons, maybe chopsticks or perhaps our fingers – which is often the most enjoyable method! During this stage we begin to interact with the food and learn more about its texture and its temperature.

Second helpings?
Some food looks delicious and appetising, but fails to taste as good as it looks. Other products taste good to begin with, but begin to lose their appeal after just a couple of mouthfuls.

All in the best possible taste
Finally, inside our mouths the taste and texture of the food either satisfy or disappoint our expectations.

The taste of a food product is sensed by the tastebuds on the tongue. These can distinguish between four groups of flavours: salt, sweet, sour and bitter.

Mouthfeel
The texture of food is an essential part of our enjoyment of the product. Food can be described by words such as crispness, chewiness, crunchiness, hardness, stickiness, etc.

Looks Good, Tastes Good

What is it that makes some foods look, sound and smell good, as well as taste good?

People respond particularly to harmony and contrast – things which go together and things which set each other off. In food products certain ingredients, textures, colours and smells work well together, while others succeed because they are completely different to each other. These harmonies and contrasts apply to:

▷ flavours (e.g. salt and vinegar)
▷ textures (e.g. a choc-ices)
▷ colours (e.g. strawberries and cream)
▷ shapes (e.g. hot dogs)
▷ smells (e.g. sweet and sour)
▷ sounds (e.g. snap, crackle and pop).

When you design or evaluate food products, you need to think about how well the ingredients, texture, appearance, smells and sounds work together to provide a satisfying mix of harmony and contrast.

Sometimes we want foods that are familiar, easy to eat and comforting. On other occasions we might want to be more adventurous and choose dishes which have a greater contrast of flavours, textures and colours

ICT ➡

Use a computer graphics program to rapidly experiment with different colour harmonies and contrasts.

Colour and taste

Colour plays a crucial role in the design of food products. We look for bright, strong and consistent colours to reassure us that the product is fresh and full of flavour.

Manufacturers spend a long time ensuring the colour is exactly right. Most of the food we eat has had its colour enhanced in some way to make it look more appetising.

For example:

▶ breads and cereals may be made to look golden brown
▶ cakes and butter may have a yellow dye added
▶ vegetables such as peas and green beans may be re-coloured after processing
▶ salt, sugar, rice and white flour may be bleached to give then the whiteness we expect.

Certain colours suggest certain flavours. Look at these colour combinations. Which taste does each suggest – sweet, salted, bitter or sour?

When the colours of familiar foods are altered, they can seem to taste completely different. A group of testers reported feeling ill after eating mashed potato which was coloured blue. Blindfolded testers often find it difficult to tell the difference between common flavours.

IN YOUR PROJECT

▶ When testing your designs, consider how the ingredients harmonise and contrast with each other.
▶ How could your product be altered to create a more appealing result?

KEY POINTS

● Food products are carefully designed to appeal to our senses.
● We evaluate food using all five senses – taste, appearance, smell, texture and sound.

Sensory Evaluation

To say that a food product is good or bad, tasty or unappetising is not very helpful. Food manufacturers need to measure the qualities of their products. They do this using sensory evaluation techniques to trial and test their products at several stages in the process of product development.

What is Sensory Evaluation?

Sensory evaluation involves the scientific measurement of the qualities of a product.

Samples from the production line are tested against specific criteria (e.g. strength of flavour). They may be compared with a control item of known quality.

Sensory evaluation is used to:

▷ check that the product matches its specifications
▷ match products against competitors' products
▷ inform decisions on reformulation or changes to existing products
▷ determine produce acceptability and to demonstrate new products to the sales team
▷ test shelf-life
▷ check standards of quality during production.

Carrying out Sensory Evaluation

Scientific principles are used to ensure **fair testing**, so that there can be confidence in the results. Conditions must be controlled, and tests are carried out by trained testers. The area must be clear of everything except the samples of food and response sheets. Testing should take place in well-lit booths in a room free from other smells.

▷ Samples of food should be in identical plain containers, and should be equal in size or quantity. They should be coded so that the tester knows as little as possible about them (e.g. Sample A, B).
▷ Water should be sipped between each tasting to clear the mouth.
▷ There should be clear instructions for the tester and a simple response sheet to fill in.

Difference Tests

These are used to determine whether there are any noticeable differences between two or more products. They include paired comparison tests and triangle tests.

Difference tests could be used when a change of ingredient or process has been made, to see if the sensory characteristics of the new product are improved or changed in any way. They could also be used to compare products with competitors' products.

Sample	1st Choice	2nd Choice	3rd Choice	Score	Order
A	✓	✓✓✓		9	2
B	✓	✓✓	✓	8	3
C	✓✓✓	✓		11	1
D		✓	✓✓✓	5	4

Paired comparison tests

Coded pairs of samples are tested for the difference of a specific characteristic. For example, the tester may be asked, 'Which of these two samples is the sweeter?'

At least six testers are needed to produce reliable results. This is the most simple test to carry out.

Triangle tests

Three coded samples are tested, two of which are identical.

Testers are asked to pick out the odd sample, without identifying the nature of the difference. Afterwards they may be asked further questions about the differences they notice.

This is a more efficient test than the paired comparison. Triangle tests are often used in quality control to ensure production and batches are the same.

Ranking Tests

A set of coded samples is given to the tester in a random order. The tester ranks the samples in order of some specific quality (e.g. sweetness) or hedonic ranking (i.e. in order of preference). A minimum of 10 testers is needed to produce reliable results. These tests are often used to screen one or two of the best samples from a group.

Rating Tests

Graphic scales such as this may be used to rate a specific characteristic:

☐ Extremely sweet
☐ Very sweet
☐ Moderately sweet
☐ Slightly sweet
☐ Neither sweet nor sour
☐ Slightly sour
☐ Moderately sour
☐ Very sour
☐ Extremely sour

For hedonic rating a numerical scale such as this may be used:

1. Like extremely
2. Like very much
3. Like slightly
4. Like moderately
5. Neither like nor dislike
6. Dislike moderately
7. Dislike slightly
8. Dislike very much
9. Dislike extremely

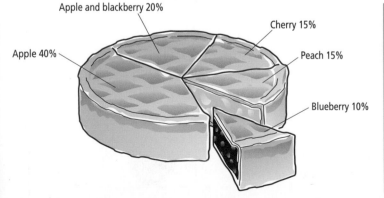

A Pie chart can be an effective way of presenting test data

Descriptive Tests or Profiling

A group of six or more trained panelists assess the flavour or texture of a product to provide a sensory profile. This is a detailed evaluation of its characteristics. A complete description of the differences between the samples helps the product developer to modify product characteristics.

A set of sensory descriptors is given for the testers to use. For example: colourful, glossy (for appearance); stale, pungent (for odour); clawing, dry (for mouth feel); floury, insipid (for flavour); brittle, mushy (for texture).

A star diagram is often used to show the results.

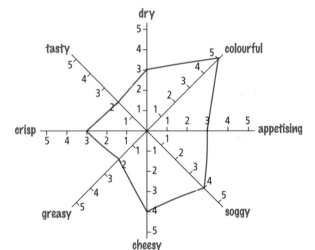

ICT ➡

Sensory evaluation results can be effectively presented using a spreadsheet program.

IN YOUR PROJECT

▶ Explain how you could use sensory evaluation during the development of your food product.
▶ How would you set up a suitable sensory evaluation booth to test your product?

KEY POINTS

● Food manufacturers use sensory evaluation to trial and test products during development.
● Sensory evaluation is the scientific measurement of the qualities of a product by the senses.
● Test conditions are carefully controlled to give accurate results.

Finding a Winner

New products appear in retail and catering outlets all the time. Where do the ideas come from, and what makes a manufacturer think its new idea will be a winner?

Producing a new product that will be successful is not easy. When developing new products, manufacturers consider consumer trends or fashions to generate new ideas.

Consumer Trends

It isn't just the clothing industry that follows fashion. There are very definite fashions or trends in food too. It's not only what people eat that determines a trend, but when and how they want to eat it, and who they will be with at the time.

Healthy eating
- ▶ Increased awareness of healthy eating has resulted from a number of official reports. .
- ▶ Many new products have a 'healthy' image which is used to make them more marketable (e.g. Birds Eye Healthy Options range).
- ▶ Low fat, low sugar, low salt, high fibre or calorie counted are often emphasised on labels.
- ▶ Healthy alternatives to existing products are demanded by the consumer (e.g. canned fruit in natural juice rather than syrup).
- ▶ Healthier preparation methods have also been introduced, such as oven baking replacing frying for crumbed fish and chips.

Recipe sophistication
- ▶ Consumer tastes are now more diverse and sophisticated.
- ▶ Increase in cookery and food programmes on television from different regions or countries.
- ▶ Increased foreign travel gives us an appreciation of food from other countries which we like to replicate at home.
- ▶ Increased consumer awareness of a wide variety of food ingredients (e.g. fromage frais).
- ▶ Products are often based on authentic ingredients rather than adaptations.
- ▶ New products or ingredients often become fashionable (e.g. sun-dried tomatoes). These generate further product ideas using them as ingredients.

Microwaves
- ▶ Many homes now own a microwave oven.
- ▶ Some foods are produced especially for the microwave (e.g. micro chips, Kelloggs Hot Krumby cereal).

Changes in lifestyle
- ▶ More emphasis is now given to leisure time.
- ▶ Family structure and size is changing. Families are often smaller now.
- ▶ More women go out to work.
- ▶ Families eat together less.
- ▶ People often 'graze' or snack rather than eat three meals a day.

Changes in the food industry
- ▶ New processing techniques (e.g. genetically engineered tomatoes used for tomato purée).
- ▶ Improved distribution methods for fresh chilled and frozen foods.
- ▶ Increased sales of own-brand products in supermarkets.

What is 'New'?

New food products may be developed in one of the following ways.

▷ An entirely new ingredient: For example, the development of Quorn resulted in a range of products including Quorn Kiev, burgers and sausages.
▷ An ingredient new to the country: such as jars of Passata, and bagels.
▷ Changes or extensions to existing ranges: new flavours, low fat versions, changes in pack sizes.
▷ New to the manufacturer: as a result of looking at competitors' products.
▷ Products using new processing or packaging systems: many ready meals previously sold frozen can now be bought as cook-chill or **ambient shelf-stable products** (with a shelf-life at room temperature).

Designing for Success

The final test of any new product will be whether it is tried, and then bought again and again by the consumer. With such a high failure rate of new food products, the designers must assess the consumer demands carefully. They must match their new products to meet those demands.

In 1992 alone, 3288 new food and drink products were launched. However, it is estimated that for every new product that reaches the shops, there are over 50 other ideas which fail. They may have failed during planning, at any stage during development or even during regional test marketing (when a product is sold in a limited area to see how successful it is).

Vegetarian products
▶ The increase in vegetarianism has resulted in a wider range of products being available in the supermarket as well as health food stores.
▶ Many non-vegetarians are now eating less red meat and more beans and pulses for reasons of health or economy.

Products for children
▶ Young children often eat different foods or at different times to the rest of the family.
▶ Children can influence their parents' purchases. Food manufacturers use advertising and marketing techniques such as promotional material, free gifts and TV tie-ins (e.g. Power Ranger yoghurts, Postman Pat pasta shapes).

Key new product areas
▶ fish and seafood (e.g. Birds Eye Fish Cuisine Range)
▶ ready meals and recipe dishes (e.g. Birds Eye World Cuisine range)
▶ frozen confectionery and desserts (e.g. McVitie's American Dream range)
▶ canned added value vegetables (e.g. ratatouille, hot and spicy mixed beans)
▶ cooking sauces in jars (e.g. Homepride Cook in Sauce range)
▶ savoury and sweet snack products
▶ sandwiches and lunch packs
▶ desserts and yoghurts.

Supermarket own brand products are also increasingly important, competing with well known brands.

Luxury products are a key growth area. Consumers now demand more products which are as close to fresh as possible.

■ ACTIVITIES

1. Working individually or in groups, make a list of all the new food products you have seen advertised over the past few months. What is your reaction to them? Did they appeal to you? Did they sound exciting and different, or just a variation of existing food products? Which new products have you tried? What did you think of them?

2. Visit a local supermarket, or go to www.newfoods.com, and find your own examples for each of the trends described on these two pages.
Study the ways in which new food products are marketed, through advertising, promotional offers and packaging.

IN YOUR PROJECT
▶ Which current consumer trend will your product be designed to meet?
▶ What is your consumer target group?
▶ How will your product meet its needs?

KEY POINTS
● New products are developed to meet consumer trends.
● Changes in lifestyles have led to the development of many products.
● Key new product areas are chilled foods and ready meals or recipe dishes.

Stages in Product Development

Manufacturers follow a clear process when a new product is being produced. A team of food technologists, nutritionalists, product evaluators, officers and marketing managers will be involved.

The New Product Development Manager co-ordinates the whole process from the initial brief to the final launch of the product.

When designing and making new food products you will need to follow a simplified version of the process used in industry.

Initial brief
This tells the product development team what is required by the manufacturer (e.g. 'a ready-to-eat cold dessert').

Market research
The team identifies possible areas for development by a variety of methods, such as evaluating existing chilled desserts, studying consumer eating patterns and shopping habits.

Design specification
Using the results of market research, the team develops a design specification for the product. This lists the general criteria the product needs to meet, (e.g. cold product, single family portion, rich in calcium, fruit flavoured, any colour).

Concept screening
From the large number of initial ideas, the team now selects five or six which best meet the specification and which are the most viable to develop further. Ideas may be rejected, for example, because of difficulties in acquiring the raw materials, or difficulties in making the product in bulk.

Generation of ideas
The team uses a variety of techniques to come up with a number of possible ideas – sometimes over fifty.

Future developments
The Brand Manager now takes over the viable product, but the development team will continue to work on ideas to extend the product. Perhaps other flavours or different pack sizes could be developed to increase sales.

First production run
The food technologist is present during the first production run to ensure large quantities can be produced to the required standards. Quality control will be carried out. Samples are tested throughout production to make sure standards are met. Quality assurance is assessed at the end of production, to ensure the final product meets the specifications. The product is then packaged.

Final product specification
The exact ingredients, recipe, processes, size, HACCP guidelines and packaging details are defined in a written specification. This ensures accuracy, safety and consistent product quality.

Product launch
Strategies are developed for targeting, pricing, promotions and advertising. Tasting stands may be used in supermarkets, or perhaps money-off coupons distributed to draw consumers' attention to the new product.

Test marketing
The product will be sold in a small area or limited number of stores to assess its potential success. Even at this stage, a product can still fail if it is unsuccessful.

Products which fail in the test market are rejected.

Product Life Cycle

Sales of most products follow a typical pattern. After the launch, sales growth is fairly slow to begin with. Production costs will be high at this stage. As the product becomes better known, sales increase rapidly and the rate of profits grows. Gradually sales level off. This is the maturity and saturation stage. A decline in sales follows eventually for all products.

Regular reviews by market researchers help keep the food industry informed about changes in consumer needs. Products may need to be be re-designed to meet the new market, or rejected completely.

First phase | Second phase | Third phase | Fourth phase

Sales

Product formulation and development
This is an intense period of activity lasting up to three months. The ideas are tried out and developed to meet the initial specifications. These are called prototypes. They will be tested in many ways before any large sums of money are spent on mass production.

Raw materials, equipment and processing techniques have to be selected. Laboratory tests and nutritional analysis is carried out. Packaging designs are made and a mock-up package will be produced. Some ideas may be dropped at this stage if they do not prove to meet the specifications.

Sensory evaluation
The prototypes are tried out on consumer taste panels using appropriate sensory evaluation tests. The results are analysed statistically to put the ideas in rank order.

Selection and modification
Two or three ideas are selected at this stage. Some changes may take place to enable the products to be made in bulk. Trials to establish the shelf-life will be started.

Consumer testing
Consumer taste panels will now select one product for final development. Small-scale production runs are carried out and the products are then tested to assess mass consumer reaction. If it meets with approval, the product will then progress towards final launch.

Products which fail consumer testing are rejected or modified.

Commercial needs
A lot of information has to be gathered to assess commercial viability. These include costs, safety, large-scale production techniques, nutrition, shelf-life, preservation, availability of raw materials, etc. Nutritional, legal and recipe information are gathered to go on the labels.

Photographs and artwork for the final package design are commissioned.

Industrial modifications
Some modifications to the design may have to be made to allow for mass production techniques. This could include the use of commercial ingredients such as flavours, modified starches, sweeteners, etc.

IN YOUR PROJECT
► Follow the stages of product development carefully when designing your product.
► How could you launch your product successfully?

KEY POINTS
● Product development follows a clearly defined process.
● The initial brief states what is required.
● Ideas can be dropped at any stage.
● Sales of a successful product will grow rapidly, then level off, before eventually declining.

Quality Counts

Consumers expect their food to be safe and of consistent quality. Food manufacturers and food service industries need to be sure that all the products they make or serve satisfy each customer's demands and expectations of that food product.

In the food manufacturing industry, quality assurance and quality control procedures are applied to ensure standards are met and maintained.

The word quality is often used these days. The consumer expects a quality product, but it is difficult to define what quality is.

▷ Quality is what gives the customer satisfaction with a particular food product.
▷ Quality helps persuade a customer to buy a food product (or service) again and again.

Quality must be planned for and built into the manufacturing process. This may include:

▷ knowing the customers' needs and expectations
▷ designing a food product to meet customer demand
▷ faultless construction of the food product
▷ using reliable materials, ingredients and component parts
▷ clear food labelling and instructions
▷ suitable packaging
▷ safe storage, transport and delivery
▷ efficient customer services.

Quality Assurance

Quality assurance is a term food manufacturers use to define the overall standard of a food product. It helps ensure that it will be manufactured consistently within quality specifications. It covers:

▷ raw materials specifications
▷ suitability of suppliers
▷ recipe information
▷ manufacturing methods and environment
▷ in-process specifications and feedback for control
▷ finished product specifications
▷ appropriate storage
▷ distribution and recall control systems.

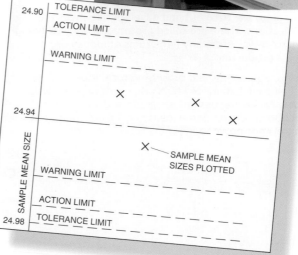

Quality Control

Quality control is part of quality assurance. It involves sampling and testing a product as it is being made. The quality control chart shown above is used to plot how close the sampled products are to the tolerance limits (see page 60). If the samples regularly start to fall close to the limits, the production production process is investigated to discover the reason why. In this way quality is maintained, and possible failure can be predicted and dealt with before a fault shuts down the whole production line.

Food Control

While the terms quality assurance and quality control continue to be used in the food industry, the difference is becoming less clear. Leading authorities are beginning to use instead the overall term of **food control**.

Production Process Systems (1)

To design a product to be suitable for manufacture, it is important to understand something about production systems and how they are planned.

Systems Analysis

A production **system** is an interconnected series of materials, components and events. Changing one part of the system will have an effect on the whole process. Careful analysis of a system can reveal more efficient ways of making it work.

The first stage in analysing a production system (or part of one) is to identify its 'inputs' (e.g. raw materials, machines, workforce), the 'outputs' (what is produced) and the 'processes' (how inputs are changed into outputs).

The next stage is to collect factual information (e.g. how long it takes for something to happen, or how often), and opinions (people's observations and comments) about how well the system works.

Finally this information can be analysed to discover if:

▷ the manufacturing process is too complicated or wasteful
▷ changing the inputs or outputs would improve performance
▷ enough quality checks are being made
▷ maintenance, emergency and safety procedures are working efficiently.

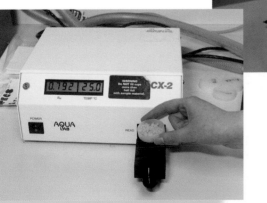

Inputs, outputs and transformation processes

All systems have 'inputs' and 'outputs'. The main purpose of a system is to change or transform the inputs into outputs. Most systems have many different sorts of input and output, and the first stage in analysing a system is to identify the inputs, outputs and the transformation processes involved.

An example might be a take-away restaurant. The inputs might include hungry customers, uncooked food, packaging materials, financial investment, etc. The outputs might include satisfied customers, take-away meals, profit or loss, etc. The restaurant is a system for transforming these inputs into outputs.

It is also possible to analyse a system in terms of a sequence of events, e.g. order food – pay – carry to table – eat – clear table.

Some transformation processes serve to maintain the 'equilibrium' or balance, of the system. Others work to improve the quantity and/or quality of the outputs. It is therefore possible to identify and analyse whether the various processes going on are maintaining the balance or attempting to improve quantity or quality.

Feedback and control

When undertaking a systems analysis it might be discovered that the quantity or quality of the outputs are unsatisfactorily in some way – poor quality print for example, or a lack of profit in a restaurant perhaps.

As a result it may be found desirable or necessary to change the inputs, or to alter the process of transformation. This is known as feedback. The means by which the inputs or processes are changed are called controls. The success of a system is judged by considering how well it transforms its inputs into outputs, and how well it is prevented from failing to work satisfactorily as a result of its feedback and control mechanisms.

As well as quality of product or provision of a service, systems analysis often focuses on achieving acceptable time delays.

Production Process Systems (2)

Most production processes involve a mixture of batch and mass production methods. Some parts might need to be individually or batch produced; others will be made continuously.

Different types of manufacturing equipment are needed for different processes. Some require special purpose tools; others require basic machines with interchangeable parts.

IN YOUR PROJECT

▶ What are the main stages of manufacture of your product?
▶ How can the production be organised most efficiently?

One-off production
It might take several hours for a chef to produce an individual food product. This is costly in terms of labour and materials, though does result in a very high quality product.

Batch production
If tasks and manufacturing equipment are shared, a team of people can produce more of an identical product, in less time than if each person worked on their own. Working in this way, they can also respond quickly to changes in market demand and switch to making a different product. This is known as **batch production**.

Mass production
If a number of workers split the manufacturing process up into a production line then they might easily be able to make a specific number of identical products very quickly for hours, weeks or months on end.
Although this reduces time and costs, the whole production stops if there is a problem. Changing the line to make a different product can take a long time.

Continuous production
Continuous production is when the production process is set to make one specific product 24 hours a day, seven days a week, possibly over periods of many years. This occurs in some areas of food manufacture (e.g. bread), where it would take a long time to stop and re-start the production process every day.

Planning Production

The first task is to identify the step-by-step process by which a product will be made. The different stages of manufacture can then be grouped together into areas of production. When planning a production line, different stages and processes of manufacture are coded using standard symbols.

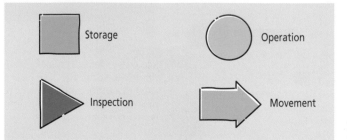

Storage

Operation

Inspection

Movement

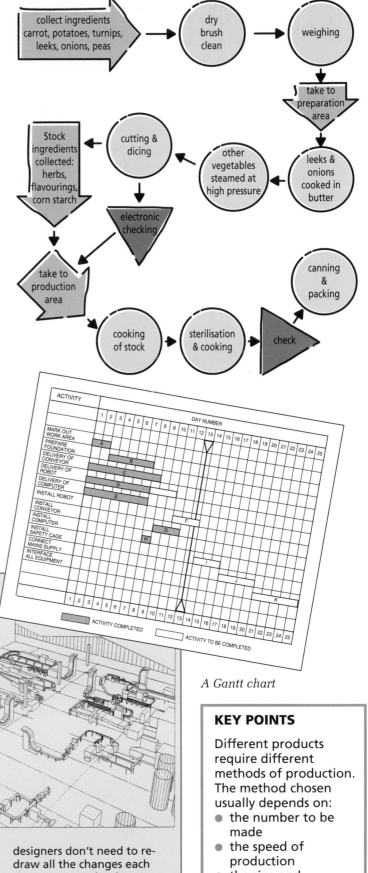

The production line

When all the operations have been identified, the next stage is to plan the layout of the production line. This is likely to involve a number of sub-assemblies – where separate ingredients have to undergo some processing before they can be added to the main production line. For example, cheese might need to be grated first.

Sub-assemblies are often made in what are called manufacturing cells. These are smaller individual units where four or five people operate specific machines or processes.

Other ways of organising a manufacturing process involve grouping similar machines and or ingredients together in one area. This has some advantages, but generally increases the distances that products need to travel within the factory.

Just in time

It is important to ensure that the correct materials and components arrive at the production line at exactly the right time and place. Many factories use a production control system called 'Just in Time' to ensure this happens efficiently.

In all types of production, a complex and accurate production schedule is essential to tell everyone when to prepare, assemble and finish the different components. A Gantt chart is often used to help plan production.

A Gantt chart

Case study:

Birds Eye Walls

Factory layouts and production scheduling can now be done more efficiently using computer-based systems.

The Birds Eye Walls CAD system has the power to allow you to fly through 3D views of the factory and see how new layouts will look in practice. Production machines are built up on screen as a series of blocks. These can be moved round quickly to see where they fit best.

Layers (like sheets of tracing paper) are used within the CAD package to hold the details of different services such as water, steam, air and chemicals.

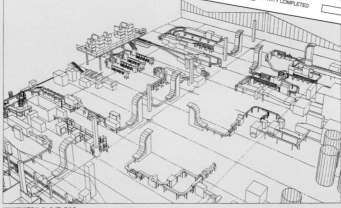

The system is much more accurate than old methods of drawing. Although the initial CAD drawing takes as long to produce, a great deal of time is saved because system

designers don't need to re-draw all the changes each time on a completely new drawing.

KEY POINTS

Different products require different methods of production. The method chosen usually depends on:
- the number to be made
- the speed of production
- the size and complexity of the product.

Unit Five: Introduction

Not so long ago, a salad meant little more than curled up lettuce leaves and tasteless tomatoes. Salads may be healthy, but unless they are appetising it can be difficult to be tempted by them.

Can you design some imaginative salads which not only do you good, but taste good and look absolutely irresistible?

Structure in Food Products (page 126)

Making it Safe to Eat (page 134)

Preparing for the Task

Read through the task on this page. Before you can start to develop and finalise your ideas for a range of salads, however, you will need to work through the sections which make up this unit.

Design specification

Product Type: a range of salads and dressings
* A variety of portions of different salads. These will be sold in lidded plastic tubs.
* A variety of dressings which can be poured over the salads and mixed while in the tub.
* The salads must make an imaginative use of ingredients such as nuts, fruit, seeds, protein and carbohydrate foods, etc.
* The flavour of the dressing should compliment the salads (e.g. a tikka flavoured dressing to go with a rice salad with red and green peppers and chicken pieces).
* The range of salads and dressings must appeal to students from different backgrounds and cultures.
* A single salad might be used to accompany another meal, or a number of different salad portions might provide a meal in themselves.
* The salads may be eaten in the tub, emptied onto a plate or dish, or be taken away.

'Since I took over as College Principal, I have become very concerned about the poor eating habits of my students. In order to find out what the students think of the college canteen I asked for some market research to be carried out. The research revealed that students:

* would like a wider choice of menu
* are looking for dishes with plenty of taste and flavour
* find the current selection of salads and other cold foods bland and uninteresting.

I have since asked the Catering Manager of the canteen to produce an outline specification which provides an indication of the new products we are looking for.

We are seeking an outside catering company to produce and supply these new items on a daily basis. Although quality is essential, so is good value.

For the well-being of the students, I also need to be assured that the potential health hazards will be strictly controlled.'

The Task

Imagine you work for a local catering company and would like to be given the contract to supply the college. Prepare some sample products, together with full costings and a hazard analysis plan for a follow-up meeting with the Principal and the Catering Manager.

First Thoughts

▷ Which vegetables would be suitable for the salads?
▷ What other ingredients could be included?
▷ Which basic recipes could be used for the dressings?
▷ What 'flavour themes' could be used?
▷ How will production be kept hygienic and safe?

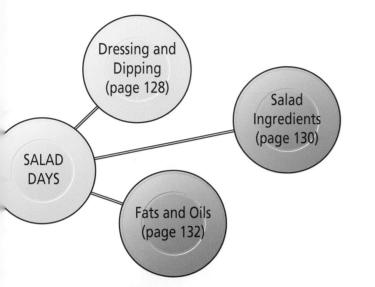

Getting Started

If possible, arrange to visit a local college and talk to the Catering Manager.

Alternatively you could approach the Canteen Supervisor in your school. You might undertake a small survey of likes and dislikes about salads.

As you work through the unit you will learn more about the structure and texture of food, salad dressings and savoury dips, vegetables and fats and oils. There is also a section on **Hazard Analysis and Critical Control Point (HACCP)**.

Developing your Ideas

Generate a range of ideas for the salads and dressings. Think about flavours, textures and colours which will compliment each other, and those which would provide contrast.

You will need to conduct some experiments and perhaps organise a taste-testing session. Choose one salad and dressing to develop further.

First consider how 100 portions of the salad would be made freshly on a daily basis. Work out a costing. What would happen if you used cheaper ingredients to reduce the cost? Could the salad be improved significantly with the addition of extra or more expensive ingredients?

Planning the Making

As well as making a final version of one of your salads and a dressing, you will also need to produce a final plan to show how 100 portions could be made. This could be in the form of a flow chart.

On the plan you will need to identify the critical points during the production process where something might happen which could cause harm to the consumer. Say what precautions will be taken at these points to reduce the risks.

You should also write out the full final specification for the salad and dressing.

Final Testing and Evaluation

If possible, take your sample product and production plans to the college, your school canteen or a local catering business and get some expert opinion. You could also set up a sensory evaluation session to get feedback from students.

Make sure you comment on your test results in your final evaluation. Do you agree with the comments made by the experts? How reliable are the results of the consumer tests?

Finally discuss how well you have worked on the task. What aspects are you most pleased with? Where could you have done better?

Structure in Food Products

When designing and making it is important to consider the structure of the foods involved. The structure affects the texture. If a food is processed, its structure will change.

Food structures can be:

▷ *plant and animal foods*
▷ *processed foods.*

Food structures can be divided into two groups:

▷ those that still contain the basic cell structure of the plant or animal from which the food comes (e.g. potatoes, cabbage, meat, fish).
▷ those foods that have been processed from the primary plant or animal source (e.g. jam, butter, ice cream, meringue). These include colloidal structures.

Plant and Animal Foods

Animals and plants are made up of cells grouped together into tissues. All cells have a soft outer membrane, but plant cells also have a rigid outer cell wall. Animal cells, and therefore animal foods, are particularly high in protein. The cellulose in plant cell walls make plant food high in carbohydrate.

Meat contains connective tissue holding the muscle cells together. These need cooking to soften the structure before eating and digesting. Fish flesh does not contain connective tissue, has a softer structure and so requires less cooking.

Some plant foods can be eaten and digested while fresh and raw (e.g. lettuce, cucumber, oranges). Others need to be cooked to soften the cellulose structure before they can be bitten, chewed and digested (e.g. potatoes, beetroot, rhubarb). Some plant foods can be eaten both raw and cooked (e.g. cabbage, carrots, apples).

Some foam can be scanned on a flat-bed scanner. This will allow you to assess the shape, volume, surface features and texture of a product.

Processed Foods

These are foods like jam or butter that have been made or processed from primary plant or animal sources (e.g. fruit, milk).

Colloidal structures

Many processed foods which have more than one ingredient have a **colloidal structure**. These consists of two parts. One part is evenly mixed into the other. The parts may be:

▷ liquid (e.g. milk, water, oil)
▷ solid (e.g. starch grains/flour, jelly)
▷ gas (e.g. air bubbles, carbon dioxide).

There are four types of colloidal structures: emulsions, foams, suspensions and gels.

Part	Part	Type of colloid structure	Food product
Solid in	liquid	suspension	flour in milk (sauce)
Liquid in	liquid	emulsion	vinegar in oil (mayonnaise)
Liquid in	solid	gel	water in fruit (jam)
Gas in	liquid	foam	air in egg white (beaten egg white)
Gas in	solid	solid foam	air in baked egg white (meringue)

Emulsions

You may have heard the saying 'oil and water do not mix'. Emulsions are formed when one liquid is made to mix with another when normally the two liquids would separate.

If oil is vigorously shaken with water, tiny droplets of water can be seen mixed in the water. It forms an emulsion but it quickly separates leaving two layers.

To stop the emulsion separating, a third substance is added to attract the two parts together. This 'matchmaker' is called an emulsifying agent. It holds the tiny droplets in position.

Examples of emulsifying agents used in food production are:

▶ lecithin (found naturally in egg yolk) stabilises mayonnaise and creamed cake mixtures
▶ glycerol monostearate (GMS) stabilises margarine.

Foods whose structure is an emulsion include:

▶ milk: oil in water
▶ cream: water in oil
▶ mayonnaise: oil in water
▶ margarine/butter: water in oil
▶ creamed cake mixture: water in oil.

Look at the labels of some commercial dressings and identify the ingredient acting as the emulsifier.

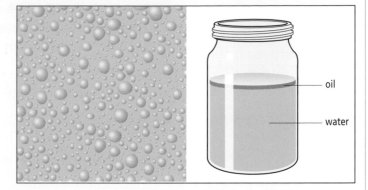

oil

water

Emulsion – Liquid in Liquid   Emulsion – Separated

Gels

Gels are formed when large amounts of liquid are set by small amounts of solid material. Examples are pectin which sets jam, and gelatine which sets jelly. Gelatine is also used to set a variety of cold sweets (e.g. lemon soufflé).

Gels are important in food preparation because they set or hold food products together. Often the food products are elastic (e.g. jelly, jam).

Foams

A foam is formed when gas (e.g. air) is mixed in a liquid (e.g. egg white). The trapped air bubbles increase the volume of the mixture. The bubbles are held in the liquid by a foaming agent. The stabiliser in beaten egg white is the protein albumen.

Beaten egg white, whipped cream and icecream are examples of foams. An example of a solid foam is meringue.

The protein albumen sets or coagulates when heated. During cooking of meringue the protein coagulates. It changes from the liquid state, becomes a solid and helps the meringue keep its shape.

Suspensions

A different colloidal structure occurs when a solid is mixed into a liquid. For example, the starch grains in flour are mixed into a liquid (often milk) when a sauce is made. Stirring the mixture keeps the solids evenly mixed in the liquid.

Heating the mixture causes the starch grains to swell, burst, dissolve in the liquid and thicken it (e.g. sauces, custard). If left to cool, a solution forms like an elastic solid (e.g. blancmange).

■ ACTIVITY

The following are products which have an egg foam in the mixture: Swiss roll, sponge flan, meringue, mousse.

Make one of these products, to demonstrate how a foam is formed and set.

IN YOUR PROJECT

▶ What type of food structure is your food product?
▶ If it is a colloidal structure, which type is it?

KEY POINTS

● The structure of a food affects its texture.
● There are two groups of food structures – plant and animal foods, and processed foods.
● Many processed foods have a colloidal structure.
● There are four types of colloidal structure.

www. ➲ For more detail go to:
www.foodtech.org.uk

Dressing and Dipping

Different dressings can create a completely new flavour in a salad. A dressing helps the salad ingredients combine together, stops them from drying out, and improves the flavour.

Various savoury dips are also available to serve with fresh raw vegetables.

Raw Ingredients

Salad dressings are made from the following basic ingredients.

Oil

Oil usually forms the basic component of any dressing. Olive oil will give the best flavour although it is expensive to buy. Some of the richer oils, such as walnut and almond, are becoming increasingly popular. They blend well with lighter oils, such as sunflower oil.

Vinegar

Most dressings combine oil with something acidic. Yoghurt, mustard and lemon can all be used but the most common ingredient is usually vinegar. Vinegars may be flavoured with garlic, herbs, wine or cider.

Other ingredients

Salt, garlic, mustard and herbs such as chopped chives, tarragon and parsley can be added to give flavour to a dressing. Spices, nuts, cheese, vegetables, cream, yoghurt and crème fraiche are other possibilities.

The two most widely used salad dressings are mayonnaise and vinaigrette. Most other dressings are derived in some way from these two. A wide range of dressings is now available such as blue cheese, thousand island, garlic and yoghurt.

Many of these dressings and dips can be bought ready-made, and the range is increasing all the time. They are not difficult to make at home, however, and would certainly cost less to produce.

Making Salad Dressings and Mayonnaise

If oil and vinegar are mixed together an emulsion will be formed, but when left to stand the oil and vinegar will separate out. A stable emulsion can only be formed if an emulsifying agent is added.

The emulsifying agent used for mayonnaise is the fat called lecithin contained in egg yolk. This also thickens the mixture.

All the ingredients used in mayonnaise should be at room temperature for best results.

■ ACTIVITY

Working in pairs, use the recipe for mayonnaise on the right as a control and compare it with samples made by:

▶ just stirring all the ingredients together
▶ beating all the ingredients together with an electric hand mixer
▶ using the ingredients straight from the refrigerator
▶ adding yoghurt, cream and other ingredients to vary the consistency and flavour of the mayonnaise.

What are the reasons for the differences in your results?

Product Range

You can create new flavours by adding other ingredients. Try using different oils or vinegars. A wide range is available. Add herbs or spices, or fruits, vegetables, seeds or nuts. Yoghurts could be thick set or Greek style, or you could try cream or crème fraiche in its place.

Storage Conditions

Mayonnaise contains raw egg which is classified as a 'high-risk' food. This is because bacteria will easily grow in it. Mayonnaise must therefore be stored below 5°C and eaten within three days.

■ ACTIVITY

The salad bar in a local delicatessen currently offers vinaigrette, mayonnaise, thousand island and blue cheese dressings. You have been asked to design a new dressing which could be added to this range.

▶ Evaluate the four products currently available.
▶ Decide which sector of the market your new dressing will be aimed at (e.g. children, vegetarians, teenagers).
▶ Generate a range of possible ideas using a variety of suitable ingredients.
▶ Write a specification for one of your ideas.

Vinaigrette – an unstable emulsion

1 level teaspoon salt
1 crushed clove garlic
1 rounded teaspoon mustard powder
1 tablespoon vinegar
freshly milled black pepper
6 tablespoons olive oil

Method
Put all the ingredients in a screw topped jar and shake until well mixed.

Mayonnaise – a stable emulsion

1 egg yolk at room temperature
125 ml oil
1–2 tbsp vinegar
salt, mustard powder and pepper.

Method
▶ Beat the dry ingredients into the egg yolk in a small basin. This will help the lecithin in the egg yolk to form a stable emulsion.

▶ Add the oil drop by drop, whisking the mixture all the time until it is thick and smooth.

▶ Add the vinegar drop by drop in the same way as the oil.

▶ The mayonnaise should look like very lightly whipped double cream.

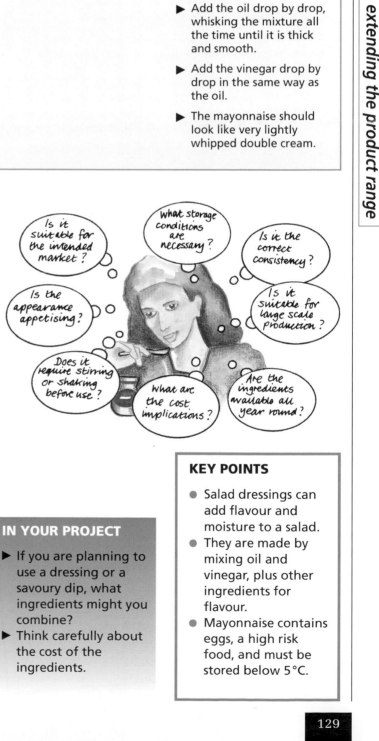

IN YOUR PROJECT

▶ If you are planning to use a dressing or a savoury dip, what ingredients might you combine?
▶ Think carefully about the cost of the ingredients.

KEY POINTS

● Salad dressings can add flavour and moisture to a salad.
● They are made by mixing oil and vinegar, plus other ingredients for flavour.
● Mayonnaise contains eggs, a high risk food, and must be stored below 5°C.

Salad Ingredients

A salad can be just about any combination of vegetables, fruit, nuts, seeds, eggs, meat and fish: the variety is endless. As well as making a meal more attractive by providing a variety of colours and textures, salads can also add many nutrients to a meal. Salads can be raw or cooked, and are usually served cold.

Salads are offered by many fast food outlets as an accompaniment to their main dishes. Coleslaw is sold at fried chicken take-aways, for example, and pizza restaurants have a salad bar.

Supermarkets sell a wide range of ready prepared salads, as well as all the vegetables and dressings to create your own. Many of the vegetables can be bought washed and prepared ready for use, although these will obviously cost more.

Seasonal raw vegetables can be used to create attractive salads at any time of the year. When lettuce is expensive in winter, cabbage can be used instead. The vegetables will be most nutritious when eaten raw, retaining the water-soluble vitamins and mineral elements which are lost during cooking. However, some ingredients have to be cooked before eating (e.g. potatoes).

Salads can also provide dietary fibre and bulk to a meal, helping to give a feeling of fullness. Two of the most popular salads are coleslaw and potato salad.

Coleslaw

The basic ingredient of coleslaw is cabbage. This belongs to the brassica family which includes cauliflower, broccoli, and sprouts. There are many varieties of cabbage which grow at different times of the year. It is a good source of vitamin C, some vitamin A and is low in calories. Winter white or red cabbages are usually used in coleslaw.

> **Coleslaw**
> 200 g white cabbage
> 1 medium carrot
> 2 sticks celery
> 100 ml mayonnaise

■ ACTIVITIES

1. Using this recipe for coleslaw as a starting point, create variations which could be served with burgers in a fast food outlet. Calculate the energy, fat and vitamin C provided by the coleslaw. Be adventurous!

2. Research the variety of ready prepared salads available in your local supermarket. Include details of ingredients, types of dressing used, costs and nutritional value.

Compare their costs with the equivalent unprepared vegetable ingredients. Do you think they are worth the extra cost?

extending the product range

Potato Salad

Potatoes are probably the most versatile of all vegetables and can be used in a wide range of dishes from soups to sweets. They are cheap to buy and still play an important part of a balanced diet.

They are an important source of vitamin C, complex carbohydrate, dietary fibre, protein and essential minerals. They are also low in calories.

Over 40 varieties of potatoes are sold – whole, in their skins, sometimes loose or packaged, washed or unwashed. The varieties differ in size, shape and colour. The texture can be floury, watery, creamy or waxy. When choosing a variety for a potato salad the texture is important. Why do you think this is?

Going Brown

Many fruit and vegetables turn brown when cut and left uncovered. This makes them very unattractive.

The cell walls of the fruit or vegetable are damaged when cut, chopped or broken. This exposes the cell contents (including enzymes) to oxygen in the air. Oxidation causes the browning effect, known as enzymic browning. Vitamin C is also lost. Browning can be reduced by removing the oxygen, for example by coating the pieces with a dressing or by changing the acidity level by adding lemon juice.

Making a Quality Product

When making salads, the size of the pieces of vegetables need to be consistent (i.e. the same size and shape). This will help to ensure a high quality, attractive product.

In industry the minimum and maximum sizes and shapes of vegetables used in salads are specified. These are known as designated tolerances.

■ ACTIVITIES

1. Working in groups, use four different varieties of potatoes to make a potato salad.

▶ Compare the results.
▶ What is the texture of the potato when cooked?
▶ Which variety was most successful?

Potato salad

350 g potatoes cut into bite-size pieces and boiled until tender

1–2 spring onions or 2 tbs chopped chives

150 ml mayonnaise

1 tbs wine vinegar

2 tbs chopped parsley

1 tsp chopped mint

2. Prepare a selection of fruit and vegetables which normally brown when cut (e.g. apples, pears, potatoes).

Cover samples of each with **a** water, **b** salad dressing, **c** lemon juice.

Leave for 30 minutes and record what has happened.

▶ Which method controlled enzymic browning most effectively?
▶ How will this affect a way the caterer prepares salads in large quantities?

3. Devise ways in which caterers or manufacturers can ensure uniformity of the size of the pieces of vegetables in their salads.

▶ Explain why this is important.
▶ What specific pieces of equipment could you use to help you?

ICT ➔

A digital camera could be used to record the stages of 'browning'.

IN YOUR PROJECT

▶ Explain how you can ensure that the nutrients of your salad product will be retained?
▶ How can you prepare ingredients which are consistent in their size and shape?

KEY POINTS

● Salads are created by combining different vegetables and fruits.
● Vegetables and fruits are most nutritionally valuable when eaten raw.
● Vegetables and fruit often turn brown after being cut.
● Browning can be reduced by coating with another ingredient or changing the acidity level.

Fats and Oils

Fats and oils are used in food products to improve appearance, flavour, colour, palatability and nutritional value. Many different types are available. Each has its own properties and uses in a wide range of food products.

Fats and Oils as Ingredients

Fats and oils can be used:

▷ to give flavour (e.g. shortbread)
▷ to enrich (e.g. sauces)
▷ as a shortening (e.g. shortcrust pastry) by coating flour particles with fat. White fats have the best qualities for this but lack flavour. They are often combined with butter or margarine.
▷ to aerate (e.g. cakes). Fat is able to trap and hold air, giving volume and a light texture.
▷ to form emulsions (e.g. in salad dressings and in sauces).
▷ to increase shelf-life. Fat helps stop baked products drying out and going stale too quickly because it emulsifies with moisture.

Fat being creamed with sugar

Fat being rubbed into flour

Fat being melted for a sauce

Oil being whisked with vinegar to form an emulsion

Fats and Oils as Cooking Mediums

Fats and oils can be used for:

▷ shallow and deep frying: to cook foods at high temperatures (e.g. chips)
▷ lubrication: to prevent food from sticking (e.g. in shallow frying or to grease baking tins)
▷ sealing: to seal food to keep moisture out (e.g. melted butter covering pâté)
▷ basting: roasted meats are basted with fats to stop them drying out and burning. This also improves colour and flavour.

■ ACTIVITIES

1. Working in groups, compare a selection of low fat spreads, butter substitutes, butter and margarine. Compare fat content, colour, texture, flavour, energy value, cost and 'spreadability'.
▶ Put your results in an appropriate table.
▶ How well do these alternative products compare with butter and margarine?

2. Look at the ingredients list on the packaging from: shortbread, individual apple pies, hot chocolate drink sachets, cheesecake.
▶ Identify the type of fat or oil used and suggest the function of the particular fat or oil in each product.
▶ Use the nutrition information panels (per 100 g) on the packaging and compare the energy fat provided from each.
▶ Use a computer to present the results in a table, e.g. a word-processor or DTP program.

Types of Fats and Oils

Although we need to cut down our intake of fat, we all need some fat to provide the vitamins A, D, E and K.

Saturated fats come from animals and are solid or semi-solid at room temperature (e.g. butter, lard).

Unsaturated fats and oils come from fish or vegetables and are liquid at room temperature (e.g. sunflower, soya, olive). They are used to make margarine.

Butter
Butter is made by churning cream. It is a popular animal fat for spreading and baking. Butter is firm and difficult to spread if refrigerated, but has a delicate flavour. It can be salted or unsalted.

Ghee
Ghee is clarified butter. It is produced when butter is heated gently until all the water evaporates and the milk solids fall to the bottom. The fat left on top is ghee.

Ghee cooks at high temperatures without burning, and is used in many Indian dishes.

Vegetarian ghee is produced from hydrogenated vegetable oils.

Compound white fats
These fats are blended from animal, vegetable and fish oils. They are aerated to give a smooth texture, and are used for pastry (e.g. Trex, Cookeen).

Low fat spreads
Low fat spreads are emulsions of blended vegetable oils and water. They were first introduced to aid weight loss but are now targeted towards the health conscious. These spreads contain about half the fat of margarine and butter and therefore have a lower energy value.

Low fat spreads are fortified with vitamins A and D. They are unsuitable for baking or frying because of the high water content (more than 16%).

Hydrogenated fats
Hydrogenation is the process by which liquid oils are changed into a solid fat. Hydrogen is pumped through a blend of polyunsaturated oils. The addition of hydrogen increases the size of the molecules of oil, and the oil hardens. It becomes a saturated fat.

Saturated fats have been claimed to increase cholesterol levels in the blood.

Very hard or very soft fats can be produced according to the degree of hydrogenation. Hydrogenated fats are often used commercially.

Oils
Oils are extracted from pressed seeds or fruits. Cold pressed oils are more expensive (e.g. olive oil).

Oils are refined in order to improve the taste and smell, remove impurities and increase shelf-life.

The flavours of oils differ according to the seed or fruit used. They can be made, for example, from maize, olives, sunflowers, soya, rapeseed, sesame, walnut, coconut or a blend of two or more. Some give a distinctive flavour to a variety of dishes.

Margarine
Margarine is blended from vegetable or fish oils or animal fats. Vitamins A and D are added by law to give a nutritional value similar to butter.

Soft margarines are produced from polyunsaturated vegetable oils. They are believed to be a healthier alternative to animal fats. Kosher margarine has no milk solids added.

Lard
Lard is made by rendering pork fat (i.e. heating until it melts). It is softer and more oily than butter or margarine, and used for shallow frying and pastry making.

Suet
Suet is made by shredding the fat surrounding beef or lamb kidneys. It is used for suet pastry and dumplings.

IN YOUR PROJECT

► What role do fats and oils play in your product?
► Could the fat or oil content be reduced to create a more healthy product, by reducing the energy content?

KEY POINTS

- Fats and oils improve the appearance, flavour, colour, palatability and nutritional value of food products.
- Fats are solid at room temperature.
- Oils are liquid at room temperature.
- There are many different types of fats and oils.

SALAD DAYS

extending the product range

Making it Safe to Eat (1)

Hazard Analysis and Critical Control Point (HACCP) is the system used for identifying the potential hazards involved in food production.

Manufacturers must identify points where hazards may occur and decide which are vital to consumer safety. Preventive action can then be established at these critical control points.

Consumers expect their food to be safe to eat. But food poisoning can easily happen if the food has not been stored, prepared, cooked or served properly.

The manufacturer needs to assess the risk of a food product becoming a health hazard. Each food product has its own particular danger points.

Manufacturers need to be able to anticipate problems if they are not to waste a lot of ingredients, time and money. Rejecting contaminated products, or even worse, receiving complaints from customers or the local health inspectors, is too late.

Risk Assessment

Risk assessment means thinking about:

▷ what could happen
▷ when it could happen and taking steps to prevent it from happening.

Risk assessment methods ensure that food operations are designed to be safe and that potential hazards are taken into account.

Hazards

A **hazard** is anything which may cause harm to the consumer. It could be:

▷ biological (e.g. *Salmonella* in chicken)
▷ physical (e.g. glass in food of any kind)
▷ chemical (e.g. cleaning chemicals in any kind of food).

These hazards can occur at any stage in food production, manufacture and/or service. For example, during:

▷ harvesting of raw ingredients
▷ production of ingredients
▷ transport to the processing plant
▷ formulation, processing and storage of the product
▷ distribution to the retail outlet and consumer.

Hazard Analysis and Critical Control Point (HACCP)

This is an important risk assessment method used in the food industry. It:

▷ identifies points where hazards may occur
▷ decides which are critical to the consumer
▷ checks the food product at critical points
▷ sets out action to be taken if not within safe limits.

Application of HACCP

The HACCP process may appear complex but it identifies simple steps to reduce health risks. If too many **critical control points** are found, then the whole production process needs to be reconsidered.

The manufacturer needs to ensure that all staff understand the system, and know why and how it is used. They will need to be trained to check things like those shown below:

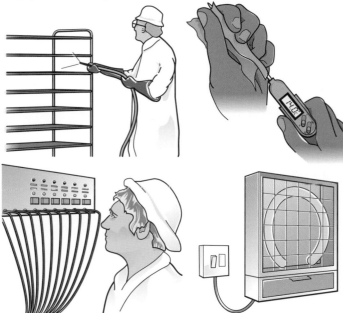

▶ keeping areas clean and hygienic

▶ wiping temperature probes before and after use

▶ the correct temperatures are being used

▶ carrying out pest control

▶ ensuring timings are accurate

▶ using stock in rotation

▶ using metal detectors at regular intervals

All checks need to be recorded carefully with the time, date, name of checker and the results of the checks.

Electronic data collection and computer monitoring systems are often used. For example, during the freezing of ice cream a print-out will show whether the temperature was maintained at the correct level throughout the process.

Hygiene regulations

HACCP should not be confused with the application of hygiene regulations. These should be in place before setting up the HACCP process. Some hygiene points will be considered as critical control points in the HACCP process.

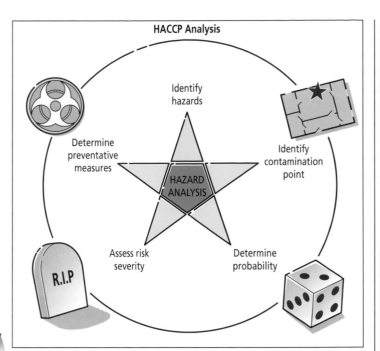

HACCP Analysis

Identify hazards

Determine preventative measures

Identify contamination point

HAZARD ANALYSIS

Assess risk severity

Determine probability

R.I.P

Stages in HACCP Study

1 Conduct a hazard analysis, identifying potential hazards and options for their control.

2 Identify the critical control points (CCPs) where hazards can be eliminated or controlled by design, automation or food operator.

3 Establish targets and tolerances which must be met to ensure the CCP is under control

4 Establish a monitoring system to ensure the control option at each CCP is being carried out properly and under control.

5 Determine the corrective action to be taken when monitoring indicates that a particular CCP is going out of control.

6 Establish documentation concerning all procedures and records appropriate to the HACCP system.

7 Establish procedures to verify that HACCP is working effectively.

ICT ➡

A chart showing the production method of your product, including HACCP, can be produced using a DTP program.

IN YOUR PROJECT

▶ Conduct a hazard analysis for a food product you are making.

▶ Select some critical control points and describe how you would prevent a hazard occurring.

KEY POINTS

● A hazard is something which may cause harm to the consumer.

● HACCP (Hazard Analysis and Critical Control Point) is a system for identifying potential hazards.

● A critical control point can be at any one stage in food production.

Making it Safe to Eat (2)

Critical Control Points

If food safety precautions are taken and checked at certain critical control points during production, potential hazards can be eliminated or reduced to an acceptable level of risk.

Critical control points can occur at any stage in the food production process. They cover a wide range of items, including: hygiene, storage, equipment, weight, consistency, temperature, foreign bodies.

Examples of some of the critical control points listed in the manufacture of cakes and pastries are shown in the table on this page. They are arranged in three categories:

▷ Safety points
▷ Quality points
▷ Mandatory points (i.e. required by law).

CCPno.	Control item frequency	Parameter range	Reaction procedure	Accountability
Safety Points				
S2	Hygiene of temperature probes – before and after use	To be wiped with alcohol before and after use	If no wipes available, inform supervisor. Do not proceed until wipes are available	Production / QA supervisor chargehand
S9	Cover ingredients – continuous	All raw materials, components and finished product to be stored covered off floor.	If container on floor or not covered, assess chance of contamination. If contamination present resieve, or reject. If not present cover and keep off floor.	Production supervisor chargehand
Quality Points				
Q1	Ingredient weighing	All materials to be weighed as per specification and recorded on tick sheet	If not correctly weighed, reject and reweigh	Storeman
Q5	Bake quality – each run	To match standards for colour and bake	If under/overbaked, reject. Alter oven settings accordingly	Production chargehand/ operative QA inspector
Q8	Mixing quality – each batch	To ensure product is mixed to specification	If undermixed, continue mixing to achieve correct consistency.	Production operative
Q16	Relaxing of pastry – each batch	Relax to avoid shrinkage	Allow pastry to relax for a maximum of 12 hours	Production operative
Q19	Recycling of pastry – continuous	To ensure a maximum of 50% scrap levels	Investigate and reject	Production operative
Mandatory Points				
M1	Food contamination	Every employee to be trained in basic food hygiene	Retrain	All departments
M3	Chill temperature – hourly	To be at 0–5°C	If not running at correct temperature, inform maintenance department to repair. Check product temperature and if necessary transfer to alternative chill. Seek laboratory advice on material rejection if product reads > 5°C	Production QA despatch

■ ACTIVITY

The table below shows the HACCP for a beef lasagne cook-chill product. It has a slightly different layout to the one on the previous page, but they both list:

▶ the critical points in the manufacturing process
▶ the hazard which may occur
▶ the control measure to be taken
▶ the limits and range which are allowed (tolerances)
▶ the monitoring procedure
▶ the action to be taken to put things right.

1. Study the CCP tables on these pages. Which of the two tables do you find easiest to follow? Why is that?

2. Working in groups, choose a food product. Make a list of the hazards that might occur during its production. Arrange your list in order of its production.

Produce a table, using a word-processor or DTP program, in which you list each critical control point, naming the hazard, and whether it is a safety, quality or mandatory point. Which controls could be linked directly to a computer?

Process No.	Event	Hazard	Control measure	Critical limit Target level	Monitoring procedure	Corrective action
22	Cook (Bechamel sauce)	Microbiological survival due to undercooking	Temperature control	Target: 80-90.5°C Critical: >72°C	Inspection by direct measurement and time. Each batch	Continue/ repeat cooking to achieve critical limits
28	Meat sauce Initial cook	Microbiological survival due to incorrect time/ temperature of cooking	Correct cooking temperatures and holding times	Heat to 70-75.5°C Hold for 3-5 minutes. Each batch	Inspection by direct measurement of sauce temp. and time. Each batch. Recorded on process sheet	Increase temp/ time required minimum specification. Reject if sauce temp fails to meet critical target
34	Final heat (Bolognese sauce)	Microbiological survival due to undercooking	Temperature control	Target: 85-90.5°C Critical: >72°C	Inspection by direct measurements of sauce temp. of each batch	Continue/ repeat cooking to achieve critical limits
36	Pasta cook	Microbiological survival due to undercooking	Temperature control	>80°C	Inspection by infra-ray or contact thermometer checked every 30 minutes	1. Reject product back to last good check. 2. Increase cook temp. to achieve minimum cook 3. Inform prod.
21	Chilled storage (minced beef)	Microbiological growth due to temperature abuse	Temperature and time control	Target < 5 °C Critical < 8°C Do not hold beyond 72hrs	Continuous temperature monitoring of chillers (with alarm). Daily chiller audits	Process operator to positively identify beef with date of batching
44	Metal detection	Physical contamination due to foreign bodies.	Metal detection in 100% product	2.5mm Fe 2.5mm Non-Fe Rejection point	Check calibration with test pieces every 30 minutes	1. Quarantine product 2. Recheck product back to last good check 3. Isolate foreign body (identify source)
48	Chilled storage (Finished product)	Microbial growth due to temperature abuse	Temperature control	Hold at –2°C to +5°C	Continuous temperature monitoring of chiller (with alarm)	1. Quarantine product above +5°C or below –2°C for technical assessment 2. Report to engineers

IN YOUR PROJECT

Each time you make a food product, select one or two of the critical points and list the following:

▶ control point
▶ control measure
▶ monitoring procedure action to be taken.

Explain if this helps ensure safety, quality, and/or legal require-ments are being met.

KEY POINTS

● Steps are taken to stop hazards occurring during food production.
● These steps are called critical control points.
● The points of risk may include hygiene, storage, equipment, weight, consistency, temperature, foreign bodies.
● The food industry sets these points out in tables.

Unit Six: Introduction

Modern lifestyles mean people eat out or use take-aways more and more. Sometimes they want a complete meal, and on other occasions just something to keep them going.

Eating Out

Every day millions of meals and snacks are eaten away from home. This has been brought about by changes in lifestyles and by developments in the way foods can be mass produced. Eating away from home occurs at work, when travelling or out shopping. It is a very convenient way to eat quickly and is a popular social activity.

A wide range of food products has been developed to meet our need to eat away from home. These meals can be bought from a wide variety of outlets, ranging from sandwich bars, take-aways and canteens to nationwide restaurant chains.

Locations of Food Services

▷ Hotels: most are open to non-residents for meals and often provide food for events such as wedding receptions.
▷ Restaurants: these range from small independent restaurants to those which are part of a large chain.
▷ Fast foods: MacDonalds, Pizza Hut and Kebab houses, for example, provide fast food.
▷ Take-aways: these include Kentucky Fried Chicken, fish and chip shops and sandwich bars.
▷ Retail stores: many large stores have coffee shops or cafés for their customers.
▷ Leisure attractions: these include theme parks, cinemas and theatres.
▷ Motorway service stations: these often provide a choice of food outlets.
▷ Public services: canteens in hospitals, schools and colleges.
▷ Industrial catering: many large factories and offices provide canteens for their staff.
▷ Transport: railways, airlines and ferries.
▷ Licensed trade: public houses, wine bars and clubs often provide lunchtime and evening meals.

■ ACTIVITY

Make a table showing the types of food services and give local examples of each.

On a street map of your local town centre, indicate all the food outlets clearly. Use a colour coding system to show each of the different types of outlet.
▶ Can you explain why these outlets are positioned where they are?
▶ Is there a need for any other type of outlet? Explain why.

WWW. ➜ Want a map of your street? Go to:
www.streetmap.co.uk

Customer Choice

There are many factors which affect our choice of food outlet. A well run outlet will try to satisfy all these considerations.

▷ The range of food and drink on offer: the type and variety available as well as the quality of the food. Special dietary needs should also be catered for.

▷ The level of service: the method, speed and reliability of the service given.

▷ Cleanliness and hygiene: of equipment, premises and staff.

▷ Price and value for money: as customers we have a perception of value for money and the price we are prepared to pay.

▷ Convenience: whenever people are away from home at mealtimes because of travel, work or leisure, they expect conveniently positioned outlets.

▷ Psychological: outlets must meet the needs of our lifestyle needs – for variety and our expectations of such things as decor, lighting and heating.

▷ If the types of customers using a food outlet are well catered for, they may return. When designing and making a new food product, the target customers need to be researched thoroughly.

Packed Lunches

Carrying food and drink around can be difficult. It can easily get squashed, spilt or too warm. The idea of a packed lunch varies in different countries.

'One of the delights of travelling in Japan is eating on the train. At 12 noon on the dot everyone brings out a small box, beautifully wrapped, and proceeds to open it and investigate the contents. The box might be round, square, or even fan-shaped, but in every case it will be divided into compartments, each holding a different sort of food. One compartment will always be full of white rice, often with a single red plum right in the middle of it – like the rising sun on the Japanese flag.

Every station in Japan has its own varieties of 'ekiben' (eki = station, ben = packed lunch), and most pride themselves on providing the specialities of the region.

A 'bento' is what every mother provides for her children to take to school for lunch'.

■ ACTIVITY

The *Omnibus* survey of 1995 showed that eating and drinking out is an activity enjoyed by many people of all ages. Study the information in this table.

▶ For the 16 to 24 age-group, list the activities in descending order. Do the same for the over-60s and the 16-and-over group.

▶ Explain why eating and drinking out appears in the positions it does for each of the age groups.

Great Britain	Hours per week					
	16-24	25-34	35-44	45-49	60 and over	All aged 16 and over
Television or radio	14	15	13	17	26	19
Visiting friends[1]	7	5	4	4	4	5
Reading	1	1	2	3	6	3
Talking, socialising and telephoning friends	3	3	3	4	4	3
Eating and drinking out	6	4	4	4	2	3
Hobbies, games and computing	2	2	1	3	3	2
Walks and other recreation	2	2	1	2	3	2
Doing nothing (may include illness)	1	1	1	2	2	2
Sports participation	3	1	1	1	1	1
Religious, political and other meetings	-	1	1	-	1	1
Concerts, theatre, cinema and sports spectating	1	1	-	-	-	-
Other	1	-	-	-	-	-
All free time	40	37	33	40	52	42

[1] This may include eating.

Source: ESRC Research Centre on Micro-social Change, from Omnibus Survey

KEY POINTS

● Many of our meals are eaten away from home.

● There are many types of food services designed to meet particular needs.

● Customers expect high levels of service, choice and hygiene.

● Market research can help businesses to meet customers' expectations.

Design and Make Assignment

At one time eating away from home usually meant a sandwich. Today there is an enormous range of food products available for people on the move. Can you come up with ideas for a new product to compete in this highly competitive market?

Fast Food Success (page 142)

Food Labelling (page 162)

Packaging Matters (page 154)

Preparing for the Task

Read through the task below. Before you can start to develop and finalise your ideas for a snack product, however, you will need to work through the sections which make up this unit.

You should refer to the sections on packaging and labelling at the end of the book and to the Project Guide at the start of the book. You may also want to review some of the sections from the previous units.

Market Research Report

Many people of all ages and lifestyles enjoy the luxury of not having to prepare food when away from home. There is always interest in trying a new product, be it either sweet or savoury. Ideally it should be something which most people would not consider making at home.

To be really successful it needs to be easy to hold with one hand. Packaging is important too – it has too be distinctive so it catches the eye in a display.

DESIGN BRIEF

As a result of our initial investigation we would like you to do some further research and development work, and come up with an idea for a new snack product.

The product might be sweet or savoury. It might be served hot or cold. To provide a range of flavours and make it economic to produce, you will probably need to use standard, ready-made components.

It will be most important to identify the target customer in terms of age, dietary need, lifestyle, and to recommend the type of places where the product would be sold.

I look forward to hearing your recommendations and tasting some sample products.

First Thoughts

▷ What are the constraints on a food which is to be eaten on the move?
▷ What combinations of savoury or sweet flavours are likely to be most acceptable?
▷ What are the most economical forms of packaging?
▷ Who is likely to purchase the product?
▷ Where could it be sold?

Getting Started

Find out more about different types of products which might be suitable. These might be savoury (e.g. cheese) or sweet (e.g. chocolate). Discover what people like to eat, where they like to eat it, and where they would buy it from. This will involve making a study of some local catering or retail outlets, and undertaking some market research.

Market research

A market research survey provides useful information about the likes, dislikes and habits of particular groups of people. This often involves the use of a questionnaire to gather specific information.

Designing a questionnaire
▶ What do you want to find out? Direct all your questions to this.
▶ Limit the number of questions.
▶ Make it easy to answer. Expected possible answers with tick boxes are simple to fill in and analyse.
▶ Compose your questionnaire using a word-processor. Make it clear and easy to read, with short simple sentences. Try out your questionnaire on a friend first. Is it easy to understand? Do you need to make any changes?
▶ Ask as large a sample of people as possible, in order to draw worthwhile conclusions.
▶ Present your results clearly. Tables, bar charts, pie charts or straight-line graphs can be produced by hand or on a computer by using a spreadsheet program.

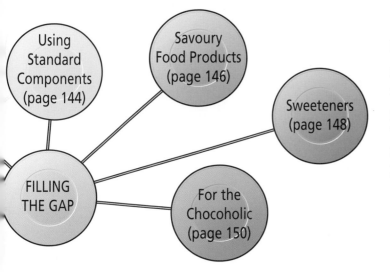

Developing your Ideas

Don't forget that most successful new products are variations of existing ideas: the shape and combinations of flavours or ingredients have been changed to appeal more to the specific needs of a target market.

As the product develops you will need to consider the ingredients and processes carefully. Test out some samples to ensure they satisfy all the requirements. For example:

▷ Is it easy to hold and eat in the hand?
▷ Is the shelf-life acceptable?
▷ Where should it be stored and for how long?
▷ If your product is to be eaten hot, what is the best method of reheating?

Analyse the nutritional value of your product using a nutritional analysis program.

Test and evaluate your product as you develop it.

Costing

As you refine your ideas you will need to think about costing. Make a table similar to the one below, or use a spreadsheet program.

Ingredients and portion quantity	Unit of purchase	Portion per unit	Unit cost	Portion cost
2 slices of bread 15g	loaf 26 slices 500g	13 33	52p	4p

Into Production

Make a small sample batch of your product. This will need careful planning.

Explain how your product would be made in quantity. You will probably need to make some changes when making a large batch, and consider food safety precautions. Think about the following points.

▷ Ready-prepared ingredients: to increase the speed of production.
▷ Quality control: equipment which could be used to produce a product of the same quality each time (e.g. a food processor to slice, grate or combine ingredients).
▷ Hygiene: manual handling during food preparation creates the possibility of contamination with micro-organisms. There is also the possibility of cross-contamination with raw, unprocessed ingredients.
▷ Temperature control: vital to prevent the multiplication of micro-organisms which cause food poisoning. Temperature needs to be controlled during preparation, storage, distribution and retail display.

Draw your system in the form of a clear flow chart to show each stage of production. You could use ICT for this.

Think about how you will present and package your product. Invent a special name to draw the customers' attention and indicate the nature of the product's contents.

Finally, write a detailed product specification.

Final Testing and Evaluation

Set up a taste panel to see what others think about your product. Ideally your tasters should represent your target market. You could also take your product to a local food manufacturer, retailer or caterer for comments.

Refer to the results of your tests in your final evaluation. Also discuss the process you followed.

▷ Was all your research worthwhile?
▷ Did you use the results of your research when designing your product?
▷ Did you thoroughly test out your ideas?
▷ Did you maintain high standards of hygiene and safety?
▷ How might you improve on your product if you were to make it again?

Fast Food Success

Fast food is big business. Take-away and home-delivery pizzas have become increasingly popular with people on the move and in a hurry. One of the essential ingredients of most pizzas is cheese.

More fast food is eaten in the UK than any other European nation. Around £30 each per year is spent on burgers, pizzas, fish and chips and other take-aways. Burgers account for over half the total sales, but pizzas now claim well over one third of the market, making them the fast food success of recent years.

Home delivery pizzas appeal to many consumers. They come in various sizes, with a wide range of toppings, and are seen as a more sophisticated product than burgers. They provide a satisfying and nourishing meal.

Pizzas are not only popular as take-aways but are also bought from the chilled and freezer sections of supermarkets, ready to heat and serve. The individual components are also available to assemble and cook at home.

The basic components of any pizza are the base, tomato purée and cheese.

The Base

This is a bread mixture formed into a flat circular base which may be thick or thin. Ready-made bases can be bought fresh or packed in a modified atmosphere to prolong the shelf-life. Various sizes are available, from individual to family size. The base provides carbohydrate.

Tomato Purée

This is a double-concentrated rich tomato paste sold in jars, cans or tubes. It provides a distinctive flavour. Various flavoured purées and pastes are available for use on pizzas but are more expensive.

Purée made from genetically modified tomatoes went on sale in the beginning of 1996. Scientists have identified the gene that causes tomatoes to become soft when ripe. Using genetic modification they have been able to remove this gene so that the tomato remains firmer for longer.

Losses during harvesting are reduced, resulting in lower production costs. The purée can therefore be sold at a lower price.

Cheese

A good flavoured hard cheese which melts well is the most successful for pizzas. It provides protein and minerals.

There are more than 500 varieties of cheese made from the milk of cows, goats, sheep or camels. Many cheeses are named after the places where they were first made. No two cheese are the same because of the variations in local grasses, herbs, climate, water and manufacturing process.

Types of cheese

Mozzarella
This is the traditional Italian cheese for pizza. It is an unripened cows' milk cheese which has a white spongy texture with a mild creamy-sour taste.

Parmesan
A very hard cheese from Italy, made from semi-skimmed unpasteurised cows' milk and matured for three to four years to give a strong flavour. It is traditionally grated over Italian dishes such as pasta and risotto.

Leicester
A hard cheese made from pasteurised cows' milk which has a distinct russet red colour and mild flavour. It melts well.

Cheddar
This cheese is mass produced in Britain and imitated all over the world. It is made from pasteurised cows' milk and has an hard, dense texture and strong flavour. It is an excellent cooking cheese.

Cheshire
This crumbly, loose textured cheese is naturally creamy white, but can be coloured with annatto to give an apricot shade (red).

Cheddar cheese production

Milk is pasteurised to destroy harmful bacteria. A starter culture of lactic acid bacteria is added to sour the milk. The temperature is raised to 30°C.

Rennet is added to coagulate the milk. Rennet contains the enzyme rennin which causes milk to clot. Rennin is found in calves' stomachs (although a synthetic version is used in vegetarian cheese).

The liquid whey separates from the curd. After 45 minutes the curd is solid. It is cut into small pieces allowing the whey to drain away more easily.

Salt is added to preserve and add flavour.

The curd is packed into moulds which are lined with coarse cloth. They are pressed to remove the excess whey and sprayed with hot water which causes a thin hard rind to form.

The cheese is then left in controlled temperatures and humidity to ripen. It is turned frequently to ensure even ripening. The cheese becomes firm in texture with a more pronounced rind. The flavour develops and strengthens the longer it is left. Mild cheddar is left to ripen for three to four months while mature cheddar is left for up to a year.

Make your own simple soft cheese:

▶ Heat 300 ml of fresh milk to 37°C.

▶ Add 1 teaspoon of rennet.

▶ Put the mixture into a bowl and leave for 15 minutes.

▶ Line a sieve with muslin and place over a second bowl.

▶ Pour the mixture though the muslin and leave to drain. The liquid is the whey. The solid left in the muslin is the curd, and is a type of soft cheese.

▶ Add seasoning to taste.

■ ACTIVITIES

One of the main features of eating food from a chain of food outlets is the consistency of product quality and portion size. A pizza take-away or restaurant has to have a system to assemble the pizzas to order, quickly and efficiently.

1. Draw a flow diagram, using a DTP or word-processor, of a production line system to produce pizzas of consistent size, depth and quantity of topping ingredients.
In industry this is known as working to designated tolerances.

▶ What equipment could be used to ensure uniformity?

▶ Identify critical control points in the system in terms of temperature, time and food safety (see page 136).

Try out your system to produce a small batch of pizzas, for example five people to make five pizzas. Is this system more efficient than each person working individually to make their own pizza?

2. A pizza take-away wishes to offer a range of up to 10 topping combinations to their customers. There is already another pizza take-away in the area, so they need to have a good range of interesting toppings to attract custom.

Working in groups or individually, list a suitable range of toppings which could be offered. Devise a short question-naire to assess the appeal of your suggested toppings.

ICT →

A visual specification of a pizza could be produced using a graphics or DTP program. The image could be annotated to show the type, number and position of ingredients.

IN YOUR PROJECT

▶ How have you ensured consistency of product quality and portion size?

▶ If your product is to be mass-produced, produce a flow-diagram of a possible production line.

KEY POINTS

● Food sold in fast food outlets is very popular.

● Pizzas account for one third of the fast food market.

● The basic components of pizzas are a base, tomato purée and cheese.

● Cheese is produced from milk by adding rennet to clot the milk, forming curds and whey.

● Many different types of cheese are produced.

Using Standard Components

Standard components are ready-prepared ingredients used during the manufacture of food products. They can be used in different ways to make different products. They can be made cheaply in large quantities and are quick and easy to use.

A **standard component** is a pre-manufactured or ready-made ingredient. It will be:

▷ a standard size or weight (e.g. pizza base)
▷ a standard shape or form (e.g. pastry case)
▷ a standard intensity of flavour (e.g. stock cube)
▷ accurate in proportion and ratio (e.g. sauce mix).

Standard components are often used to save time, and because they will be of a consistent and reliable quality. They are widely used in the catering trade. For example a pizza take-away outlet can save time by using ready-made mass produced pizza bases. At the same time it can be sure that the size, depth and quality will always be the same. Other ingredients (which may also be standard components) are then added to make a range of final products.

Some other examples of using standard components include:

Standard component	Final product
Shortcrust pastry case	quiche lorraine
Meringue nest	fruit pavlova
Sponge fingers	sherry trifle

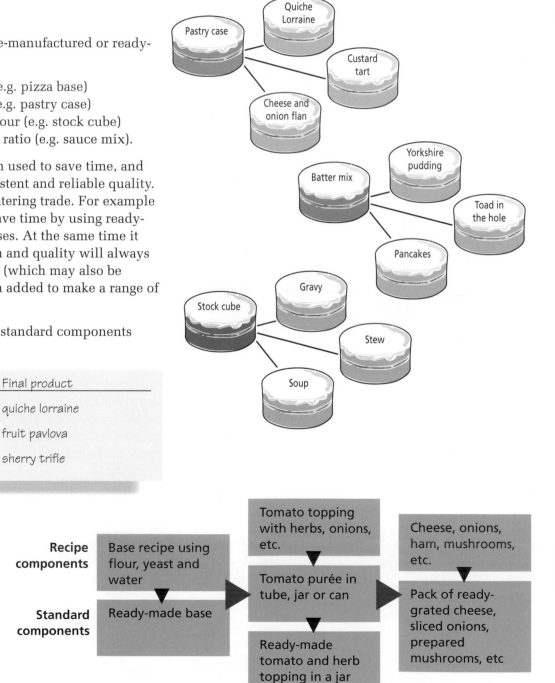

■ ACTIVITIES

Re-draw the table above. Add in other examples of final products made using the same standard components.

What other standard components and final products can you think of?

Recipe components	Base recipe using flour, yeast and water	Tomato topping with herbs, onions, etc.	Cheese, onions, ham, mushrooms, etc.
Standard components	Ready-made base	Tomato purée in tube, jar or can	Pack of ready-grated cheese, sliced onions, prepared mushrooms, etc
		Ready-made tomato and herb topping in a jar	

Making a Standard Component: Pizza Bases

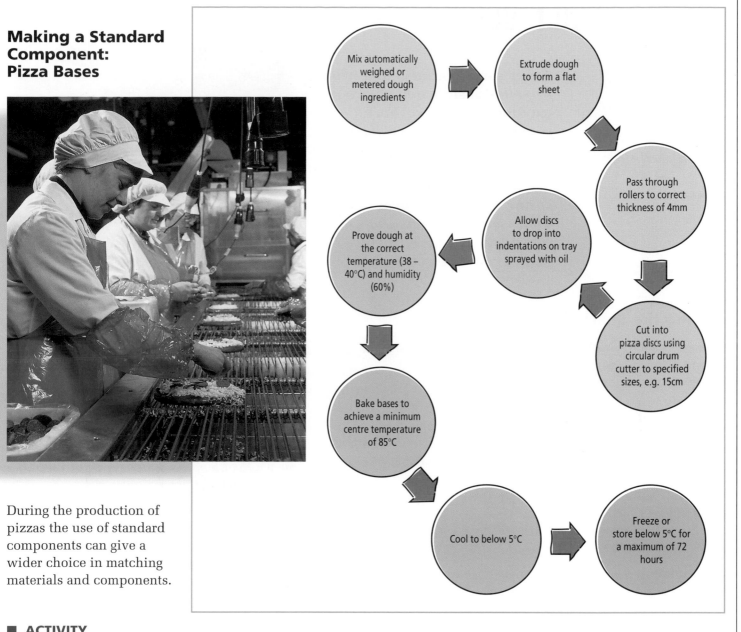

During the production of pizzas the use of standard components can give a wider choice in matching materials and components.

Flow chart contents:

- Mix automatically weighed or metered dough ingredients
- Extrude dough to form a flat sheet
- Pass through rollers to correct thickness of 4mm
- Cut into pizza discs using circular drum cutter to specified sizes, e.g. 15cm
- Allow discs to drop into indentations on tray sprayed with oil
- Prove dough at the correct temperature (38 – 40°C) and humidity (60%)
- Bake bases to achieve a minimum centre temperature of 85°C
- Cool to below 5°C
- Freeze or store below 5°C for a maximum of 72 hours

■ ACTIVITY

Choose a product that could be batch-baked in a small catering outlet. The product must use a standard component (e.g. large or small pastry cases, sponge flan case, basic white sauce for use with pasta).

Specify the details of your chosen standard component and the variety of final products:

- ▶ the type and quantity of ingredients
- ▶ the times for mixing, stirring, cooling, etc.
- ▶ the time and temperature for baking
- ▶ the number to be made
- ▶ the range of different final products.

Produce a flow chart to plan the production of the standard component using ICT if possible.

Prepare a second flow chart to plan the production of the different product varieties.

IN YOUR PROJECT

- ▶ Could standard components be used in the mass production of your food product?
- ▶ If you specify a standard component, how will it be stored until needed on the production line?

KEY POINTS

- ● Standard components are ready-made ingredients of consistent size, shape and flavour.
- ● They save time and money and help ensure consistency.

Savoury Food Products

Today's multicultural and widely-travelled society demands a more exciting range of savoury snacks than sausage rolls, pork pies and pasties. The food industry has responded by developing products from different cultures, such as samosas, spring rolls, tikka slices and bhajis. There is also a wide range of lower fat snacks for increasingly health conscious customers.

Cracking the Snack

The crisp, nut and snack market has grown rapidly owing to a worldwide trend towards 'snacking'. The savoury snack market was valued at £639 million in 1994. There was a 40% rise over five years.

Ethnic foods, particularly Indian and Mexican, are part of this increased market. Mexican tortilla chips, for example, are estimated to have annual sales of more than £12 million.

New products

The consumer's idea of a snack has broadened with the development of new snack products.

Manufacturers are keen to explore new flavours, shapes and textures. However, potato crisps remain the number one favourite, with a variety of flavours and special types, including reduced fat.

Do you think people now prefer snack products and savoury bagged snacks, rather than traditional confectionery, bakery or light meals?

3D snacks

Three-dimensionally shaped snacks can now be made by extruding or squeezing a soft mixture through a specially shaped die. It emerges in a continuous strip which is then cut into smaller slices and cooked. A cooker extruder can make expanded three-dimensional snacks at a rate of 500 kg per hour. The process has enabled manufacturers to produce snacks such as Onion Rings, Wotsits, Quavers and Monster Munch.

Less Fat

Lots of savoury snacks have a very high fat content. But many consumers today expect a healthier choice. Diets high in fat, particularly saturated fat, can result in heart and blood vessel disease. Any fat not used for energy is stored as body fat, which can lead to weight problems.

The Government's *Health of the Nation* report of 1992 set the following targets for the year 2005:

▷ to reduce the average percentage of food energy derived by the population from saturated fatty acids by at least 35% (to 11%).
▷ to reduce the average percentage of food energy derived by the population from total fat by at least 12% (to no more than 35%).

How could traditional recipes be adapted to produce snack foods with a lower fat content?

Extruded snacks are a key area for research and development. The process is increasingly being used for breakfast cereals such as Honeynut Loops and Weetos.

WWW. ➡

For more details go to:
www.nutrition.org.uk
www.foodstandards. gov.uk

Future Snacks

Health trends have influenced manufacturers to be more aware of the use of fats and additives. Fried snacks are gradually being replaced by baked savoury snacks and fat-free snacks. Baked savoury snacks is a new market being developed by manufacturers.

Overall the fastest growth in the snack market is in extruded savoury snacks and tortilla chips.

■ **ACTIVITIES**

1. Working in pairs, carry out a survey to find out the popularity of different types of bagged savoury snacks with different age groups (e.g. young children, teenagers, adults).

Present your findings as graphs, using a spreadsheet if possible. Compare your results and report your findings.

2. Find out where and how bagged savoury snacks are sold locally.

▶ Which outlet has the smallest range available? List the range.
▶ Which outlet has the largest range?
▶ What does the range include?
▶ What multicultural flavours are included?

3. Evaluate the range of savoury foods sold locally to familiarise yourself with the product range. Traditionally, some foods are associated with a particular area (e.g. Cornish pasties).

▶ How do you think the range might differ in other parts of the country?
▶ Who are the products aimed at?
▶ Produce a chart comparing the type and amount of fat in each product.
▶ For each product, suggest any other ingredients that might increase the fat content.
▶ Suggest ways in which each of the products could have their fat content reduced.

For more details go to:
www.snackfoods.com

IN YOUR PROJECT

▶ What market is your product aimed at? Why will it appeal to potential customers?
▶ How could you adapt your recipe to produce a product with a lower fat content?

KEY POINTS

● The range of savoury food products includes recipes from different cultures.
● Three-dimensional snacks are made by a process of extrusion.
● Many snack products have a high fat content.
● Recipes can be modified to reduce their fat content.

FILLING THE GAP

extending the product range

147

Sweeteners

Sugar is found in a wide range of sweet and savoury products. It is commonly known as a sweetener but has many other uses in food product development.

Manufacturers often use sugar substitutes in order to meet current dietary recommendations.

If you want more information go to:
www.britishsugar.co.uk
www.tateandlyle.co.uk

Sugar

There are two sources of sugar:

▷ cane sugar grown in the tropics
▷ beet sugar grown in mild climates.

All white sugar is refined. This means that the impurities are removed and the sugar is separated from its molasses (a sticky syrup).

Brown sugar may be refined or unrefined. Unrefined sugars have the best flavour and aroma.

Sugar is a simple carbohydrate. It is quickly absorbed and metabolised by the body. This produces an instant but short-lasting boost of energy. One 5 g teaspoon of sugar provides about 19 calories, (392 kcal/1670 kJ per 100 g).

Type of sugar	Name	Found in
Monosaccharides (single sugars)	glucose	fruits, vegetables, honey, glucose syrup
	fructose	fruits, vegetables, honey
Disaccharides (double sugars)	sucrose	fruits, sugar cane, sugar beet
	maltose	malt, germinating cereals, honey
	lactose	milk and dairy products

■ ACTIVITY

Investigate the amount of sugar per 100 g or per portion in the following products: canned vegetables, tomato ketchup, baked beans, pudding mixes, jam, breakfast cereal.

▶ Present your findings as a bar chart on a spreadsheet.
▶ What do your findings show?
▶ Can you identify the role or function of the sugar in each product?

Sugar beet

Sugar cane

Using Sugar

During the preparation of food, sugar can:

▷ be used as as a sweetener
▷ contribute to energy value
▷ develop colour and flavour in baked products and some savoury foods
▷ contribute to food texture
▷ prevent the development of gluten in cakes and pastry, giving a softer product
▷ encourage rising and aeration in yeast cookery and cake making
▷ help the fat to incorporate more air in cakes
▷ prevent drying out in baked products
▷ improve the quality of frozen products such as fruit and cream (e.g. has a stabilising effect in sorbets)
▷ act as a preservative in jams, jellies and marmalades, reacting with pectin to form a 'set'.
▷ be used in preparing many sweets (e.g toffee, fudge).

Sugar Commodities

Granulated
This general purpose sugar is the most common and the cheapest. It is refined from cane or beet sugar and has medium crystals.

Caster
Caster sugar has small white crystals which dissolve easily. It creams easily in baking.

Icing sugar
The fine, white powdery sugar dissolves instantly. It is used for icings and confectionery, and has an added anticaking agent (calcium phosphate).

Demerara
This unrefined cane sugar has large, golden brown crystals. It is less suitable for baking.

Muscovado
This raw cane sugar has soft, fine brown grains with a strong, distinctive flavour. It is used in rich fruit cakes, gingerbread, Christmas puddings, etc.

Ingredients: Flour, Vegetable and Animal Fats, Sugar, Wholemeal Flour, Cane Syrup, Raising Agents (Sodium Bicarbonate, Tartaric Acid), Salt.

Ingredients: Milk Chocolate, Vegetable Fat, Wheatflour, Sugar, Dried Whey, Cocoa, Maize Starch, Dextrose, Salt, Colour (Caramel), Raising Agent (Sodium Bicarbonate).

Sugar Substitutes

In response to current Government dietary recommendations, many manufacturers have developed alternative products which are lower in sugar. This is done by reducing the total amount of sugar in the product or by using a sugar substitute.

There are two types of sugar substitutes:

▷ hydrogenated sugars
▷ non-nutritive or intense sweeteners.

Hydrogenated sugars are sweet but are not absorbed by the body. They include sorbitol, mannitol, hydrogenated glucose syrup and xylitol.

Non-nutritive or intense sweeteners are sweet but supply little energy. They include saccharin, thaumatin, aspartame and acesulfame K. Saccharine is the most widely used – it is 300 times sweeter than sugar. These sweeteners:

▷ are used in smaller quantities
▷ lack the bulk which is sometimes necessary in the manufacture of confectionery
▷ may sometimes leave a bitter after-taste
▷ do not have the same properties of sugar necessary in many cooking processes
▷ reduce the palatability and shelf-life in products.

■ ACTIVITIES

1. Find out about the production of sugar from beet or cane. At what stage are golden syrup and treacle produced? List a number of food products that use syrup or treacle as ingredients.

2. Set up a taste test (see page 114) to compare one or two products with their reduced sugar alternatives. Use a ranking method. Draw conclusions about your results. Do the reduced sugar versions taste as good as the standard version?

Healthy Choices?

We often choose products made with sugar substitutes as a healthier choice to chocolate bars or savoury snacks. Manufacturers sometimes use sugar substitutes:

▷ to lower the calories in biscuits and cakes for slimmers
▷ to create a 'diet' product such as cordials or fizzy drinks, yoghurts
▷ to promote a food for dental health, as in sugar-free gum and lollies.
▷ to market food for 'diabetics' such as jams and chocolates.

■ ACTIVITY

A bakery company wishes to extend its range of tray bake products to appeal to the health conscious. It wishes to produce lower sugar varieties.

Develop and produce a suitable product by adapting recipes and substituting ingredients.

Carry out product evaluation to assess its acceptability.

Would the changes have any effect on the selling price of the product?

IN YOUR PROJECT

► Identify the sugar in your product and its role in the recipe.
► Experiment with the use of sweeteners used in place of sugar to create a product with fewer calories.

KEY POINTS

● Sugar is produced from cane or beet.
● Sugar is a carbohydrate, which provides us with energy.
● There are many types of sugar, each with a particular use.
● Sugar substitutes contain fewer calories.

For the Chocoholic

Chocolate is used in a wide range of food products such as cakes, biscuits, puddings and desserts. There is also a huge variety of chocolate bars.

To create the desired finished, product manufacturers need to know about cocoa (the raw material), how it is made into chocolate and the correct processing techniques.

If you want to learn more go to:
www.cadbury.co.uk
www.nestle.co.uk
www.rowntrees.co.uk

Cocoa Production

Cocoa comes from the beans of the tropical cocoa tree. The beans are harvested from October to December. They are fermented for 5–6 days to develop the flavour, then transported all over the world for processing. **1**	The beans are sorted, cleaned and roasted in revolving drums at a temperature of 135°C. If the beans are to be used for cocoa powder they are roasted for longer than if they are to be used for chocolate. **2**	The beans are broken down into small pieces by a process called 'knibbling' and the brittle shells are blown away by a process called 'winnowing'. **3**	The nibs or small pieces are ground into a thick brown liquid known as 'mass'. The mass contains 55% cocoa butter. It is cooled to a solid. **4**

▷ Cocoa powder is produced by removing half the cocoa butter from the mass and grinding this into a fine powder. It is used for drinks and is the cheapest way to produce a chocolate flavour in cooking.

▷ Drinking chocolate is 25% cocoa with sugar and natural flavourings added.

▷ Malted chocolate drinks have malt extract added.

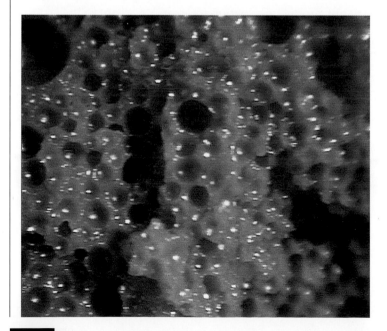

Chocolate Production

For milk chocolates the 'mass' is mixed with sugar and full cream milk and sugar which has been condensed to form a rich creamy liquid.

Plain chocolate uses the same process but is a mixture of cocoa mass, sugar and cocoa butter.

White chocolate is made with cocoa butter, milk and sugar.

Conching

The resulting liquid is dried to form a crumb. This is ground with more cocoa butter then beaten to develop the flavour and to coat individual particles with fat. By law all chocolate sold in the UK must contain at least 25% fat, to ensure an acceptable flavour and texture.

Tempering

The liquid chocolate is heated, cooled to crystallise, then reheated to 28–30°C. At this temperature unstable crystals melt, leaving the desired 'seed' crystals for a smooth texture. Without tempering, large crystals would form and give the chocolate a gritty texture. The gloss would turn to a dull grey bloom.

Cooking with Chocolate

Dessert chocolate with a high percentage of cocoa solids will give a better flavour and texture in cooking.

▷ Luxury continental chocolate contains 75% cocoa solids.
▷ Luxury plain chocolate contains 45% cocoa solids.
▷ Milk chocolate contains 30% cocoa solids and 20% milk solids.

Chocolate-flavoured cake coverings have very little cocoa solids or butter and a high percentage of animal fats and synthetic flavourings.

Melting Chocolate

Chocolate will burn if placed over direct heat. The easiest method is to use the microwave.

The Bain Marie method uses a double boiler or a bowl suspended over hot, but not boiling water.

Remove from the heat immediately and use while still warm. Leave to set in a cool dry place. Rapid cooling in a damp place such as the refrigerator may cause a white 'bloom' to appear on the surface.

Carob: a chocolate alternative

Carob is made from the Mediterranean carob bean. The beans are harvested then knibbled, roasted and ground to produce carob powder.

This chocolate substitute is used in snack bars, confectionery and sold as a powder for cooking. It is marketed as a natural, healthy product and is available from health food shops.

Carob is naturally sweet, allowing the quantities of sugar in recipes to be reduced. It resembles chocolate but has a distinctive flavour and different nutritional value.

■ ACTIVITIES

1. Working in pairs, select a recipe for chocolate biscuits or chocolate cake. Make one batch using carob and another using cocoa. Evaluate the finished results using a sensory evaluation technique (see page 114).

2. Compare the nutritional value of carob with cocoa powder. You will find this information on the labels of the products. Is carob a healthier alternative to cocoa?

3. Carry out a product evaluation on a range of chocolate confectionery. Consider the variety of shapes, textures and flavour. Sensory work could be presented as star diagrams.

▶ How do you think these effects are achieved?
▶ What are the ingredients?
▶ What is their function in the finished product?

Chocolate Confectionery

There are two types of chocolate confectionery:

▶ **Moulded products**: liquid chocolate is poured into moulds to form bars. A filling is poured into a chocolate shell, and then finished with a base layer of chocolate (e.g. Mars bars).

▶ **'Countline' products**: In these the chocolate covers a filling. This is called 'enrobing'. The solid centres pass under a curtain of chocolate liquid which coats them as they move through on a continuous belt (e.g. Lion bars).

IN YOUR PROJECT

▶ Experiment with your ingredients to make sure you have selected the most suitable ones.
▶ If you have chosen chocolate, which type have you specified in your product?
▶ Give clear reasons for your decision.

KEY POINTS

● Chocolate, cocoa and drinking chocolate are produced from the cocoa bean.
● Chocolate can be moulded into shape or used to coat or enrobe a filling.
● Chocolate with a high percentage of cocoa solids gives a better flavour and texture in cooking.
● Carob can be used in place of chocolate.

Examination Questions

Before spending between one and two hours answering the following questions you will need to have learnt about sensory evaluation, food product development, salad products and HACCP. This has been covered in Units Four, Five and Six.

Write your answers on A4 paper. You are reminded of the need for good English and clear presentation in your answers.

1. This questions is about product evaluation. *See page 106.*

Gathering information is an important starting point for research.

(a) List five items of information gained from existing products that would be useful to a food product designer. *(5 marks)*

(b) Explain how electronic media can be a useful when gathering and using this information. *(4 marks)*

2. This question is about consumer trends. *See pages 116 and 138.*

Over recent years there has been an increase in the number of meals eaten away from home.

(a) Give reasons for this current trend of eating out. *(4 marks)*

(b) What are the disadvantages of eating ready prepared and processed meals. *(4 marks)*

3. This question is about materials and components. *See page 144.*

(a) Explain the term 'standard food component'. *(2 marks)*

(b) What standard food components may be purchased to aid the production of take-away pizzas? *(4 marks)*

(c) Discuss the disadvantages of using standard food components. *(4 marks)*

4. **This question is about quality control and assurance.** *See pages 120–121.*

(a) Explain the meaning of quality control. *(2 marks)*

(b) Refer to the recipe on page 130. Using notes and sketches describe the Input, Process and Output in the production system for a coleslaw. Show where Feedback will take place following quality control checks. *(10 marks)*

(c) Routine control checks show the following faults. Explain why each has occurred and how to prevent the fault.
i) vegetables are outside of designated tolerances *(4 marks)*
ii) oxidation has taken place *(4 marks)*

(d) Modified starch is a new material used in the industrial production of mayonnaise.

What is the function of modified starch in this product? *(2 marks)*

5. **This question is about production systems.** *See pages 134–136.*

HACCP is a system for making sure that all possible risks have been identified and controlled during the production of a food product.

(a) Using notes and sketches describe the production system for a chicken curry. You will be awarded marks for identifying risks and showing the CCP's needed to overcome them. *(10 marks)*

(b) Name two items of industrial equipment that would be used when:
i) chopping onions for the curry sauce *(2 marks)*
ii) testing the temperature of the finished dish. *(2 marks)*

6. **Environmental influences.** *See pages 160–165.*

Manufacturers have a responsibility to ensure that packaging used for food products benefits both the consumer and the environment.

(a) Describe how careful choice of packaging can benefit the environment. *(4 marks)*

(b) What are the legal requirements for food labelling? How do these help the consumer? *(8 marks)*

Total marks = 75

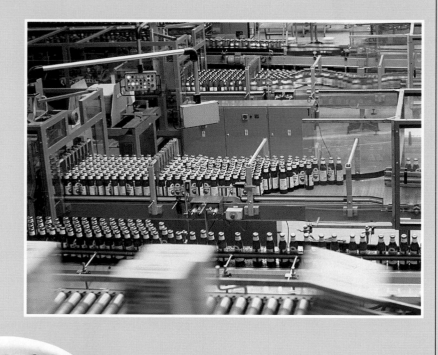

Checking the temperature of fried chicken pieces in a food processing factory. Rigorous hygiene and temperature control are essential to prevent organisms such as salmonella.

Packaging Matters (1)

Informing The Consumer

Nearly all the food we buy today is packaged.

▷ *What are the benefits to the manufacturers and the consumers?*
▷ *What materials can be used?*
▷ *How is packaging designed?*
▷ *How is it made?*

Billions of pounds are spent each year on packaging food products. Sixty per cent of all packaging produced is for the food industry. At the beginning of this century most food was sold loose. It was weighed or measured out and put in paper bags or directly into the customer's shopping bag to carry home.

Packaging materials and methods have changed over the years as new technologies have been introduced. Perhaps the package needs to be microwavable, or be stored in the freezer. Lighter materials can be used to keep transportation costs down. Packaging design goes hand in hand with product design. In fact, it is sometimes the packaging idea that offers opportunities for new product design.

Government Food Regulations

These state that food packaging must not:

▷ be hazardous to human health
▷ bring about the deterioration of the food
▷ cause unacceptable changes in its natural substance or quality.

■ ACTIVITY

Identify three foods which have changed their packaging (e.g. tomato ketchup changed from glass to plastic bottles).

▶ Why do you think the changes have been made?
▶ What are the benefits to the manufacturer and the consumer?

The Purpose of Packaging

Although it is eventually thrown away, packaging has a number of important functions. To be effective, packaging must protect, contain, preserve and identify the product, and prevent tampering.

Protection

Packaging protects food products from:

▷ physical damage during transportation and storage so that the product reaches the customer in perfect condition. This is particularly important for delicate foods such as soft fruits, eggs, etc.

▷ deterioration due to high or low humidity, the effects of temperature changes, insect or rodent attack, mould growth, oxidation and moisture loss. It guarantees food safety and hygiene.

Containing

Packaging contains the contents so that they can be transported, stored and displayed easily. The shape and size must suit the filling method as well as the crates, trays or pallets used to transport the packages. Packaging can help make awkwardly shaped products easy to handle.

Preserving

Packaging can be part of the process of preservation, for example tin cans and modified atmosphere packaging (see page 157).

Identification

Packaging describes and identifies the contents. A description and all the labelling information can be printed on the packaging. This helps consumers choose exactly what they want.

Good packaging design gives a brand image and links other products in the range, increasing sales appeal. Customers scan 5000 items in an average visit to the supermarket. Manufacturers want their product to stand out. Some colours stand out more than others. Orange and yellow have a higher colour recognition value, while designs with large areas of blue are very popular.

Preventing tampering

Packaging helps stop the tampering of goods. Products are sometimes contaminated by people opening the packaging, tampering with the contents, then reclosing the package.

It is almost impossible to make packaging tamper-proof, but it can be designed so that it is obvious if the package has been opened.

IN YOUR PROJECT

► How will your food product be packaged?
► What purposes will the packaging have?
► How will tampering be prevented?

KEY POINTS

● Most food items need to be packaged.
● Food safety regulations also apply to packaging.
● Packaging helps protect, contain, preserve and identify its contents.
● Packaging can help stop tampering of goods.

WWW. ➡ For more details go to:
www.jakeh.demon.co.uk

Packaging Matters (2)

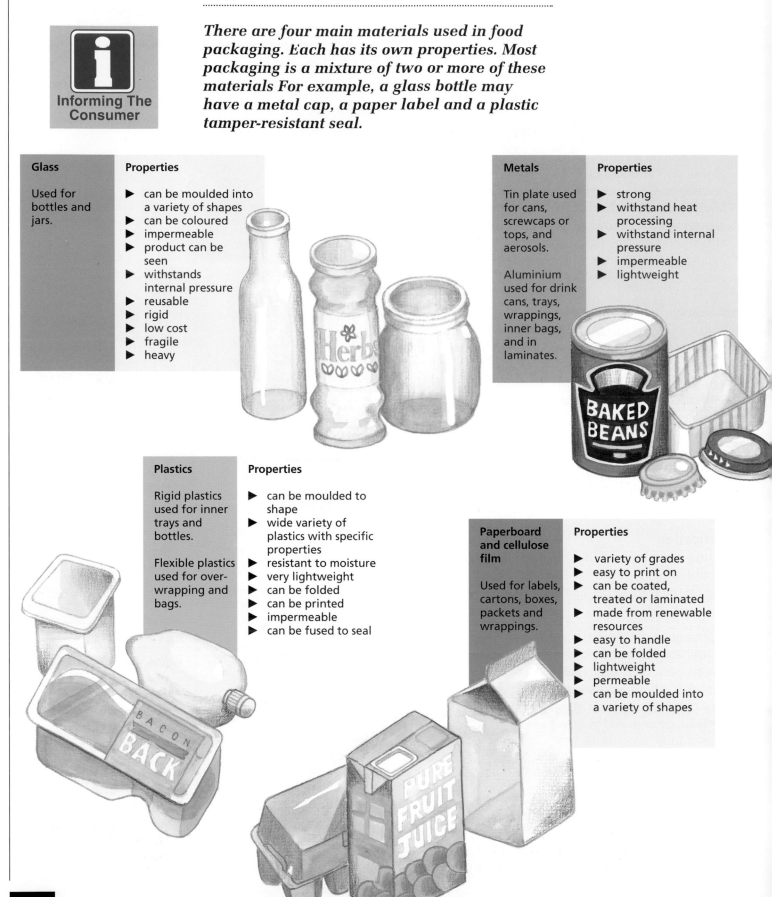

Informing The Consumer

There are four main materials used in food packaging. Each has its own properties. Most packaging is a mixture of two or more of these materials For example, a glass bottle may have a metal cap, a paper label and a plastic tamper-resistant seal.

Glass

Used for bottles and jars.

Properties

▶ can be moulded into a variety of shapes
▶ can be coloured
▶ impermeable
▶ product can be seen
▶ withstands internal pressure
▶ reusable
▶ rigid
▶ low cost
▶ fragile
▶ heavy

Metals

Tin plate used for cans, screwcaps or tops, and aerosols.

Aluminium used for drink cans, trays, wrappings, inner bags, and in laminates.

Properties

▶ strong
▶ withstand heat processing
▶ withstand internal pressure
▶ impermeable
▶ lightweight

Plastics

Rigid plastics used for inner trays and bottles.

Flexible plastics used for over-wrapping and bags.

Properties

▶ can be moulded to shape
▶ wide variety of plastics with specific properties
▶ resistant to moisture
▶ very lightweight
▶ can be folded
▶ can be printed
▶ impermeable
▶ can be fused to seal

Paperboard and cellulose film

Used for labels, cartons, boxes, packets and wrappings.

Properties

▶ variety of grades
▶ easy to print on
▶ can be coated, treated or laminated
▶ made from renewable resources
▶ easy to handle
▶ can be folded
▶ lightweight
▶ permeable
▶ can be moulded into a variety of shapes

INFORMING THE CONSUMER

starting point

Specialist Packaging

Ovenable paperboard

This is designed for use in microwave ovens. Paperboard is coated with heat-resistant plastic and formed into trays. It allows microwave energy to pass through.

Paperboard is able to withstand temperatures from −40°C to +230°C, so the product can be stored in the deep freeze and then cooked in the tray, in either a conventional or microwave oven.

Paperboard is convenient and hygienic, and is used for many ready meal and recipe products. A special laminate can be added which helps browning or crisping of food in the microwave.

Heat-resistant plastics

Containers designed to be put in the oven used to be made of aluminium. Now heat-resistant plastics are widely used. The plastic does not soften when heated. Sheet plastic is vacuum formed to create a shaped tray with two or three compartments to contain a whole meal.

ICT ➡ A digital camera could be used to photograph different styles of food packaging.

Modified atmosphere packaging

This new technique is used to prolong the shelf-life of all sorts of fresh foods. The food is placed in plastic trays which have lids or bags that are impermeable to air. The food is 'flushed' with a mixture of gases designed to delay the deterioration of the food. The contents are sealed by fusing the plastic together.

Each food type needs different proportions of nitrogen, carbon dioxide and sometimes oxygen to keep them fresh longer. Meat, fish, fruit and vegetables packaged in this way will keep for up to 10 days rather than the usual two or three days. Fresh pasta will keep up to three months.

Modified atmosphere packaging is being used for an increasing variety of foods to meet the demand for fresher products (e.g. smoked fish, cold meats, cheese and fruit).

Carbon dioxide

Carbon dioxide gas is used to delay the growth of bacteria. The more that is used, the longer the shelf-life. However this can cause damage to the food, so the amount used has to be controlled carefully. Most foods absorb carbon dioxide. This could cause the package to collapse.

Nitrogen

Air contains about 80% nitrogen and 20% oxygen. Some oxygen is necessary to keep meat red, help fruit 'breath' and stop certain micro-organisms growing on fish and vegetables. But too much oxygen causes oxidation (a chemical reaction) which makes some foods go bad. Nitrogen does not react easily, unlike oxygen. If part of the oxygen in air is replaced with nitrogen, oxidation slows down.

IN YOUR PROJECT

▶ Which materials would be most suitable for your packaging?
▶ Would modified atmosphere packaging help to prolong the shelf-life of your product?

KEY POINTS

- Paper, board, glass, metals and plastics are the main materials used for food packaging.
- Each has particular properties and uses.
- Ovenable paperboard and heat-resistant plastics have been developed for 'ready-meal' products.
- Modified atmosphere packaging prolongs the shelf-life of many fresh products.

Packaging Matters (3)

Informing The Consumer

The Functional Requirements of Packaging

The food manufacturer needs to match the type of food with the most appropriate type of packaging. It is important to develop a clear design specification for the packaging.

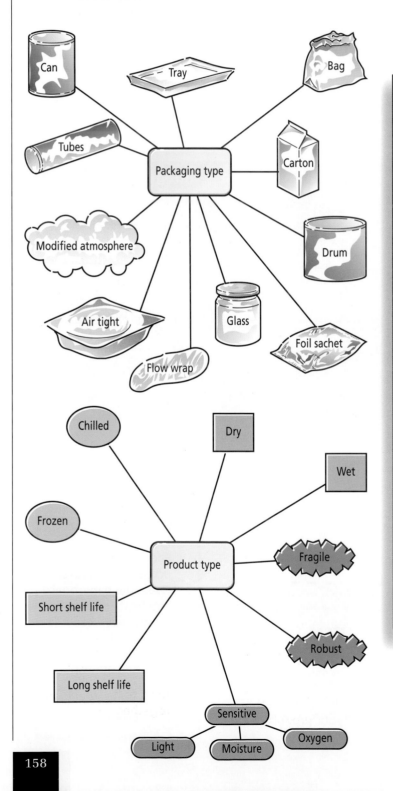

FOOD PACKAGING DESIGN CHECK-LIST

Is the package:

✓ compatible with the food (i.e. will not affect the flavour, etc.)

✓ cost effective

✓ fit for purpose (e.g. microwavable)

✓ airtight (to prevent dehydration and weight loss)

✓ providing a moisture barrier

✓ unaltered by change in temperature (e.g. boil in the bag)

✓ strong enough to allow stacking in storage and on shelves

✓ lightweight (e.g. for airline catering, weight is particularly important. Glass bottles, for example, are five times heavier than plastic bottles.)

✓ firmly sealed, yet convenient for the customer to open when required

✓ acceptable for food legislation tests

✓ able to allow customers to see the product they are buying (this could make the package more expensive: e.g. cellophane windows in boxes increase the cost)

✓ aesthetically acceptable as part of the overall product range?

Matching the Product with the Package

Product	Cornflakes	Fresh meat	Instant freeze-dried coffee
Product is:	light, moisture and oxygen sensitive, fragile, cheap and has a relatively long shelf-life at ambient temperatures	oxygen sensitive, short shelf-life due to microbiological contamination, relatively fragile and wet, requiring chilled storage	fragile, sensitive to oxygen, moisture and temperature, and very expensive
Packaging should provide:	impact protection, protection from light, moisture and oxygen, and also be cheap	impact protection, oxygen barrier properties, possibly with a modified atmosphere to prolong shelf-life, and be suitable for chilled storage (cost is less important than with cornflakes as it is a more expensive product)	moisture and oxygen barrier properties and impact protection
Packaging solution:	an airtight bag inside a cardboard carton provides all of the above desired properties while still being cheap	a plastic tray, with a heat-sealed oxygen barrier covering, with or without a modified atmosphere	a glass jar with a seal inside the lid provides more than adequate protection, and gives the perception of a high quality product (the relatively high cost is justified by the product image)

■ ACTIVITY

Using the same headings as the table on the left, select other foods and detail the characteristics, packaging requirements and packaging solutions.

IN YOUR PROJECT

► Remember to write a detailed design specification for the packaging for your product.
► Make sure you carefully match the food product with the most suitable packaging.

KEY POINTS

● The type of packaging used for food is determined by the nature of the product.
● A packaging design specification is produced.
● In many packages different materials need to be combined together.

■ ACTIVITY

Collect different types of packaging from a range of food products.
► Suggest the target group of consumers for each product (e.g. vegetarian, elderly, children).
► Decide if each product is a luxury or everyday item. How can you tell from the package?
► Which packages allow the food to be seen? Why is this important?
► Record your comments about each package design in terms of the advantages to the consumer and to the manufacturer.

WWW.
If you want more details on packaging design go to:
www.dtonline.org.

Packaging Matters (4)

Informing The Consumer

Green Packaging

Environmental issues are important when designing packaging. Making packaging requires energy and uses up natural resources such as trees, oil, sand and metal ores. Some expanded polystyrene packaging used to be made using CFCs which damage the Earth's atmosphere, but are now subject to strict controls.

At the end of the day, most packages are simply thrown away: a third of all rubbish is packaging! Using materials which can be re-cycled is one solution, although this can be expensive in terms of energy and the cost of collection and sorting. Another approach is to use biodegradable products, such as untreated paper, which decompose more quickly.

CHECK-LIST

Does the packaging:

✓ use the least materials and energy

✓ use recycled materials

✓ use biodegradable materials where recycling is not possible

✓ use sustainable resources

✓ encourage the consumer to recycle the packaging or dispose of it correctly? This is particularly important for take-aways.

Plastic packages can be recycled but need to be sorted according to their type. Symbols help identify the different types.

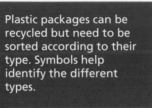

Recyclable symbols

a alu PLEASE RECYCLE

b RECYCLABLE STEEL PLEASE RECYCLE

c PLEASE RECYCLE (glass)

d THIS PACKAGING USES A MINIMUM OF XX% RECYCLED BOARD

Plastics symbols

e 1 PETE   2 HDPE   3 V   4 LDPE   5 PP   6 PS   7 OTHER

Take-away Packaging

Packaging for take-away products must:

▷ keep food hot and moist
▷ contain its contents without leakage or spillage
▷ stand up to the temperature of the food without softening or melting
▷ protect the food during transportation home
▷ be easy to dispose of.

■ ACTIVITIES

1. Collect a range of fast-food containers and packages. Evaluate each one for its suitability, as described above.

2. Find some packages which include the recycling logo and/or the plastic identification logo.

Packaging Production

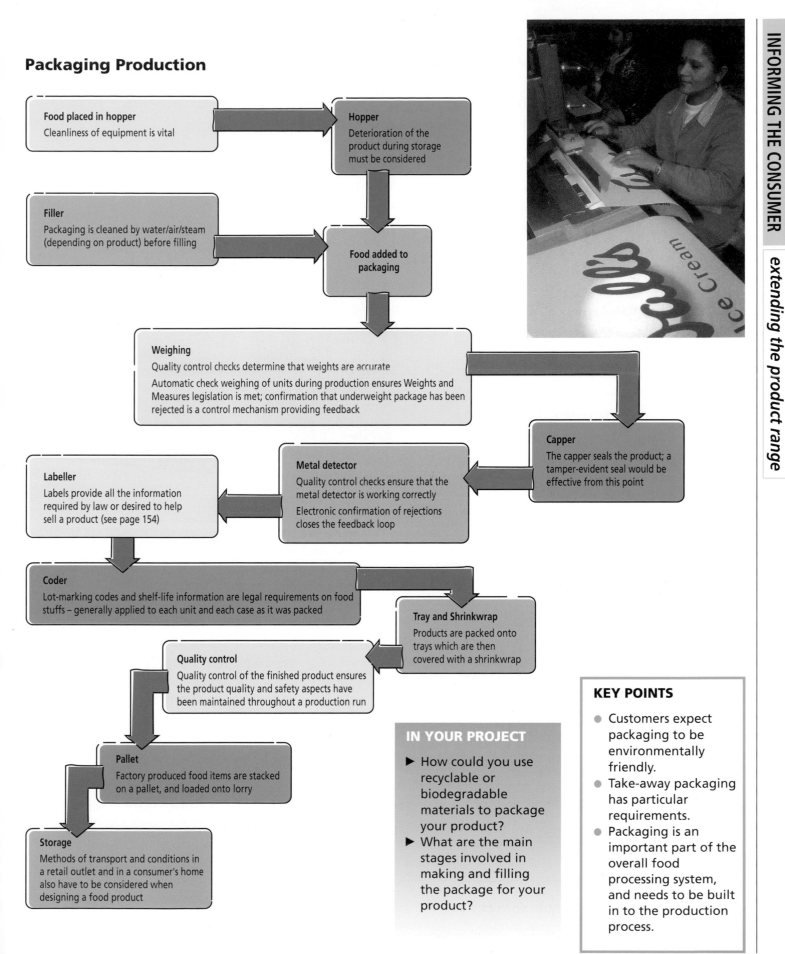

Food placed in hopper
Cleanliness of equipment is vital

Hopper
Deterioration of the product during storage must be considered

Filler
Packaging is cleaned by water/air/steam (depending on product) before filling

Food added to packaging

Weighing
Quality control checks determine that weights are accurate
Automatic check weighing of units during production ensures Weights and Measures legislation is met; confirmation that underweight package has been rejected is a control mechanism providing feedback

Capper
The capper seals the product; a tamper-evident seal would be effective from this point

Metal detector
Quality control checks ensure that the metal detector is working correctly
Electronic confirmation of rejections closes the feedback loop

Labeller
Labels provide all the information required by law or desired to help sell a product (see page 154)

Coder
Lot-marking codes and shelf-life information are legal requirements on food stuffs – generally applied to each unit and each case as it was packed

Tray and Shrinkwrap
Products are packed onto trays which are then covered with a shrinkwrap

Quality control
Quality control of the finished product ensures the product quality and safety aspects have been maintained throughout a production run

Pallet
Factory produced food items are stacked on a pallet, and loaded onto lorry

Storage
Methods of transport and conditions in a retail outlet and in a consumer's home also have to be considered when designing a food product

IN YOUR PROJECT

▶ How could you use recyclable or biodegradable materials to package your product?
▶ What are the main stages involved in making and filling the package for your product?

KEY POINTS

● Customers expect packaging to be environmentally friendly.
● Take-away packaging has particular requirements.
● Packaging is an important part of the overall food processing system, and needs to be built in to the production process.

Food Labelling (1)

Informing The Consumer

Consumers today expect a great deal of information about food products. This enables them to make informed choices and allows them to compare similar products.

Strict legal regulations exist to ensure that we can tell from a label exactly what it is we are buying.

Labelling and the Law

In recent years legislation has been passed which makes it compulsory for certain information to be given on all prepacked food. This acts as a safeguard for the consumer.

By law, the following information must be provided on a label:

▷ the name of the food
▷ the name and address of the manufacturer or seller
▷ storage instructions
▷ cooking or preparation instructions
▷ weight or volume
▷ a list of ingredients
▷ any special claims.

Many labels also contain nutrition information, but this is voluntary, unless a nutrition claim is made.

The name of the food

All prepacked food must display a name which will tell consumers what the pack contains. This is one of the most important pieces of information on the label. For example, it is not sufficient to just say 'paté' because there are so many different types: the label or a notice on the shelf must say what sort of paté it is.

The name must also give information about any processing the food has undergone (for example, UHT milk, smoked salmon, dried apricots). Any pictures that are used must not be misleading. A strawberry yoghurt that gets its flavour from artificial sources and not mainly from fruit is not allowed to have a picture of strawberries on the pot.

A few well known foods are allowed to keep the names by which we all know them. This is because we are not likely to be misled. For example, we all know that cream crackers do not contain cream, and that Swiss rolls do not have to come from Switzerland.

The name and address of the manufacturer or seller

All food products must carry this information on the label. For branded products (e.g. Heinz, Cross and Blackwell) this is the name and address of the manufacturer. For own label (e.g. Sainsbury, Asda, Tesco) this is the name of the retailer.

Storage instructions

Almost all food must carry an indication of how long the product will keep. This is done using date marking. The dates marked on food labels are an important safeguard against food which may be unfit to eat. They help to maintain the safety and quality of food. They also enable us to identify and use safely both high risk foods and those which have a longer shelf-life. There are two ways of doing this:

▷ The '**use by**' datemark is for foods of a highly perishable nature, which could be a food safety risk (e.g. cook-chill meals and some meat and fish products). 'Use by' is a clear instruction and it means that the food should be used by the end of the date given on the label. Keeping food beyond that date could pose a hazard to health. 'Use by' does not always mean 'eat by' because cooking or freezing food before its 'use by' date can extend its life.

▷ The '**best before**' datemark is used on foods that can be kept safely for a longer period of time. However when the date has expired, it does not mean that that food will be dangerous, but rather that it may no longer be at its best. Dried, canned and frozen foods will deteriorate over a period of time. Manufacturers must put the datemark in a place where it can easily be seen on the package. You will normally find the date alongside the 'best before' or 'use by' mark.

Food Labelling (2)

Informing The Consumer

Cooking instructions

Following the instructions for preparing and cooking food also helps to protect against illness.

Defrosting and cooking times and temperatures are tested by food manufacturers to find the best conditions that will kill harmful bacteria as well as give a successful end product.

Weight or volume

All prepacked food must carry either a weight or volume declaration. Metric units (e.g. grams and litres) must be used.

The large e placed alongside the amount indicates that it is an average quantity.

A list of ingredients

Almost all prepacked food products must carry a statement of their ingredients. These must be listed in descending order of weight at the time of their use in the processing of the food. The list does not have to give the amounts of any ingredient. A fruit yoghurt that lists sugar and then fruit may only have a small amount of fruit in it.

All additives (see page 100) must be stated on the ingredients list. The company can show the name of each additive, or a UK number, with an 'E' if it has also been approved by the European Union, or both.

Before each name, the label must say what sort of additive it is, for example 'preservative'. For flavourings, the label must either say if they have been used or give their names.

Uncle Ben's
Wholegrain Rice
Packed in a foil sachet to maintain perfect freshness

COOKING INSTRUCTIONS

1. Bring water to the boil. Stir in the rice, add salt if required.

2. Cover and simmer for 18 - 20 minutes.

3. Drain well and serve.

Portion	2	4
Rice	125g	250g
	1	2
Water	750ml	1500ml
Salt	1/2 tsp	1 tsp

Total Absorption Method (2 portions) Bring 2 cups of water to the boil. Add 1 cup of rice. Cover and simmer until all water is absorbed (18 - 20 minutes).

Ingredients as Served (greatest first)

Water, Rice, Onion, Carrot, Peas, Chicken, Modified Starch, Hydrogenated Vegetable Oil, Curry Powder, Flavouring, Yeast Extract, Maltodextrin, Caseinates, Salt, Emulsifiers (Sodium Tripolyphosphate, E471, E472), Flavour Enhancers (Monosodium Glutamate & Sodium 5'-Ribonucleotide), Sugar, Stabiliser (Potassium Orthophosphate) and Citric Acid. Less than 10% meat as served.

Special claims

If a food label makes a special claim about the product (for example 'with extra chocolate') the label must show the minimum amount of that ingredient.

Unwrapped foods

Food that is sold unpackaged, for example from a delicatessen counter, does not need to carry an ingredients list. Instead, a nearby ticket or notice must show its proper name, and the type of any main additives in it: for example, 'this product contains preservative'.

Nutrition Information

Nutrition labelling on food is voluntary, except when a nutrition claim is made. However, as more and more people become interested in healthy eating, manufacturers and retailers are being encouraged to produce full information on labels.

Nutrition information is given in a standard way so that people can easily compare the nutrient content of one food with another.

The information should be in a table where space on the label permits.

There are two basic formats which can be used:

▷ Group 1: energy, protein, carbohydrate, fat
▷ Group 2: energy, protein, carbohydrate, sugars, fats, saturates, fibre and sodium.

The label can also show the amount of monosaturated and polyunsaturated fat, cholesterol and starch, plus a selection of vitamins and minerals if the food provides a significant proportion of the amount people need each day. This is sometimes shown as the Recommended Daily Allowance (RDA) on the label.

Consumers need as much information as possible to make an informed choice. The information on a label must be given per 100g or 100ml of the food. Consumers can then compare the value of similar products.

Smart Codes

Most food product labels include a barcode. This is used to identify the product for pricing and stock-taking.

In the future many food packages will carry a more sophisticated electronic data barcode. This will be updated during the processing and storage of the product. It will store detailed information about the source of its ingredients, its production stages and batch, as well as its datemark.

Nutrition information for your products can be quickly calculated using a nutritional analysis program. Nutrition information panels can be professionally produced using a DTP or word-processor. A digital image, or clipart, of your product could also be added.

NUTRITION INFORMATION
100g of Drained Product gives

Energy	1188KJ / 286kcal
Protein	22.0g
Carbohydrate	0g
(of which sugars)	0g
Fat	22.0g
(of which saturates)	3.5g
Fibre	0g
Sodium	0.4g

Ingredients: Sardines, Olive Oil, Salt.

Princes is a Registered Trade Mark of Princes Holding (Rotterdam) B.V. and is sold under licence in UK by Princes Limited.

PRODUCT OF PORTUGAL 120 g ℮

© PRINCES LIMITED

■ ACTIVITIES

1. Look at the nutrition information on three different packets of breakfast cereal. Compare the way in which the information is given on each, and record your findings.

If your breakfast cereals were to be included as part of a slimming diet, which product would you recommend and why?

What advice would you give to a manufacturer about ways in which it could improve the presentation of the nutritional information on the package?

2. Using the information that you have been given on these pages, design and make a label which could be used on the sleeve of a cook-chill product, and that could be presented to a retailer who is hoping to launch a new product range. Remember to include all the information which must appear on the label by law. You could use a graphics or DTP program for this.

IN YOUR PROJECT

► What information must you include on the label of your food product?
► What additional information will you give to help consumer choice?

KEY POINTS

● Good labelling helps the consumer to make informed choices.
● Some information must be included by law.
● Foods sold unpackaged must have the information displayed by it on the shelf or display cabinet.

Glossary

Additives (pages 100–1)
Natural or artificial substances added to food in small quanitites for a particular purpose e.g. preservative emulsifier, colour etc.

Aerate (pages 38–39)
To incorporate air into a mixture

Ambient shelf stable products (page 117)
Products which will remain unchanged when kept under normal conditions in a retail outlet. They do not require freezing or chilling

Bacteria (pages 63, 64, 95)
One celled simple living organisms

Batch production (pages 60, 122)
To produce a quantity of the same item at the same time

CAD / CAM (page 13)
Computer Aided Design / Computer Aided Manufacture

Commodity (page 32)
Goods or produce to be bought or sold

Contamination (pages 64–65, 95)
The accidental or deliberate infection or pollution of a food

Cook chill (pages 68–70, 98)
A method of food preservation where food is prepared, cooked, rapidly chilled and kept in a chilled cabinet for reheating at a later stage

Critical Control Point (C.C.P) (page 136)
A step which if controlled will eliminate or reduce a hazard to an acceptable level.

Cross contamination (page 64)
The transfer of bacteria from raw to cooked foods

Decision tree
A sequence of questions to decide whether a disease-causing micro-organism is potentially hazardous within a food handling or processing system

Dehydrate (page 99)
To remove water, to make dry, a method of preserving food.

Designated Tolerances or Parameters (page 60)
The values which are above and below a target level but which are still acceptable

Emulsion (page 127)
A mixture of an oil and water

Enrobing (page 78)
To coat or cover e.g. a biscuit covered with chocolate

Fair testing (pages 114–115)
Used in sensory evaluation to make sure you are comparing like with like. All conditions are the same e.g. size, temperature, equipment